Thomas Hughes, John Malcolm Forbes Ludlow

A Sketch of the History of the United States

From Independence to Secession

Thomas Hughes, John Malcolm Forbes Ludlow

A Sketch of the History of the United States
From Independence to Secession

ISBN/EAN: 9783744749626

Printed in Europe, USA, Canada, Australia, Japan

Cover: Foto ©ninafisch / pixelio.de

More available books at **www.hansebooks.com**

A SKETCH

OF THE

HISTORY OF THE UNITED STATES

FROM INDEPENDENCE TO SECESSION.

By J. M. LUDLOW,

AUTHOR OF "BRITISH INDIA, ITS RACES AND ITS HISTORY;" "THE POLICY OF THE CROWN TOWARDS INDIA," &c.

TO WHICH IS ADDED,

THE STRUGGLE FOR KANSAS.

By THOMAS HUGHES,

AUTHOR OF "TOM BROWN'S SCHOOL-DAYS;" "TOM BROWN AT OXFORD," &c.

Cambridge:
MACMILLAN AND CO.
AND 23, HENRIETTA STREET, COVENT GARDEN,
London.
1862.

LONDON
BRADBURY AND EVANS, PRINTERS, WHITEFRIARS.

PREFACE.

THE History of the United States has yet to be written. It could not have been written hitherto; or rather, to speak more strictly, it might have been *prophesied*, it could not have been narrated. It is Secession which has torn the veil that lay upon the facts of which it is composed, and has shown them in their true character, proportions, and bearings.*

---

* Since the above was written, and whilst the present work was passing through the press, I have obtained a copy of Quackenbos's "Illustrated School History of the United States" (New York, 1861), a work which appears to have been printed in 1857, but which did not appear in the booksellers' catalogues some months ago, when I vainly inquired for some such publication. I have been able to avail myself of it for a few corrections and additions, but the entire difference of scope between it and the present work is sufficiently shown by the following figures : of its 458 pages of history, 188 are taken up with the colonial history of the United States, which I have disposed of in 8 pages ; 120 with the War of Independence and the Confederation, which take up 14 of mine ; 44 with the war with England, making 9 of mine ; 17 with the Mexican war, which occupies with me about 5 ; whilst, on the other hand, the Missouri compromise is disposed of in half a paragraph, the period between the treaty with Mexico and Mr. Buchanan's election, to which I have devoted 51 pages, in 16, &c., &c. In short, everything that I have cut short is treated of at length, and almost everything that I have considered in detail is summarily dismissed. The work stops, moreover, at Mr. Buchanan's election.

The present work, so far as my share in it is concerned, is essentially what it professes to be, a sketch. It is put together, with additional developments, from the materials for two lectures delivered by me at the Working Men's College, on the 23rd and 30th August, and 9th November, 1861, which were followed, on the 23rd November, by a lecture from my friend Mr. Hughes, on Kansas, also included in the present volume, as being a branch of the same subject. My own work leaves on one side many important aspects of American history, such as that of the religious and literary development of the nation, and barely glances at various others. In preparing it, I have not had leisure to consult either the proceedings, or even the Acts, of Congress. My principal authorities have been —besides Bancroft's "History of the United States," Elliott's "New England History," and Anderson's "History of the Colonial Church," for the colonial period, and the War of Independence,—Holmes's "Annals of America," extending to the year 1826; the "President's Messages" (of which, however, I have had no complete collection at hand since the date of General Harrison's presidency, 1840); Benton's "Thirty Years' View, or a History of the Working of the American Government," 1820-1850, supplemented by Mr. Palfrey's "Chapter of American History," published (without his name) in 1852; and for the last few years, the "Annuaire des Deux Mondes." Story on the "Constitution of the United States," has afforded me many valuable details; Tocqueville's

"Démocratie en Amérique" a few; I have borrowed others from the biographies of American Presidents in the "Penny Cyclopædia," from Mr. T. R. Cobb (of Georgia)'s "Inquiry into the Law of Negro Slavery in the United States of America," and from two admirable articles on American slavery, published by M. Elisée Reclus, in the "Revue des Deux Mondes," 15th December, 1860, and 1st January, 1861. The details of naval events are taken from Chamier's edition of James's "Naval History," checked by Fenimore Cooper's "History of the American Navy." For treaties, and most other diplomatic papers, I have consulted, I think invariably, Martens or his continuators, or Hertslet; some of the diplomatic correspondence is, however, quoted from Dr. Wheaton's "History of the Modern Law of Nations."

As a rule, I have endeavoured to consult no publications issued since the date of Secession, or if any, those only by sympathisers with the South; which will account for my not referring to Mr. Motley's well-known pamphlet. The only exception has been Mr. Olmsted's "Journeys and Explorations in the Cotton Kingdom," which, as being in the main a condensation (or rather, unfortunately, a somewhat hasty reduction) of his three former works, and more likely than the originals to be accessible to my readers, I have freely referred to. No one who seeks to understand the subject can indeed overlook Mr. Olmsted's testimony but at his peril.

Where I have derived facts from other sources than

those above indicated, I believe I have always referred to them (as, indeed, I have often done in respect of the above-named works themselves),—except, perhaps in the case of some statistical data, to be found in almost any of the "Statesman's Manuals," or "Constitutional text books," &c., &c., so copiously produced in America.

And if I be asked why I have put forth a work which I earnestly trust to see one day superseded, I answer that I have had to learn so much in drawing it up,—I find the ignorance of my countrymen on the subject of which it treats so general, and feel that ignorance to be so dangerous in the feelings which it allows to grow up, and the conclusions to which it allows them to be led by newspaper writers, too often quite as ignorant as their readers, but only more audacious, that I have ventured to think no time should be lost in supplying some elementary but, I trust, correct data on which a safer judgment may be formed by any who choose to think for themselves. As for my own opinions on the questions at issue, I have not affected to disguise them. I think but little of the man who should be able to go through the task I have done, without forming some opinion upon those questions; and I believe that it is not the free expression of opinion, but the concealment of it, which is the real hindrance to the discovery of the truth. You may easily make allowance for an avowed preference, but a secret bias may poison almost every statement of fact, almost beyond cure.

I am not ashamed to confess, however, that, on one point, at least, my own previous opinions have been greatly modified by the study of the subject. I came to it, as I suppose nine-tenths of European readers would do, with a strong prejudice against Jackson, and with a special distrust of his partisan Benton. I rose from it, with a conviction that " Old Hickory" has been erroneously undervalued, and that Benton's two huge and most ill-digested volumes are yet a far more reliable repertory of historical facts for the period of which they treat than might be supposed. The fact is, from his peculiar position as a strong Southern Unionist, aided by his impartial intolerance of wellnigh all that was not T. H. Benton, the "Hawk of Missouri," was able, with singular clear-sightedness, to point out the faults and blunders of both the North and the South; whilst his loyalty (for I can call it by no other name) to Jackson enables him to bring out in full relief the vigorous and massive character of his chief. Certain it is, that on passing from his work to the collection of Webster's speeches, I could not help feeling that I was in presence of a partisan at least as unscrupulous as himself, less reliable, because more adroit, and whose whole policy, except so far as it coincided with Jackson's, has been most signally confuted by events. The latter work, indeed, I have not once quoted, for I have borrowed nothing from it.

Mr. Spence's much praised work on "the American Union," I should observe, only came into my hands when my own task was finished. Had I met with it before, I might have quoted some of its statements of fact; I certainly should not have altered one jot or tittle of the views I have expressed. Mr. Spence warns us, indeed, of his being "strongly adverse" to the "doctrines and actions of the Northern party;" and I must own that I never met with an instance in which a studied moderation of tone has more successfully shielded from hostile criticism not only extreme one-sidedness of view, but the most glaring contradictions in point of argument. I had to read the volume twice through before I could believe that, in devoting a whole chapter of forty-eight pages to the "right of Secession," Mr. Spence had not thought it worth while to refer even once to Jackson's elaborate arguments against it, which yet he must have had ready to his hand, through the large quotations from them contained in "Justice Story's admirable Commentaries." I had even more trouble in realising the fact, that whilst setting forth the Constitution of the United States at full length, with its careful provision (Art. V.) for the framing of amendments to that Constitution, Mr. Spence should have treated a mere resolution of Congress (never ratified by a single state), for proposing an amendment against interference with slavery, as being an actual amendment (pp. 140, 141), and should have coolly tagged it as such in his Appendix to the amendments legally passed. Whilst apparently acquainted with the difference between a "state" and a "territory," he assumes, without a scruple, that the provision of the

Constitution (Art. V., sect. 3), for the recovery of persons "held to service or labour" in a "state," extends to "territory," although the latter is specifically named, in distinction from "state," in the very next section; wholly overlooking on this head the absence of all provision for the recovery of slaves in the Articles of Confederation, and as wholly ignoring both Jefferson's attempt absolutely to exclude slavery from all "territory" in 1784, and the ordinance of 1787, prohibiting it north-west of the Ohio,—circumstances which seem to show that, in the intention of the framers of the Constitution, the provision in question was never meant to apply to territory. Mr. Spence, indeed, accepts the Dred Scott decision at one gulp, boldly defying any uninterested person to view it as being otherwise than in accordance with the Constitution. Quoting Benton repeatedly, he nevertheless indorses the common slave-owner's fallacy, which Benton has himself exposed, that because human flesh is held as property in one state, therefore it must be such in another, where it is expressly prohibited so to be held.

But Mr. Spence's self-contradictions are even more surprising than his assertions. At page 23 he declares, that had those who are struggling to maintain the Constitution "*really acted in its spirit*, no convulsion would now have occurred; the evils of the country arise from the fact, that the Constitution has not really been maintained." I turn the leaf, and lo! on page 24, speaking of the same Constitution, I find the words:

"Our view is, that circumstances are so widely altered, that it suits them no longer, *even if fairly interpreted.*" At page 114, speaking of the chances of avoiding the conflict, he says: "There is, indeed, one means of escape. It is possible for the Southerner to surrender all power to the North, to abandon all defence of what he holds to be his rights, to emancipate his slaves, not at the instigation of his own conscience, but in obedience to the conscience of other men. If that emancipation be gradual, he may place himself under the direction of Northern men, who will regulate his affairs; if sudden, he can risk his life, and those of his children; and should his property be destroyed, he may emigrate." A single-minded reader would probably infer from this that the South secedes to avoid forced emancipation. Not a bit of it. By page 135 Mr. Spence declares that, "so far as slavery is concerned, the South has every possible reason for remaining in the Union." It may be said, he adds (page 136), "that the accession of the Republican party to power produced an apprehension that the strength of the North might be eventually exerted to abolish slavery, and that the South have acted in this anticipation. *But this theory can only be entertained by those who are unacquainted with American politics.*" (!) At page 136, after asking what the Southerner has to gain by leaving the Union, he says: "Instead of the whole power of the continent to support him, two-thirds will be lost to him —perhaps arrayed against him. In place of the Northern states to prevent, to act as a prison wall to the escape of his slaves, and return them at his bidding, he makes them foreign and jealous powers. Instead of Abolitionism being the doctrine of a small sect, regarded as fanatical by the great majority of the North, he will have it adopted as an article of the general creed. It is difficult to imagine a change more dangerous, more disastrous, to his interests as a slave-owner." Read on to pages 161, 162, and the following passage stares you in the face: "It is argued that when the North becomes a foreign power, it will be impossible to prevent the escape of slaves, and that this must ensure the downfall of the system. *This impression* is a natural one, on a cursory view of the subject, but *will not bear examination.* The relative position of the slave and free states will be the same. . . . One of the most material changes that will result from a separation, will be the formation of a strong government in the North. A very prominent condition of peace will doubtless be the rendition of slaves. But such a condition would then be enforced by a strong government, and demanded by a rival power. Again, the agitation against slavery, though it will continue, will cease to be a matter of party politics, and this will remove from it the main element of its power." Mr. Spence dilates upon hostile tariffs as one of the causes of disruption,—though indeed, he does in one place admit them to be perhaps the "least active agent" in that behalf; speaks of the South having protested against them "for thirty years in vain." Yet he admits that the South maintained its original political supremacy, "not only long after the change in relative population had removed its solid foundation, but down to the present day" (page 104); admits that "the Northerner has been practically excluded from the rule of his own country" (p. 317). The Abolitionists are spoken of, at page 136, as standing "apart in their action from that of the Washington government," and as being "one of its most perplexing difficulties;" whilst at page 311 they "are now in favour, they are useful, they give an impetus, they work in the common direction," &c., &c.

Once on our guard, indeed, against a writer so variable in his reasoning, we may find much that is valuable in Mr. Spence's book. His two first chapters on the effects of the Union, although little more than a development of Tocqueville carried down to the present day, with the substitution of the word "Union" for "Democracy," afford much matter for reflection. The difficulties of the "struggle to maintain the Union" are in Chapter VII. ably forecast. But I venture to think, that no unprejudiced man can read his book without feeling that it leads simply from fallacy to fallacy to that crowning one of supposing that a stable government can ever be formed on the basis of a right of secession; that freedom is to be promoted by the triumph of the slaveholders—that the evil tree is to bring forth good fruit.

For those who may recollect that I have written on another historical subject before, I may add, that for years I have been accustomed to consider American slavery and Indian reform as interdependent. You cannot do justice to India without striking a blow at the fetters of the American slave; you cannot free the latter without giving an enormous impetus to the development of India. This truth, seen many years ago, by Thomas Clarkson, and which a long defunct and forgotten society (the "British India Society"), of whose workings I was a close spectator, endeavoured for some years, at great expense to a few earnest men, to keep prominently before the public mind nearly a quarter of a century ago, is fast becoming universally recognised, and by the force of things, self-evident.

One word more. I have retained the form of lectures in the present publication, although much of the work was not delivered orally at all, and much of it delivered in a different shape and connection. To those who may dislike the form, I will only say, that it is pleasanter for me by means of it, to feel myself still addressing my friends, the students of the Working Men's College, than merely to write for an unknown, impalpable, indefinite public; and I trust that my pupils themselves will in like manner take the book itself, so addressed primarily to them, as some compensation for the haste and imperfection which marked, I am well aware, my actual lectures.

POSTSCRIPT.—The above pages (except so much as relates to Mr. Spence's work) were written long before the intelligence reached England of the stoppage of the "Trent" by the "San Jacinto," and the carrying off of the Southern Commissioners. The mischievous absurdity of the act was to none more painful than to those who, like myself, confess to an absolute want of sympathy with the Southern cause. In doing so, America, as she has herself since practically admitted, belied the whole tradition of her past history, and that staunch maintenance of the rights of neutrals which alone gave once a character to her foreign policy. Americans are proverbially touchy in matters affecting the national honour; and it required but common sense to feel that we, their kinsmen, could not brook such an outrage as Captain Wilkes chose to perpetrate. They should have known that, in the face of an affront to a policy, which the interests of liberty throughout the world require to be preserved inviolable, there could be no distinction of parties, no selection of sympathies, in England, but a full reliance on the sense of national honour in the Government, and a full determination to support it in any measures which it might deem fit for vindicating that honour. The consciousness of England's strength was the only consideration which could enable an Englishman to bear with some calmness an act so irritating in form and in substance, and which the folly of the American press and American Congress contrived to render yet more offensive. But since a war,—than which none could be more pernicious to the best interests of mankind,—has been averted by the timely release of the Commissioners, and by a return to better feeling on the part of the American people,

I trust that same consciousness of strength will avail England still to look on unmeddling, whilst this dread battle is being waged, where the cause is so great, and its champions seem yet so small,—knowing that God can use the most unworthy instruments to fulfil His ends of love,—knowing that the Judge of all the earth shall do right.

J. M. L.

LINCOLN'S INN,
 Feb. 6th, 1862.

CONTENTS.

LECTURE I.

CHARACTER OF THE HISTORY OF THE UNITED STATES—THE DECLARATION OF INDEPENDENCE—THE CONFEDERATION (1776-1789) . . 1

LECTURE II.

THE CONSTITUTION OF THE UNITED STATES—SLAVERY, AND THE ORDINANCE OF 1787 23

LECTURE III.

FROM THE CONSTITUTION TO THE MISSOURI COMPROMISE (1789-1820)—THE INDIAN WARS—PARTIES—THE PURCHASE OF LOUISIANA—THE WAR WITH ENGLAND 52

(Washington, 1789-97; J. Adams, 1797-1801; Jefferson, 1801-9; Madison, 1809-17; Monroe, from 1817.)

LECTURE IV.

FROM THE MISSOURI COMPROMISE TO THE PRESIDENCY OF GENERAL JACKSON (1820-1829)—THE SLAVERY QUESTION AS RESPECTS THE TERRITORIES 100

(Monroe, to 1825; J. G. Adams, 1825-9.)

LECTURE V.

FROM THE PRESIDENCY OF GENERAL JACKSON TO THE END OF THAT OF MR. VAN BUREN (1829-1841)—THE DEMOCRATIC PARTY IN POWER—SOUTH CAROLINA NULLIFICATION—THE SLAVERY QUESTION AS RESPECTS THE TARIFF AND CONSUMPTION—THE UNITED STATES' BANK 130

(Jackson, 1829-37; Van Buren, 1837-41.)

LECTURE VI.

FROM THE CLOSE OF VAN BUREN'S ADMINISTRATION TO THE FUGITIVE SLAVE LAW (1841-1850)—THE ERA OF MEDIOCRE PRESIDENTS—THE NATURE AND RULE OF THE SLAVE POWER—THE ADMISSION OF TEXAS—THE MEXICAN WAR—CALIFORNIA . . 186

(Harrison, 1841 ; Tyler, 1841-5 ; Polk, 1845-9 ; Taylor, 1849-50 ; Fillmore, from 1850.)

LECTURE VII.

FROM THE FUGITIVE SLAVE LAW TO THE JUDGMENT IN THE "DRED SCOTT" CASE (1850-1856)—RESISTANCE TO THE FUGITIVE SLAVE LAW—FILIBUSTERING—REPEAL OF THE MISSOURI COMPROMISE—KANSAS—THE REPUBLICAN PARTY—FREMONT'S CANDIDATESHIP 236

(Fillmore, to 1853 ; Pierce, from 1853.)

LECTURE VIII.

FROM THE JUDGMENT IN THE DRED SCOTT CASE TO SECESSION (1856-1861)—THE SLAVE-POWER AND THE SUPREME COURT—FREE-SOIL VICTORY IN KANSAS—OFFICIAL SCANDALS—HARPER'S FERRY—BREAK-UP OF THE DEMOCRATIC PARTY—ELECTION OF LINCOLN—NATURE OF THE PRESENT CONFLICT . . . 268

(Pierce, to 1857 ; Buchanan, 1857-61.)

THE STRUGGLE FOR KANSAS. 319

ADDITIONS AND CORRECTIONS.

Pp. 118 and 127. The treaty with Spain of 1819 is erroneously referred to as if never ratified. From the minutes of cession of Florida, it appears that the ratifications were "duly exchanged at Washington" on the 22nd February, 1821.

P. 181. Van Buren's Sub-Treasury Act, it should be observed, was repealed under Tyler. But it had done its work, and the Executive was never more threatened by an overbearing money power.

P. 207. The Ashburton treaty. There are stories of withheld maps in reference to this treaty which, I think resolve themselves into nothing. According to the version with which we are familiar, the United States' Government was in possession of a map authenticated by a note in Franklin's handwriting, besides one found in Jefferson's collection, showing the exact line contended for by Great Britain, and even conceding something more. According to the American version, as set forth amongst ourselves in the House of Lords by Lord Brougham, England was in possession of the map used by Oswald, the British Commissioner in 1783, with a note upon it probably in the handwriting of George III., and giving the American line, and not the British. The simple fact seems to be, that at the negotiations of 1783, there had been an exchange of maps, each party being put in possession of, and retaining

c

the one showing his adversary's claim. The whole wrangle on the subject seems thus to be one about a mare's nest.

P. 214. The second treaty of Washington was dated "June" 15, 1850, and not "January." It is also quoted from an incorrect text. The main portion of its first article runs as follows:—

"From the point on the 49th parallel of North Latitude where the boundary laid down in existing treaties and conventions between Great Britain and the United States terminates, the line of boundary between the territories of Her Britannic Majesty and those of the United States shall be continued westward along the said 49th parallel of North Latitude to the middle of the channel which separates the continent from Vancouver's Island, and then southerly through the middle of the said channel and of Fuca's Straits to the Pacific Ocean."

P. 248. The Ostend Conference. I am assured that this proceeding was actually directed by the American Government, and that, though Mr. Buchanan drew up and signed the minutes, he went to the conference most reluctantly. The actual place of meeting moreover, it appears, was Aix-la-Chapelle.

P. 250. The proposed treaty with the Dominican republic is alleged by the Americans to have been rejected at the instigation of France and England, on account of an intended cession to the United States of a coaling station at Samana; probably a very fair ground of opposition, considering the slave-trading and annexation propensities of the then dominant faction in America.

ERRATA.

P. 57, line 13 from bottom, for " Miamis," read " Miami."

P. 178, line 10 from top, and p. 179, line 15 from top, for " Pennsylvania Bank of the United States," read " United States' Bank of Pennsylvania."

P. 186, line 7 from top, for " Taylor, 1849," read " Taylor 1849-50."

SKETCH

OF THE

HISTORY OF THE UNITED STATES, FROM INDEPENDENCE TO SECESSION.

LECTURE I.

CHARACTER OF THE HISTORY OF THE UNITED STATES — THE DECLARATION OF INDEPENDENCE — THE CONFEDERATION (1776—1789).

In undertaking to lecture to you on the history of the United States of America, my chief object has been to enable you to understand better the nature and drift of the present crisis. It is for this reason that I leave on one side not only the colonial history of the United States, but the War of Independence, and although starting from the Declaration of Independence in a political point of view, do not mean to chronicle the subsequent events of the war, the most momentous, in a military point of view, of all. My task would have been far easier as well as far more interesting, had I chosen to dwell on that earlier history. Documents respecting it abound. The Americans are never tired of telling and retelling the story of both their colonial and revolutionary periods. But there is absolutely no standard work for the later period, and the unexpected difficulty I have found in my task has painfully convinced me of its utility.

But without dwelling on the colonial history of the United States, there are certain broad facts which it is necessary for us to bear in mind in reference to the settlement of the country. Whatever other elements may have been mixed up in forming the American people, there is no doubt that the so-called Anglo-Saxon one has remained the largely and unquestionably predominant one; that the great republic of the west is in the main an English colony separated from the mother-country. But we should never overlook how vast a portion of the area over which it extends was originally settled, or at least more or less ruled and overrun, by other European races. The dominion of the Spanish race has extended from ocean to ocean,—from the extreme East of Florida and Carolina to the shores of the Pacific, and the dislodgment of that race by the Anglo-Saxon one belongs entirely to the present century, and has been in the main accomplished within the last twenty-five years (independence of Texas, 1836). Where that dominion was broken, it was broken by that of the French race, which almost cut in two the whole present area of the United States. Through the great colonies of Canada and Louisiana (then a single province, now a whole congeries of states), it had command of the basin of the St. Lawrence, and that of the Mississippi and its affluents,—its hunters and trappers, who easily amalgamated with the Indian tribes, venturing already even into the wilderness of the west,—and seemed likely to hem the Anglo-Saxon race within limits which would embrace only a fraction of its present area of habitation. The presence of these widely-spread foreign elements, in blood, in legislation, in religion, in habits, should always be borne in mind, however they may have been overgrown by the Anglo-Saxon one. Nor should we forget that, when a man leaves his country for one subject to a foreign rule, it must in general be either that he does not care for it, or that it does not care for him; it must either be that he is so little attached to the institutions of his own country that he is willing to submit to those of another, or that he despises the latter sufficiently to look forward to replacing them by those of his own. Wherever, therefore, the soil of the United States was once occupied by Spain or France, we may be sure that a set of bold and hardy adventurers,—often mere outlaws,—formed at least a large portion of the first representatives within it of the now dominant Anglo-Saxon element, and have left more or less impressed upon the community the stamp of their own character. And this overgrowth of the Anglo-Saxon element, we must also bear in mind, has in the main taken place at second-hand from the mother-country; not always, indeed, at second-hand in blood, but always in point of political influence. The whole West of America, however many Englishmen may have settled there, is yet an American colony, not an English one; for the English settler has gone there, not as the citizen of an

English colony, but as the citizen, actual or prospective, of the United States.

Again, if we confine our attention to the genuinely English portion of the United States territory, or, say to the thirteen states that originally formed the Union (although even here we must recollect that there are in several places substrata of foreign blood, as the Dutch in New York and New Jersey, the Swedes in New Jersey and Delaware), we must distinguish between two widely different currents of immigration, in the North and in the South. Speaking broadly, the North was settled by religion,—the South by adventure and cupidity. The desire to worship God in freedom in such form as they deemed most acceptable to God, led the Pilgrim Fathers to Plymouth harbour, and planted the group of New England states in the most ungenial portion of the present American territory. Rhode Island was founded on the principle of absolute religious toleration; Pennsylvania (in the grant of which was originally included Delaware, whilst New Jersey was also purchased by the "Friends") represents the most important contribution by Quakerism to the history of the world. If, in the midst of these communities founded upon the religious principle, New York stands upon a less exalted footing, it represents to the present day emphatically the commercial element in the republic, and its city, the great fitter-out of slavers in modern times, has always been marked by its sympathies with the slave-owners of the South.

With the exception of Georgia, whose early history

is much mixed up with that of the rise of Wesleyan Methodism, we find no such predominance of the religious element in the South. The history of the colonisation of Virginia is indeed interesting, from the strong national feeling which it excited from the first in the mother-country, and the high station and remarkable character of many who took part in it. Maryland, once a lordship of Lord Baltimore's, had equally much noble blood poured into it, and was remarkable for the tolerant spirit of its administration under a Roman Catholic nobleman, at a time when a stern and narrow sectarianism prevailed in New England. Carolina, too, the grant of which extended originally to the Pacific, between the 29th and 36th parallels of north latitude, numbered a Lord Chancellor and a Chancellor of the Exchequer among its first "Lords Proprietors," and had a Constitution penned for it by Locke. But the milder climate, the richer soil of the South, offered a far greater temptation to human cupidity than those of the North; above all, by their better adaptation to the labour of tropical races, they offered a strong incentive to the introduction of slavery. For that southern soil, teeming with the elements of wealth, teemed equally with those of death. The swampy lowlands, which are best adapted to the growth of rice,—the tangled tropical forests which had to be cleared away to make room for the tobacco, or eventually for the cotton plant, were such as none but the hardiest and most reckless adventurers generally would affront, nor then elsewise than through the yet untamed slave labour of the newly imported African. Thus, the early colonists of Virginia in 1607 sought for gold. The first negro slaves were introduced there in 1620. Nor must we forget, as a set-off to the high blood of which Virginia boasts, that that colony was for a length of time a place of penal transportation. And though Jefferson, anxious to vindicate the purity of descent of his fellow-citizens, limits to two thousand at the utmost the number of convicts transported, and gives us to understand that few of them can have left descendants, the proudest of the southern states probably received in her colonial days more sentenced criminals than she did squires' sons.

We must therefore bear in mind, that, whilst the original thirteen states of the American Union were mainly peopled from this country, the tide of serious, organised, religious emigration flowed almost exclusively to the North, and especially toward the New England colonies of the North-east,—the high blood and the desperadoes sought the South, the convicts were carried thither; and that slavery and the slave-trade were introduced into the country from England; the former indeed continuing to be forced upon Virginia, after the express request of its legislature that it should be discontinued. Nor should we forget that the spirit in which these colonies were ruled from England was one, in the main, of intense selfishness. The answer of Seymour, an English Attorney-General, under William and Mary, or towards the close of the seventeenth century, to the request of Virginia for a college, when her delegate begged him to consider that the people of Virginia had souls to be saved as well as the people of England, "Souls! damn your souls! plant tobacco," * is scarcely an unfair exponent of that spirit.

Now, although I look upon the New England states as forming the very kernel of the American nation, and trust to see them taking more and more the lead in its counsels, until the young populations of the West have grown to full maturity, there could be no greater error than to suppose that during the colonial period they had attained anything like the prominence which they have now reached. During this period, the North was mainly struggling to live by tilling the ground for food; supplying all wants which it could not meet from the soil itself by the produce of its timber, its whale and cod fisheries, and its ship-building. The main element of wealth in the South, on the other side,—as you may have inferred from the rough speech of Attorney-General Seymour,—was tobacco; till within the latter half of the eighteenth century, it was literally the currency of Virginia and Maryland, that in which taxes, tithes, salaries, fees, &c., were officially paid; † in fact, although latterly rice began to be grown, and sugar made in the South, it was emphatically the era of tobacco for North America, as the present is of cotton.

* "Franklin's Correspondence," vol. i. p. 155.
† See Anderson's "History of the Colonial Church," vol. iii. p. 117, and *passim*.

But tobacco was and is mainly grown, not in the extreme southern districts, but in the central ones,—in what are now called the "Border Slave States," such as Virginia and Maryland. Now, these were precisely the ones of the South into which, on the whole, the healthiest emigration had been poured, as well as the most aristocratic. We need not therefore be surprised to find that, at the time of the revolution, they stood really at the head of the revolted colonies, so that Virginia in particular enjoyed the distinction of giving to the new republic four out of its five first presidents, and thus directing its destinies during thirty-two of the thirty-six first years of its existence, dating from the constitution.

Of the War of Independence I need only say that it was one of the great struggles of the world's history, fit to rank with that of Greece against Persia, of Switzerland against Austria, of the Netherlands against Spain; the successful resistance of two or three million of colonists against the forces of a whole empire. Great indeed, not in its details, since its most sanguinary battles would have been but skirmishes in the wars of the first Napoleon; but unspeakably so in its results. And it is a remarkable feature of American history, that the shadow of this war projects over it, so to speak, far into long years of peace,—the Government having been, for half a century after it, almost exclusively directed by those who, either as soldiers, or as statesmen, had taken a prominent part in the revolution. The spirit of those days is, however, so alien to that of the present,—the tendency to union which characterised it having given way to the jarring passions which have now broken out into open warfare, that, perhaps, if I were to seek the most prominent result of the War of Independence still lingering in the American people—over and above, of course, the roughly shaken fabric of the Federal authority itself,—I should point out above all that national vanity which the success of the war left behind it, and which, by feeding year after year, every 4th July, on its recollections, has swelled till it has become enormous.

Starting, therefore, simply from the fact that certain English colonies in North America wrested their independence in the last century from the mother-country, —if we consider the subsequent history of the United States, we shall observe one remarkable difference in it from most other histories with which we may be acquainted. With other nations, history turns chiefly on external relations and the events which give rise to them, and especially upon wars; or upon internal revolutions. To take a striking instance from what is passing on under our eyes: the present dilemma of Louis Napoleon between the priests and the people of France, the false position into which he has got through his occupation of Rome, and, as connected therewith, one of the great causes of complication in the politics of the world,—all these things are absolutely unintelligible, unless we go back to a particular event of the fifth century, the conversion of a petty Frankish chief to the orthodox form of Christianity, then represented by the Bishop of Rome, rather than to the Arian one, embraced by all the other leading barbarian chiefs. The relation thus established between France and the Bishops of Rome, the title of eldest sons of the Church thus earned by the rulers of France, will lead us on, through the sanctioning by the popes of the Carlovingian sovereigns,—through the crowning of Charlemagne at Rome, and his or his father's donations of territory to the Pope,—through many an Italian war of France, —through all internal religious persecutions and struggles,—through St. Bartholomew's day, and Hugonot wars, and revocation of the Edict of Nantes, and Camisard insurrection,—through the endeavours of a new Charlemagne in our own fathers' days to mould the Romish papacy into an instrument of his policy,—down to the Roman expedition of the French republic, and all that we now see. You cannot separate the history of France from that relation with Rome and its consequences; without it, such history becomes a riddle. So, again, the Italian and German conquests of Charlemagne serve to explain the French pretensions over Italy—over the Rhine. So the wars with England are the real forming of the French nation. So the wars of Louis XIV. are necessary to explain the French Revolution of 1789; so the wars of the Republic and of Napoleon I. explain alone the phenomenon of Napoleon III. In England, on the other hand, though our great foreign invasions—the Roman, the Saxon, the Danish, the Norman—really form the race, though subsequent features of our foreign relations—such as the French wars, the struggle with Spain in the sixteenth century—are of momentous importance, internal struggles and revolutions, mostly bloody ones, assume generally the prominent place. The war of the Barons founds the constitution. The wars of the Roses break the power of the aristocracy. The Reformation revolutionises society. The civil war of the seventeenth century and the Revolution of 1688 create constitutional monarchy. The Reform Bill founds the power of the middle classes.

But in America, during about three-quarters of a century which have elapsed since the revolutionary war, beyond some early quarrelling with Barbaresque powers, there are only two wars worth speaking of—that with England in 1812-14, and that with Mexico. The former was quite indecisive, and uninfluential except so far as it promoted domestic manufactures; the other, though important both in its character and results, yet only precipitated a crisis which was sure to come, so that literally the history might be told without saying more than a word of either. And during the same period there were no civil wars, nor do I suppose a dozen men were killed in the various small insurrections which took place.

The interest of the history, then, is altogether elsewhere. It lies in the gradual development of a nation, till it has stretched from ocean to ocean, across the breadth of a great continent; in the working of a freely accepted constitution and laws, unfettered by foreign influences or domestic catastrophes; in the character of those men, forming one of the ablest groups of statesmen in history, by whom that working was long guided and fostered; lastly, in the slow evolving of those causes of dissolution which were contained in the very vitals of the constitution itself, and which, when fully expanded, have snapped the whole fabric of government asunder. Of that history, the battles of Hastings, or of Waterloo, are simply votes of Congress, or even those of bodies called "conventions," altogether unrecognised by law, and with none but a purely voluntary authority; the decision of a court of justice becomes equivalent in it to a *coup d'état*. And as such history unrolls itself under the finger of God, it seems to do so on purpose to show us how, in spite of perfect national freedom without, and unbounded material prosperity within, one false principle may vitiate the whole existence of a nation; one seed of wrong, tolerated by the wisest and best men, may grow till it seems on the eve of bringing all to the ground.

The "Declaration of Independence" (4th of July, 1776), penned by Thomas Jefferson, of Virginia, and afterwards but slightly altered from his draft, affords the true starting-point of the history of the United States as such.

"When," it says, "in the course of human events, it becomes necessary for one people to dissolve the political bands which have connected them with another, and to assume, among the powers of the earth, the separate and equal station to which the laws of nature and of nature's God entitle them, a decent respect to the opinions of mankind requires that they should declare the causes which impel them to the separation."

Accordingly, after setting forth certain rights to which it alleges men to be entitled, it enumerates the violations of such rights by the king of Great Britain, and the vain endeavours of the colonists to obtain redress, and then concludes as follows:—

"We, therefore, the representatives of the United States of America, in general Congress assembled, ... do, in the name and by the authority of the good people of these colonies, solemnly publish and declare, that these united colonies are, and of right ought to be, free and independent states; that they are absolved from all allegiance to the British crown, and that all political connection between them and the state of Great Britain is, and ought to be, totally dissolved; and that, as free and independent states, they have full power to levy war, conclude peace, contract alliances, establish commerce, and do all other acts and things which independent states may of right do."

American constitutional writers are fond of pointing out that, before the date of this Declaration there were only in North America certain colonies, not pretending to be sovereign, united together by community of origin, and by subjection to a common mother-country; that the states, as such, and the nation were born together, and sprang alike from the Declaration. The time was when such doctrine was freely insisted on in South Carolina itself. The time was when one of the revolutionary statesmen, C. C. Pinckney, could thus express himself in the debates of the South Carolina Legislature (January, 1788) :—" This admirable manifesto sufficiently refutes the doctrine of the individual sovereignty and independence of the several states. . . The several states are not even mentioned by name in any part, as if it was intended to impress the maxim on America that our freedom and independence arose from our union, and that without it we could never be free or independent. Let us then consider all attempts to weaken this union, by maintaining that each states' is separately and individually independent, as a species of political heresy which can never benefit us, but may bring on us the most serious distresses."

It is important for us, whilst we are contemplating a Secession, founded expressly on the doctrine of "state rights," of the individual sovereignty of the several states, to bear such words in mind. Only through the conviction which they express, and which has now become traditional, for a large number at least of Americans, for three-quarters of a century, that the states and the nation were born at one birth, can we understand the deep horror of many at the North for the present Southern movement.

But, is the view a correct one? When we recollect that the author of the Declaration was himself, in afterlife, the foremost champion of states' rights (though he would certainly have turned away with abhorrence from the consequences to which these have since been driven), we may well hesitate to accept it without qualification. And if we turn to the text of the Declaration itself we shall find, I think, that it affords at least as much argument for the one view as for the other. It is true that the paper itself has its origin expressly in the obligation to explain why it has become " necessary for one people to dissolve the political bands which have connected them with another." It is true that it is only as "*united* colonies" that the states declare themselves "free and independent." But, on the other hand, it is equally true that they do not declare themselves "*a* free and independent state," or "people," or "nation," but distinctly "free and independent *states ;*" the plural "states" being twice repeated subsequently, and standing in strong contrast to "the *state* of Great Britain." The simple facts seem to be, that when the Declaration was put forth, still in the very thick of the war, the Americans were far more preoccupied with achieving their independence than with constituting their nationality. The forcible rhetoric of Jefferson, which entirely fitted in with the passions of the struggle, should have been suffered to become mere matter of history when that was closed. Whereas, by means of the annual celebration of the 4th of July, and of the fearful amount of spouting which this has kept up yearly, for more than two whole generations, it has, I believe, tended much to perpetuate that turgid declamation which characterizes it, and which so repels an Englishman to this day, in American speaking and writing; and through its want of logical precision, and the opposite constructions to which it thereby seems to lead, it has equally tended to keep open in public opinion a chasm, which the Constitution in later years, as we now see, vainly endeavoured to fill up, and only, in fact, bridged over for the time.

But, whatever may be the exact bearing of the Declaration of Independence on the question of state rights, no thinking man can doubt that it was conclusive as to the question of slavery. "We hold," it says, "these truths to be self-evident;—that all men are created equal; that they are endowed by their Creator with certain inalienable rights; that among these are life, liberty, and the pursuit of happiness; that to secure these rights, governments are instituted among men, deriving their just powers from the consent of the governed; that whenever any form of government becomes destructive of these ends, it is the right of the people to alter or to abolish it." Evidently, the only logical issue for the slave-holder out of positions like these is to deny the negro to be a man; and this, we know, is now the favourite dogma of Southern physiologists. It is remarkable, indeed, that the original draft of the Declaration, as prepared by Jefferson, was still more explicit. One of the grievances it alleged against the King, in its usual rhetorical style, was that he had "waged cruel war against human nature itself, violating its most sacred rights of life and liberty in the persons of a distant people, who never offended him, captivating and carrying them into slavery in another hemisphere, or to incur miserable death in their transportation thither. . . . Determined to keep open a market where man should be bought and sold, he has prostituted his negative for suppressing every legislative attempt to prohibit or restrain this execrable commerce. And that this assemblage of horrors might want no fact of distinguished dye, he is now exciting those very people to rise in arms among us, and to purchase that liberty of which he has deprived them by murdering the people upon whom he obtruded them,—thus paying off former crimes committed against the liberties of one people, with crimes which he urges them to commit against the liberties of another." Men who freely quote and strain Jefferson's authority in favour of states' rights, should in fairness allow it its due weight on the subject of slavery.*

But, to return to the question of states' rights, certain it is, and we are too apt to forget it, that the plan of the individual sovereignty of the states was fairly tried, and altogether failed. By the " Articles of Confederation," adopted by Congress in November, 1777, but not signed or ratified by any state till July, 1778,

---

* It is commonly stated, and on Jefferson's own authority, (see Bancroft, vii. 299), that the clause above referred to was omitted in deference to the feelings of some of the delegates from slaveholding states. Mr. C. W. Elliott, in his 'New England History,' vol. ii. p. 195, denies this, and states that it was omitted as not being technically true of George III.

nor finally adopted by the thirteen original states* till 1781, it was expressly declared (Art. II.) that each state retained its sovereignty, freedom, and independence, and every power, jurisdiction, and right, which was not by that confederation expressly delegated to the United States in Congress assembled, whilst, by the third article, the states severally entered into a firm league of friendship with each other for the common defence, the security of their liberties, and their mutual and general welfare. They were not, without the consent of the United States, to send or receive embassies, nor were any two states, without the consent of Congress, to enter into any treaty, confederation, or alliance with each other, nor to lay imposts or duties interfering with any proposed treaties, nor to grant commissions or letters of marque and reprisal, except after a declaration of war by Congress; and their union was to be perpetual. No provision, it may be observed, was contained in these articles for the recovery of fugitive slaves. As respects the slave-trade, already on the 6th April, 1776, it had been resolved by Congress " That no slaves be imported into the thirteen colonies."

You will see at once that even under these Articles of Confederation, since superseded by the Constitution, —a far more precise and stringent document,—such a confederacy as the present one of the Southern States,

---

* The thirteen original States : New Hampshire, Massachusets, Rhode Island, Connecticut, New York, New Jersey, Pennsylvania, Maryland, Delaware, Virginia, North Carolina, South Carolina, Georgia.

and the acts which have emanated from it, such as the flooding the seas with privateers, were expressly prohibited. Still, it is true, no doubt, that the Articles of Confederation only formed in the main a league of states. As such, indeed, the Confederation had the glory of conducting to its close the revolutionary war, through Lord Cornwallis's surrender of York Town (19th October, 1781), and the provisional treaty of peace (30th November, 1782). Weak as might be its bonds, it was yet sufficient to bring out, at least among the leaders of the people, the feeling of nationality. Thus, as early as 1778, overtures of peace from British commissioners were rejected, as being derogatory "to the honour of an independent nation," and as supposing "the people of these states to be subjects of the Crown of Great Britain." The nationality of the United States was indeed practically asserted in every treaty that was contracted,—with France (1778), with Sweden, Denmark, Spain, Russia (1783), with Great Britain (1782-1783), with Prussia (1785), with the Cherokee Indians (1785), who acknowledged themselves to be under the protection of the United States, and of "no other sovereign whatsoever." Statesmen of authority like Dr. Rush, Franklin's colleague in the representation of Pennsylvania, and afterwards his successor as Minister of the United States to France, went so far as to assert the actual sovereignty of Congress. Washington wrote in 1783: "Whatever measures have a tendency to dissolve the Union, or contribute to violate or lessen the sovereign authority, ought to be considered hostile to the liberty and independence of America, and the authors of them treated accordingly."

But matters were fast coming to a dead-lock under the league-of-states plan. Congress had only a power of recommendation, both as respects taxation and the raising of troops. It had no power of enforcing its own laws. It was, to use the words of Colonel Benton, of Missouri, in his "Thirty Years' View," "powerless for government, and a rope of sand for union." By 1787, the following is described as the state of affairs under it:—There was an enormous debt, with public credit in the last stage of depreciation. A system of taxation had been devised and recommended, but only partly adopted, and never put in operation. The ordinances of Congress were disregarded, the several states neglecting or refusing their quotas of expenditure. Treaties, particularly that with Great Britain, were disregarded or openly violated. England, in return, refused to give up the possession of forts on American frontiers. There had been repeated mutinies in the army. Under the burthen of a heavy debt and heavy taxes, with money scarce, and trade and manufactures decaying, an insurrection had broken out in 1786 in the Puritan stronghold of order and religious faith, Massachusetts. It had spread through four counties, taken possession of court-houses, defied the governor's proclamations. The flame had extended to New Hampshire, where the General Assembly had found itself surrounded by a mob, clamorous for paper money.

Although stifled in the latter state, it had only been put an end to in Massachusetts (1787) by force of arms, and three insurgents had fallen dead under the fire of the troops. "In this state of things," we are told, "it was the opinion of the wisest citizens that an energetic system of national government only could revive the ruined state of commerce, restore public and private credit, give a national character to the states, secure the faith of public treaties, and prevent the evils of anarchy and civil war." As early as 1783 Washington had recommended "an indissoluble union of the states under one general head," as one of the "pillars on which the glorious fabric of our independency and national character must be supported."

From this need of practical union—of a strongly-organized nationality—sprang the American Constitution. And nothing proves the absolute and imperative nature of that need more than the seemingly fortuitous character of the steps by which its fulfilment was brought about. The two states of Virginia and Maryland, in 1785, appointed commissioners to frame a compact between them as to the navigation of the rivers Potomac and Pocomoke, and of Chesapeake Bay. The commissioners met,—found their powers inadequate to the need,—were led on to the wider subject of the trade of the country in general, and how it should be regulated. So the next year (1786), Virginia appointed commissioners who should meet those from other states, to consider the trade of the United States, and how far a uniform system in commercial relations was necessary to the common interest, and to permanent harmony. Five states met by their commissioners at Annapolis (September, 1786)—New York, New Jersey, Pennsylvania, Delaware, Virginia. They met, and again the object in view expanded before them. They demanded greater powers, and recommended the appointment of commissioners to consider the situation of the United States, and to devise provisions to render the constitution of the Federal Government "adequate to the exigencies of the Union." New commissioners from twelve states met accordingly in convention, and adopted a constitution (17th September, 1787), which was soon ratified in separate conventions by eleven out of the twelve.

Such, then, was the history of the United States' Constitution. From the petty necessities of two neighbour states as to the use of a water-line there sprang a document under which, but last year, some thirty millions of the most enterprising people on the face of the earth were peaceably ruled. The story is a very homely one, but, through its very homeliness, I think, strangely impressive.

LECTURE II.

THE CONSTITUTION OF THE UNITED STATES—SLAVERY, AND THE ORDINANCE OF 1787.

THE subject of the present lecture may not seem an inviting one. Constitutions are not lively reading. An old Frenchman, who had been a school-boy at the time of the first French revolution, once said to me, "When they told us there were to be no more Sundays, we threw up our caps and cried, '*Vive la République,*' thinking that we should have no more catechism to learn, and no more rappings over the knuckles for not knowing it. But we found that on the '*décadis*' (the tenth days of the revolutionary week) we had to learn the constitution, and were rapped over the knuckles all the same for not knowing it, and it was *much more stupid still* than the catechism: so we found we had only lost by the change."

Dull or not, however, no man who wishes to understand the present crisis can avoid looking into and trying to master the American Constitution. So far from its being of less importance now than it was, its importance is simply doubled for the future. Having been copied, with a few variations, by the Seceders, it is now the law, not of one country alone but of two;

claiming, however, to interpret it upon an entirely different principle. Such a phenomenon is one, so far as I am aware, unparalleled in history, and surely deserves careful investigation.

"We, the people of the United States, in order to form a more perfect union, establish justice, ensure domestic tranquillity, provide for the common defence, promote the general welfare, and secure the blessings of liberty to ourselves and our posterity, do ordain and establish this Constitution for the United States of America."

So begins the American Constitution. It proceeds to enact (Art. I. sec. 1, § 1). That all Legislative powers "herein granted" shall be vested in a Congress of the United States, consisting of a Senate and a House of Representatives, the latter being chosen (sec. 2, § 1) every second year by the people, and their qualifications being that they should be twenty-five years of age, should have been for seven years citizens of the United States, and should inhabit the state for which they are named. The principle of representation is peculiar. "Representation and direct taxes shall be apportioned among the several states which may be included within this union, according to their respective numbers, which shall be determined by adding to the whole number of free persons, including those bound to service for a term of years, and excluding Indians not taxed, three-fifths of *all other* persons" (§ 3). By "other persons" you are to understand slaves. The ratio of representation is determined every ten years, according to the results of the census, but not more than one representative is, by the Constitution, to be allowed for every 30,000 souls, nor less than one for any single state. The House of Representatives so constituted has the sole power of impeachment (§ 5).

The House of Representatives represents population; the Senate represents state interests. Large or small, each state (sec. 3) sends two senators, elected by its legislature for six years, but one-third of the whole number going out every second year. The senators must be thirty years old, must have been for nine years citizens of the United States, and must inhabit the states which they represent. The Vice-President of the United States is President of the Senate, but with only a casting vote. The Senate tries impeachments sent up by the House, and convicts by a majority of two-thirds; but the penalties for impeachment are only removal and disqualification for office. The legislatures of the several states (sec. 4) may prescribe the time, place, and manner of holding elections for senators and representatives, but except as to "the places of choosing senators," Congress "may, at any time by law, make or alter such regulations."

Congress, thus constituted, meets once at least in every year; on the first Monday in December, unless otherwise ordained by law (sec. 4, § 2), Each House keeps and publishes journals of its proceedings, except as to such parts as may require secrecy (sec. 5, § 3). Neither House, during the Session of Congress, may adjourn without the consent of the other for more than three days, nor to any other place of meeting.

On the provisions as to the compensation to be paid to members, or as to their privileges, I need not dwell. No senator or representative is to be appointed to a civil office created or increased whilst he is such, nor is any office-holder to be member of Congress (sec. 6). Bills for raising money are to originate with the House of Representatives, but the Senate (freer, in this respect, than our House of Lords) may propose or concur with amendments to such bills (sec. 7).

Every bill which has passed both Houses of Congress is to be presented to the President, who signs it, if he approves of it, and thereby gives it force of law. If he disapprove of it, he sends it, with his objections, to the House where it originated. If, on reconsideration, it be approved once more by that House, and by a majority of two-thirds, it is sent on with the President's objections to the other House, and if approved here also by a majority of two-thirds, becomes law without the President's sanction; the votes in such case being taken by "yea" and "nay," and the names of members voting being entered on the journals. Again, if a bill is not returned by the President in ten days it becomes law, unless Congress adjourn meanwhile (sec. 7, § 2). Every order, resolution, or vote, to which the concurrence of both Houses is necessary (except as to adjournment) follows the same course (§ 3).

You will see from what precedes to what extent the President is to be considered as part of the sovereign authority of the United States. Practically, though he has no share in originating legislation, and his veto is only a suspensive one, his controlling power is considerable. For it is very seldom that there can exist a majority of two-thirds in *each* House to force upon him a law which he disapproves of. Let him only secure the support of somewhat over one-third in either, and his power of obstruction is absolute. Whilst, by procuring his supporters to fight against time, so as to put off the final passing of a bill till within the last ten days of the usual period of closing the session, he may make use, and has made use ere this, of the provision which allows him by implication ten days for making up his mind upon a measure, to throw it over, by simply retaining it.

The main share of the supreme authority, however, belongs undoubtedly to Congress. Congress, it is enacted by the Constitution (sec. 8), " shall have power, 1. To lay and collect taxes, duties, imposts and excises, to pay the debts and provide for the common defence and general welfare of the United States" (but all duties, &c., to be uniform;) " 2. To borrow money on the credit of the United States; 3. To regulate commerce with foreign nations, and among the several states, and with the Indian Tribes; 4. To establish an uniform rule of naturalisation, and uniform laws on the subject of bankruptcies throughout the United States; 5. To coin money, regulate the value thereof and of foreign coin, and fix the standard of weights and measures; 6. To provide for the punishment of counterfeiting the securities and current coin of the United States ; 7. To establish post-offices and post-roads ; 8. To promote the progress of science and useful arts, by securing for limited times to authors and inventors the exclusive right to their respective writings and discoveries ; 9. To constitute tribunals inferior to the Supreme Court ; 10. To define and punish piracies and felonies committed on the high seas, and offences against the laws of nations ; 11. To declare war, grant letters of marque and reprisals, and make rules concerning captures on land and water ; 12. To raise and support armies ; but no appropriation of money to that use shall be for a longer term than two years ; 13. To provide and maintain a navy ; 14. To make rules for the government and regulation of the land and naval forces ; 15. To provide for calling forth the militia, to execute the laws of the Union, suppress insurrections and repel invasions ; 16. To provide for organising, arming, and disciplining the militia, and for governing such part of them as may be employed in the service of the United States ; reserving to the states respectively the appointment of the officers, and the authority of training the militia according to the discipline prescribed by Congress ; 17. To exercise exclusive legislation in all cases whatsoever over such district (not exceeding ten miles square), as may by the cession of particular states and the acceptance of Congress become the seat of the government of the United States ; and to exercise like authority over all places purchased by the consent of the legislature of the states in which the same shall be, for the erection of forts, magazines, arsenals, dock-yards, and other needful buildings; and 18. To make all laws which shall be necessary and proper for carrying into execution the foregoing powers, and all other powers vested by this constitution in the government of the United States, or in any department or officer thereof."

Few, if any, of the essential characteristic prerogatives of sovereignty are omitted in the foregoing enumeration. A single one, that of coining money, is sufficient to prove such sovereignty; " Render unto Cæsar the things that are Cæsar's." And yet the very enumeration shows that that sovereignty is meant to be a limited one. You may hunt up and down our statute-book till the end of time without effect for any legislative enumeration of the powers of parliament, as you would no doubt hunt in vain in the Russian laws for an enumeration of the powers of the Czar; simply because in either case the sovereignty is absolute, and has nothing earthly beyond. Here, on the other hand, the sovereignty of the Federal authority is essentially a qualified one. It is absolute only for specified purposes; only within the four corners of the Constitution. But among the specified purposes we must not forget that the "calling forth the militia to execute the laws of the Union," and to "suppress insurrection," is included. It is worthy, moreover, of remark, that Congress is less fettered than is our own government as respects standing armies. With us the mutiny act, as well as army appropriations, are continued only from year to year; whilst the army appropriations of Congress may be for two years.

Next to the powers of Congress come the limitations to those powers (sec. 9). It was not to prohibit the slave-trade before the year, 1808. This is wrapped up in the following language, ashamed as it were of its own meaning :—" The migration or importation of such persons as any of the states now existing shall think proper to admit shall not be prohibited by the Congress prior to the year, 1808," but a tax may be imposed on such importation (§ 1). Habeas Corpus is not to be superseded "unless where in cases of rebellion or invasion the public safety may require it." There is to be no bill of attainder or *ex post facto* law, no capitation or direct tax except in proportion to the census; no tax or duty on articles imported from state to state, no preference shown to the ports of one state over those of another, &c. No money is to be drawn except by legal appropriation, the accounts being published. No titles of nobility are to be conferred, nor is any person holding an office of profit or trust to accept, without the consent of Congress, any present, emolument, office, or title from a foreign power. Some of the above prohibitions, it will be seen, are general, and cannot be construed strictly as limitations on the powers of Congress.

The limitations to the powers of the states are next enumerated (sec. 10). " No state shall enter into any treaty, alliance, or confederation, grant letters of marque and reprisal, coin money, emit bills of credit, make anything but gold and silver coin a tender in payment of debts, pass any bill of attainder, *ex post facto* law, or law impairing the obligation of contracts, or grant any title of nobility" (§ 1). "No state shall, without the consent of the Congress, lay any imposts or duties on imports or exports, except what may be absolutely necessary for executing its inspection laws; and the net produce of all duties and imposts laid by any state on imports or exports shall be for the use of the Treasury of the United States, and all such laws shall be subject to the revision and control of the Congress. No state shall, without the consent of Congress, lay any duty of tonnage, keep troops or ships of war in time of peace, enter into any agreement or compact with another state, or with a foreign power, or engage in war, unless actually invaded, or in such imminent danger as will not admit of delay" (§ 2).

The executive power is vested in a "President of the United States of America" (Art. II. sec. 1, § 1), who holds office, as well as a Vice-President, for four years. The mode of election for both is peculiar. Each state is to appoint, in manner directed by its legislature, a number of persons equal to the whole number of senators and representatives in Congress; but no senator or representative, or person holding office of trust or profit under the United States, is to form part of the persons so appointed. These persons meet, and vote for the President and Vice-President, the mode of election enacted by the Constitution having been somewhat altered by a subsequent amendment (Art. XII.) to it.

The vote is by ballot, and the result of the ballot is sent up sealed to the President of the Senate, who counts the votes in presence of both Houses of Congress. The candidate obtaining a majority of the votes is the President; but if no person obtains an actual majority, the House of Representatives chooses by ballot one of the three candidates having the highest number of votes. If it cannot agree in its choice before the 4th March following the election, the Vice-President acts as President. The latter is elected in like manner, except that for default of an absolute majority the right of choice lies with the Senate, not with the House of Representatives. The Congress (§ 4) determines the time of choosing the presidential electors, and the day of their voting, which must be the same throughout all the United States. The President must be a natural-born citizen (or one who was a citizen at the time when the Constitution was adopted), must be thirty-five years old, and must have resided fourteen years in the United States. In case of his removal, death, resignation, or inability to fulfil his functions, his place is supplied by the Vice-President, power being given to Congress to provide by law for the like case as respects the latter (§ 6). The President receives a compensation for his services, but which is not to be increased or diminished during his term of office, nor can he receive any other emolument. He solemnly swears or affirms " that I will faithfully execute the office of President of the United States, and will to the best of my ability, preserve protect, and defend the Constitution of the United States" (§§ 8, 9).

The President (Art. II. sec. 1) is Commander-in-Chief of the army and navy of the United States, and of the militia of the several states when called into the actual service of the United States. He may require the opinion, in writing, of the principal officer in each executive department on any subject relating to the duties of his office; he grants reprieves and pardons for offences against the United States, except in cases of impeachment. With the consent of the Senate (by a majority, as to treaties, of two-thirds of the senators present), he makes treaties, appoints ambassadors, ministers, consuls, judges of the Supreme Court, &c.; but Congress may vest in him alone the appointment to inferior offices: he fills up vacancies by temporary commissions. From time to time (sec. 2) he gives information to Congress of the state of the Union, and recommends measures for adoption; on extraordinary occasions he convenes both Houses, or either; he adjourns Congress when the two Houses disagree on the point; he receives foreign ambassadors and ministers; "he shall take care that the laws be faithfully executed;" he commissions all officers of the United States. The President, Vice-President, and all civil officers of the United States, are removable on impeachment for treason or other high crimes and misdemeanors (sec. 4).

It will be obvious to you that the power of consent given to the Senate as to treaties and appointments to high office affords considerable opening for unpleasant friction, where the President and Senate fall out,—as the subsequent history will show. I suspect that this limitation to the President's patronage as to the higher offices has led to that abuse of it as to the lower, which, especially of late years, has made a "clean sweep" of office at each Presidential election. It is because the President is never certain of having the men of his choice in the really responsible offices, that he is driven to fill every custom-house and post-office with his creatures. Let it be remembered that his term of office is four years only, and that, if he has a meagre power of addressing Congress directly through messages, his ministers, by accepting office, exclude themselves from Congress, so that they can neither defend nor promote their policy by personal action upon it, and it will be seen how little of cordiality there must often be between the President and his Cabinet,—how often he will be likely to prefer having his most efficient friends rather as his defenders in Congress than as his fellow-workers in office, nay, how through such friends he may actually counterwork his own cabinet,—how, above all, the short term of the Presidency tends to be further wasted by the struggle for re-election, not only when the President is simply ambitious, but when he is far-seeing, and feels that he has a work in hand which four years will not allow him to carry through. When we consider this, I think we shall feel that the American Constitution— as was not unnatural at the issue of a revolutionary war,—through distrust of the President as the executive power,—through seeing in him mainly a pseudo-king, —has tended to degrade him into a mere popularity-hunter, such as, till Mr. Lincoln, have been more than one of the men elected of late years to his office.

A peculiar feature of the Constitution of the United States is what the Americans term its "judiciary." The judicial power of the United States (Art. III. sec. I.), is vested in one Supreme Court, and in such inferior courts as Congress may create, the judges holding office during good behaviour, and receiving a compensation for their services which may not be diminished whilst they hold office. "The judicial power," it is enacted (sec. II.) "shall extend to all cases in law and equity arising under this Constitution, the laws of the United States, and treaties made or which shall be made under their authority,—to all cases affecting ambassadors, other public ministers and consuls; to all cases of admiralty and marine jurisdiction ; to controversies to which the United States shall be a party; to controversies between two or more states—between a state and citizens of another state" (this jurisdiction was modified by subsequent amendment)—"between citizens of different states— between citizens of the same state claiming lands under grants of different states,—and between a state or the citizens thereof, and foreign states, citizens or subjects" (a provision also modified subsequently by amendment). Its jurisdiction is original (that is to say, the procedure is first commenced before it) in all cases affecting ambassadors, &c., and those in which a state shall be a party. In all other cases it acts only on appeal, both as to matters of law and fact. We may say in short that, according to the scheme of the Constitution, afterwards slightly modified, the Supreme Court has exclusive jurisdiction in all questions of constitutional, international, and if I may venture the term, interstate law. All trials are to be by jury (except in cases of impeachment), and in the state where the crime was committed, or if it were not committed in a state (*e.g.*, if committed in a "territory"), then at such places as may be decreed by law. "Treason" (sec. III.) "against the United States shall consist only in levying war against them, or in adhering to their enemies, giving them aid and comfort;" it must be proved by two witnesses to some overt act, or by confession of the offender in open court. Congress declares the punishment of treason, but there is to be no corruption of blood, nor forfeiture, except during the life of the attainted person.

Some almost miscellaneous provisions, though some of them very important, follow (Art. IV. sec. I.). Full faith is declared due to all the acts, records, and judicial proceedings of the several states. "The citizens of each state shall be entitled to all the privileges and immunities of citizens in the several states" (§ 2). All fugitives from justice are to be mutually delivered up from state to state. "No person held to service or labour in one state under the law thereof" (*i.e.*, no slave) "shall, in consequence of any law or regulation therein, be discharged from such service or

ADMISSION OF NEW STATES. 37

labour, but shall be delivered up on claim of the party to whom such service or labour may be due" (§ 4).

Provision is made for the expansion of the Union. New states (sec. III.) may be admitted by Congress, but may not be formed or created within the jurisdiction of another state, nor by junction of two or more states or parts of states, without the consent of the legislatures of the states concerned, as well as of Congress. It is this provision, you will observe, which has till now prevented the Federal Government from recognising Western Virginia as a separate state under its new name of Kanawha. Congress may dispose of and make all needful rules and regulations respecting territory or other property of the United States, and nothing in the Constitution is to prejudice any claim of the United States, or of any particular state thereto. Those who penned this clause little foresaw the violent debates it would occasion, as to the limited or unlimited power of Congress to legislate over vast territories, larger than European empires.

The United States (sec. IV.) guarantee to every state in the Union a republican form of government, and protect each one against invasion, and, on the application of its legislature, or of its executive, where the legislature cannot be convened, against domestic violence.

Provision is made (Art. V.) for the amendment of the Constitution. If a majority of two-thirds in each house deem it necessary, amendments may be proposed by Congress; or, on the application of the legislatures of two-thirds of the states, it must call a convention for proposing amendments, which, when ratified by the legislatures of three-fourths of the states, or by conventions of the people in three-fourths of them, obtain force of law (with certain limitations as to the power of amendment, respecting the slave-trade, and direct taxation, prior to 1808). But no state is without its consent to be deprived of its equal suffrage in the senate. This power of amendment is alleged by the Southerners or their English advocates, as a main justification of secession, on the ground that in ten years[*] three-fourths of the states will be unanimous in seeking to amend the constitution, so as to destroy the slave-power.

After a provision adopting the debts and engagements of the Confederation, it is enacted (Art. VI. § 2), that the Constitution, the laws made in pursuance of it, and treaties concluded under the authority of the United States, shall be the law of the land, and that the judges in every state shall be bound thereby, "anything in the constitution or the laws of any state to the contrary notwithstanding." All senators (§ 3), representatives, members of state legislatures, executive and judicial officers, both of the United States and of the several states, are to be bound by oath or affirmation to support the Constitution; but no religious test for office is ever to be required.

---

[*] See Dr. Lempriere's "American Crisis Considered," p. 131.

We may as well consider at once the few amendments to the Constitution adopted not long afterwards. Most of them, except the first and three last, simply embody some provision of Magna Charta, of the Bill of Rights, or some rule of our common law.

Congress (Art. I.) is to make no laws respecting an establishment of religion, or prohibiting the free exercise thereof, abridging freedom of speech, or of the press, or the right of the people peaceably to assemble and petition Government for redress of grievances. The right of the people to keep and bear arms is not to be infringed (Art. II.); no soldier in time of peace is to be quartered on any premises without the owner's consent, or in war but as prescribed by law (Art. III.). There are to be no unreasonable searches or seizures; all warrants for such purposes are to be issued on probable cause, to be supported by oath or affirmation, and shall particularly describe the place to be searched, and the persons or things to be seized (Art. IV.). There are to be grand juries before trial for any capital or infamous crime, except in the land or naval forces, or in the Militia when on active service. No person is to be twice put in jeopardy of life or tried, nor forced to bear witness against himself in a criminal case, nor deprived of his life, liberty, or property, without due process of law, nor is private property to be taken for public use without compensation (Art. V.). In criminal prosecutions, there is to be a speedy and public trial by an impartial jury of the state and the district where the crime was committed; the accused is to be informed of the nature and cause of the accusation, to be confronted with the witnesses, to have a compulsory process for obtaining witnesses in his favour, and to have the assistance of counsel (Art. VI.). In common-law suits for a value exceeding twenty dollars, a jury is granted, and no fact tried by a jury is to be re-examined in a court of the United States, except according to the rules of the common law (Art. VII.). There is to be no excessive bail, no excessive fines, nor any cruel and unusual punishments (Art. VIII.). Very admirable provisions mostly, if honestly carried out, but which Judge Lynch, with his burnings alive, hangings, tarrings and featherings, and the like, has long since set at nought in the South, and sometimes in the West, and seems to be brushing aside now in the North itself.

The following provisions are somewhat insidious, and are pervaded by the ultra-democratic, states-rights doctrine.

By Art. IX. it is enacted that the enumeration in the Constitution of certain rights is not to be construed to deny or disparage others retained by the people. By Art. X. "the powers not delegated to the United States by the Constitution, nor prohibited by it to the states, are reserved to the states respectively, or to the people." By Art XI. the judicial power of the United States is not to extend to a suit in law or equity against a state by the citizens of another state, or the citizens or subjects of a foreign state. Art. XII. amends the provisions of the Constitution as to the election of President and Vice-President. I have given you the effect of it already.

Such is the Constitution of the United States—a document under which the government of the United States has been carried on, without interruption, from the 4th March, 1789, the date of the assembling of the first Congress, to the present crisis, a period of nearly three-quarters of a century. Except the few amendments I have mentioned, the very machinery of government has scarcely varied, the only alterations which have taken place consisting in the substitution of messages for the speeches in which the Presidents used at first to address the Congress, and in the addition of a few members to the cabinet as originally framed. Yet that Constitution, as we see now, has come to a dead-lock. Let us try to find out its weak place.

It is *not* weak, let Secessionists or their advocates write or say what they please, in establishing the nationality of the people of the United States, in asserting the supremacy of the Federal power, for all purposes connected with the welfare of the Union. Nothing but blind prejudice or sheer dishonesty can make Secession anything else than an open and positive violation of the Constitution. Take even that amendment which is expressly framed to guarantee the privileges of the states (Art. X.) Nothing is reserved to the states but " the powers not delegated to the United States by the Constitution, nor prohibited by it to the states." It does expressly prohibit to them the entering "into any treaty, alliance, or confederation," such as the so-called

"Southern Confederacy." It does expressly prohibit to them the granting "letters of marque and reprisal," such as those under which the "Sumter" and a host of such quasi-pirates are now scouring the seas. It does expressly prohibit to them the making "anything but gold and silver a tender," as the seceding states have done, in authorizing their banks everywhere to suspend specie payments. It does expressly prohibit to them the making of laws "impairing the obligation of contracts," as the seceding states have done, in forbidding the payment of debts due at the North. It does expressly prohibit to them the keeping troops or ships of war, such as the army that fought and won (though strangely) at Bull's Run. And, lest there should be any pretence that rights are reserved to the states, paramount to the express provisions of the Constitution, it is enacted that the Constitution shall be the law of the land, and that the judges in every state shall be bound thereby, "anything in the constitution or in the laws of any state to the contrary notwithstanding;" whilst all senators, representatives, members of state legislatures, executive and judicial officers of the states, are made to swear to support the Constitution. It is obvious that no rights inconsistent with the Constitution could possibly be reserved by the several states, as is alleged by some partisans to have been done, without violating this provision.

Do not, I pray you, treat as now superfluous the point we are considering. To some, I know, the discussion of the constitutional question of secession appears as valueless as the question of the rights of the Stuarts to the British crown. The secession, they say, is accomplished, or if it can be reversed, it must be by a reconquest, and the proof of the argument must be by the sword, not by law. Grant all this, if you please, with reference to the present secession. But upon the question of the right or wrong of secession turns the further question, whether *both* the American republics shall be ropes of sand, or only one. If secession be a right, then there is nothing to prevent either from splitting again and again. If it be a wrong, the one that proclaims it such, though it should fail in enforcing that proclamation by the sword, has yet a bond of union, a basis of nationality; the one that asserts it as a right, though successful for the time, is devoid of both.

The American Constitution, then, has not broken down through want of sufficient clearness in defining the functions of the central authority, nor yet through want of sufficient power to fulfil them. The lesson supplied by the history of the Confederation had been too sharp not to meet the necessity of this. It has, I believe, been seriously weakened by its undue distrust of the executive, and by its machinery of presidential election, both of which causes combined have tended at once (as the experience of the last thirty years nearly has proved) to thrust mediocrity forward, and to keep aloof the really foremost men of the time. It has, perhaps, been weakened still more by that exclusion of all office-holders from Congress, which morally decapitates every party in turn through the very consummation of its victory. Realise, if you can, the absurdity of such a rule, by imagining, not only Lord Palmerston and Mr. Gladstone, Lord Russell and Lord Westbury, but even to the very last Whig underling, now excluded from either House of Parliament; Lord Derby and Mr. Disraeli the undisputed rulers of their respective Houses, with no one pitted against them but Whig third-rates unfit for office, or better men who should hold it and have forgone it for the sole purpose of defending their official friends, and who, in any case, have to be crammed for the occasion, whenever the Government requires spokesmen, and are thus at all times rather counsel speaking from a brief than responsible organs of a policy; and lastly, the excluded Whig chiefs, when desirous of personal utterance, obliged to resort to all manner of irregular channels, public meetings, letters, answers to addresses, &c. Could you conceive of a machinery more calculated to lower at once both the Government and the Parliament? to destroy all harmony between them? to hamper and paralyse the really able and honest minister? to screen the dishonest one from public castigation? and at the same time to encourage the utmost virulence of cowardly slander against an unpopular one?

But the weakest point in the Constitution lies yet elsewhere. It lies in that truckling to the slave-power which is obvious in it, when one compares it with the "Declaration of Independence." It lies especially in that singular provision for what is termed "black" or "slave" representation, whereby, alone amongst all species of property, that in human flesh is made a source of political power.

At the time of the War of Independence, it is scarcely too much to say that the slave-trade and slavery were abhorred by every eminent mind throughout the Union, and were looked upon as death-doomed within a brief period. They were considered, as Jefferson's suppressed paragraphs in the "Declaration" show, as an accursed inheritance from the tyranny of the mother-country. The dangers of both were vividly enforced upon the minds of men by the appeals of the British to the negroes to rise against their masters,— appeals to which Virginia had replied by recalling her repeated attempts to abolish the slave-trade, and by declaring that "the present masters of negroes in Virginia would willingly, not only prevent any more negroes from losing their freedom, but restore it to such as had already unhappily lost it."* The slave-trade, as I have already shown, had been declared prohibited, without limit as to time, and Congress had even been memorialised for the abolition of slavery.† So far was the North from entertaining its present prejudices as to colour, that free negroes served in the revolutionary armies, shoulder to shoulder with the white man, and this in spite of the opposition of Rutledge of South Carolina, and other Southern delegates.‡ For some years after shaking off the yoke of the

* Bancroft, vol. vii. pp. 136-7.
† *Ibid.*, pp. 202-3.
‡ *Ibid.*, pp. 60, 141-2.

mother-country, the same feelings continued to prevail. We have seen that no provision for the recovery of fugitive slaves was contained in the Articles of Confederation. The proclamation of human equality, of the right of all men to life and liberty, contained in the " Declaration of Independence," was adopted, with slight variations in the words, in most of the Northern State constitutions, and even in that of Virginia. The true bearing of those words was shown to have been felt in Massachussetts, when they were judicially construed to have abolished slavery within that state (1783). Connecting still more expressly political with civil liberty, Pennsylvania " in justice to persons heretofore denominated negro and mulatto slaves, and in grateful commemoration of our own happy deliverance from that state of unconditional submission, to which Britain would have reduced us," emancipated her slave population (1784). Connecticut emancipated her slaves to be born after a given date, at fifteen (1784). Yet more striking is it that, on the accidental absence of a single delegate, turned the question of the absolute arrest of any future development of the slave power. The story is so curious a one that it is worth while giving its detail.

Many of the states possessed large tracts of land either uninhabited, or thinly inhabited, by white settlers, or covered by a squatter population, little observant of the claims of property, or claiming under contested titles. In some instances whole communities had thus sprung up, as that of Kentucky in the west of Virginia, and that of Vermont in the north of New York; and the history of Vermont's struggle for independence,* in particular, forms a lively passage in the colonial history of America. These new and as yet unrecognised communities had all sided with the popular party in the revolutionary struggle, and had contributed their share of heroes to its annals. When it was over, it became necessary to close old feuds, and one mode of doing so was by cession of unoccupied or disputed territory from the states to the Union at large. Virginia, in particular, ceded over to the Union the whole of her North-West territory; and a resolution was proposed the same day (11th March, 1784,) by Mr. Jefferson, that "after the year 1800," there should be "neither slavery nor involuntary servitude" in any of the states into which the territory of the United States should hereafter be formed. This was in the old Congress, under the Articles of Confederation, where the states were represented by delegates, a majority of states (not of delegates) being required, and no state vote counting unless both its delegates concurred. Of twenty-three delegates present, sixteen were for the resolution, seven against. The sixteen votes for, represented six states; the seven against, three; the vote of North Carolina being neutralized; Delaware and Georgia were not represented. New Jersey finally voted for the resolution by a single dele-

---

* See Elliott's "New England History," vol. ii. pp. 110 and following.

gate, his colleague (who agreed with him in opinion) having been called away by some necessary business. The resolution thus failed, and through the absence of a single New Jersey delegate, it may be said, slavery was enabled to cross the Alleghanies, behind which it should otherwise have remained confined.*

From this moment, it may be said, dates the growth of the slave-power. By 1787 an ordinance is passed, which, in later days, was inveighed against as excessive, prohibiting slavery indeed in the territories; but only north-west of the Ohio river. Then comes the Constitution, which virtually admits slavery without the name, with its provisions for the representation of slave property, for the recovery of fugitive slaves. The want of this latter provision, under the Confederation, we are expressly told,† "was felt as a serious inconvenience by the slaveholding states, since, in many states, no aid whatever would be allowed to the owners, and sometimes they met with open resistance." The principle of representation requires now our special consideration.

When we say that slave property is represented under the Constitution of the United States, it is not meant that a slave-owner votes in respect of his slaves, as with us a freeholder in respect of his freehold. Had this been the rule, I believe the mere influx of white population in the slave-states would long since have

* See Palfrey's "Chapter of American History," Boston, 1852.
† Story, vol. iii. pp. 676-8.

abolished it. No; the mischief of the rule is far more subtle. Since, for the purpose of reckoning the amount of population sufficient to confer the right of representation, three-fifths of the slaves are added to the free, it follows that every white man in a slave-state acquires a collective interest in the existence of slavery. Suppose 300,000 be the figure of population required to return a representative, then, whilst 300,000 freemen of the North are required for the purpose, 30,000 Southerners, owning collectively 450,000 slaves, or fifteen on an average (many plantations employing hundreds) are their equals politically, and every " poor white," however ignorant and miserable, has his vanity gratified by standing at the ballot-box the equal of his richest slave-holding neighbour, whilst each of them is equally invested with ten times the political power of the Northerner, be he never so steady, never so wealthy, never so able. But if, again, the slave-holders, to whom, in process of time, the very neighbourhood of a non-slave-holder of their own colour becomes an eyesore and a danger, succeed in a district in buying or shutting out all poor whites, they may come to wield as one man the whole political power of that district for the purposes of their own slave-holding interest.

Nor does the mischief stop here. The provision as to the representation of slave-property grated upon the feelings of the North. To reconcile the non-slave-holding states to it, the apportionment of direct taxation was fixed on the same basis, and in the same clause.

But thereby two-fifths of all slave-property became exempted from direct taxation. Now, direct taxation has always been impatiently felt by the American people. In forty years it was only resorted to three times (1798, 1813, 1815). Least of all could the North feel in favour of it, seeing that the South must enjoy such a handsome discount upon it, in exact proportion to its wealth in slaves. Thus the South obtained the constant benefit of the three-fifths rule as respects representation, but escaped the burthen of direct taxation.* What has been the consequence? The machinery of the United States government has had to depend almost exclusively upon indirect taxation. The North, by the force of things, has become manufacturing; the south, agricultural. Thus import duties have fallen more heavily on the South, while the North has had an interest at the same time in raising them. The crack in the American constitution, produced by slavery, has been widened by American tariffs, till at last we have seen Pennsylvanian iron-masters take indecent opportunity of the present fearful crisis to pass a piece of Protectionist legislation for their own advantage. It should be stated, indeed, that the South was mainly reconciled to certain provisions in the Constitution, especially to the power of regulating trade by a bare majority, through the provision as to slave-representation.† Thus, complain as it may of

---

* See Story, vol. ii. pp. 107 and following.
† Story, vol. ii. p. 113.

Northern tariffs, it has had its pound of flesh. That the South has grossly exaggerated the mischief to it of a high tariff, I shall perhaps be able to show you hereafter.

At the date of the Constitution, indeed, the dangers to be apprehended either from jarring commercial interests, or from slavery, were yet far. Looking back from the Constitution to the Declaration of Independence, we may see that the spirit of freedom was losing ground; that peace, by lulling to sleep the more generous impulses, by removing the dangers of slave insurrections, by increasing the value of slave-property, was beginning to give a new direction to public feeling. Yet when we look back from the present day to the Constitution, we are struck by its difference of tone from anything we see now. It is morbidly ashamed, as you have observed, of using the words "slave" and "slavery," which the new Confederate States, copying mostly, word for word, the old Constitution, have now inserted, unabashed, in their own. It never speaks of the slave as a property, but as a person; the only right of property which it recognises in its fugitive slave clause being one in the *services* of the man, not in the *man* himself. Evidently, in the view of the framers of the Constitution, slavery was still only a disgraceful sore, to be hidden, as far as possible, till it was healed.

LECTURE III.

FROM THE CONSTITUTION TO THE MISSOURI COMPROMISE (1789—1820)—THE INDIAN WARS—PARTIES—THE PURCHASE OF LOUISIANA—THE WAR WITH ENGLAND.

(Washington, 1789-97; J. Adams, 1797—1801; Jefferson, 1801-9; Madison, 1809-17; Monroe.)

ON the 4th of March, 1789, the first Congress met under the Constitution. The first President of the United States was the man to whom all public opinion pointed as the one who should fill the post. George Washington, the Virginian, born in 1732, stands out in the history of the world as one of the very purest characters that it has to show to us. Leaving school before sixteen, at all times unacquainted with the classical languages, with never more than a smattering of French, he began life as a surveyor, and surveyed for Lord Fairfax his wild lands in the Alleghanies. Even at school he had been fond of playing at war; at nineteen he was commissioned as "major" of a frontier district, and had eventually to visit and inspect a division comprising several counties. At twenty-one we find him sent as commissioner to confer with a French officer on the Ohio. At twenty-two he made his first campaign, as second in command, against the French, became commander by the death of his chief, and received the thanks of the House of Burgesses of his colony for his operations. At three-and-twenty, in a disastrous campaign of General Braddock's against the French, he distinguished himself by his wise counsel and determined bravery. Then we find him appointed to reorganize the provincial troops, and projecting a chain of forts. At twenty-five (having succeeded to a brother's property at Mount Vernon), he threw up his commission as commander of the provincial troops, and retired into private life. We now see him marrying a wealthy widow, sitting in the House of Burgesses, practising hospitality, exporting his produce, importing such goods as he required, keeping his own books, sought for as arbitrator. From the year 1769, being consequently then thirty-seven years of age, he takes part in the resistance of the colonists. In 1775 he is elected Commander-in-chief by Congress. As such he wins no great victories, performs no dashing feats of war, His greatness is shown by doing much with little, organising armies without money and without arms, keeping the enemy at bay without powder; always ready to profit by opportunities, never quailing under reverses, and so by degrees inspiring universal confidence. Naturally slow in forming his opinions, he had entered into the struggle without at all realizing its probable issues. "When I first took the command of the army," he has said himself (1776) "I abhorred the idea of independence." But by the time he thus spoke he was " fully convinced that nothing else will save us." Having carried that war to a successful issue, through the surrender of Lord Cornwallis, he was ready, on the demand of Congress, to disband his army after the peace. Unpaid, unclothed, unprovided for a day's maintenance, the victorious troops were dismissed by their Commander-in-chief. And now he was invested with the highest office in the state, which, of his own free-will only he was to lay down. John Adams was Vice-President under him. His first act was to renounce all personal emoluments, beyond the repayment of such expenses as the public good might require. Jefferson was his secretary of state,—as we should say, his prime minister.

The events of Washington's Presidency (the term of which was renewed in 1793), are very few. As we read his addresses (the form of messages had not been yet adopted), we find but little variation in the topics they treat of. New states are admitted, Vermont, 1791; Kentucky, 1792; the latter to be followed by Tennessee, 1796. There are treaties with European powers, (with England particularly, 1795); wars and treaties with Indian tribes. Public credit and prosperity revive and develope themselves; the home debts are funded, to a great extent paid off, partly out of surplus revenue, partly by means of new loans contracted on more favourable terms,—Holland and Belgium being the great storehouses of accessible capital abroad. Capital accumulates at home; the third annual address records the foundation of a Bank of the United States, and that the subscriptions to it were completed in one day (1791). Means are taken for organising the defence of the frontier, and relations of trade with the Indian tribes. Incessant recommendations are made to establish the militia on a satisfactory footing, to establish standards of weights and measures, to develope the postal service and post-roads, which latter indeed grow apace year by year. Trade is expanding, and requires regulation; in the Mediterranean in particular, protection against Barbaresque pirates; some amount of war-navy has already to be created for this purpose. There is a growing tide of immigration from Europe, and laws for the naturalisation of foreigners are required. A consular establishment has to be organised; the judicial system to be improved; a uniform currency to be introduced; the sale of waste lands to be regulated. The first census is carried out, and gives a population bordering upon four millions. The district of Columbia is ceded to the Federal power by the states of Maryland and Virginia, and the city of Washington laid out.

Strange as it may seem to us now, the great business of the American people at this period was really to establish their supremacy over the Indians, and obtain from them room for development. I believe no greater mistake can be made than that often committed by travellers of the present day, who, finding the Red Indians nothing but a set of degraded savages, imagine they have never been anything else. On the contrary, all early accounts show clearly that, however far behind their brethren of Mexico and Peru, the Indians of North-Western America were, two centuries and a half ago, in a far superior condition to anything we now find. Strachey's "Historie of Travaile into Virginia Britannia," reprinted by the Hakluyt Society, exhibits them to us as a settled people, semi-agricultural,* having " square plots of cleared ground round their houses," planting their fields in the spring, and living part of the year chiefly on the produce of their cultivation, at other times chiefly on the fish caught in their rivers. They had temples " sometimes twenty foot broad and a hundred in length," containing various images. They had " such government as that their magistrates for good commanding, and their people for due subjection and obeying, excel many places that would be counted civil." There were regular gradations of authority; so that one of the noted chiefs of early days, Powhattan, is described as an emperor ruling over many kings. Nor had the lapse of nearly two centuries, at the time we are speaking of, erased many of the main features of this picture. In the early wars of the newly emancipated American colonists with the Indians, we find Indian sovereigns ruling over vast tracts of country, bringing large bodies of men into the field, often engaging the Americans with success and extorting concessions from them. In the war of 1790 with the Indians, North-West of the Ohio, the Americans suffered two repulses,—at the first encounter their militia fled at the very appearance of the enemy. The Creeks,

---

* Tocqueville, in treating of them as mere hunters, simply repeats a vulgar error.

under the guidance of a celebrated chief named Alexander McGillivray, who had been brought up by a Missionary, and knew not only English but Latin, saw their opponents solicit peace of them, and obtained the relinquishment of a large territory claimed by the state of Georgia. In the following year (1791), a still more disastrous defeat was inflicted by them on the white men. The numbers engaged were nearly equal, 1400 on the American side, 1000 to 1500 on the Indian. Out of the American force, thirty-eight commissioned officers were killed, 593 non-commissioned officers and privates killed and missing, twenty-one commissioned officers and 242 non-commissioned officers and privates wounded; in other words, about two-thirds of the American force were put *hors de combat*. It was only three years later (20th of August, 1794), that a decisive victory was obtained (near the river Miamis) by the Americans, which may be said to have broken the Indian power. The forces in the field were 3100 on the American side, about 2000 on the Indian, but only about 900 Americans were actually engaged. Even here the advance battalion was compelled to retreat in the first instance, and a charge was required to carry the Indian position. After the victory, the Americans burnt all Indian villages and standing corn within fifty miles of the river, and laid all the country waste. It is from this period chiefly that date the treaties with the Indians and cessions of land by them, which ended in their final removal.

I believe that nothing was further from Washington's

mind than to oppress or circumvent the Indian tribes. He knew them well by personal intercourse; he had fought them, and fought with them. In all his addresses there is to be traced a constant solicitude for their welfare. He is always anxious to avoid coercive measures or to terminate the use of them. He is perfectly aware of what the Indians have to suffer from lawless white men. He denounces the "wanton murders" committed by citizens of Georgia on Indian hunting parties. He is urgent for "more adequate provisions for restraining the commission of outrages upon the Indians, without which all pacific plans must prove nugatory." Again he urges that the steps heretofore taken for protecting the Indians "from the violence of the lawless part of our frontier inhabitants" are insufficient. His darling plan is the establishment of commercial relations with them through salaried government agents. Next to a "rigorous execution of justice on the violators of peace," nothing, he thinks, is more likely to conciliate their attachment. But such trade "ought to be conducted without fraud, without extortion, with constant and plentiful supplies, with a ready market for the commodities of the Indians, and a stated price for what they give in payment and receive in exchange." Of course, his plan failed eventually altogether.

In addition, however, to what I have mentioned, there is one somewhat remarkable event of internal history to be chronicled during Washington's administration;— nothing less than an insurrection. In order to raise a revenue, duties had been laid (1790) on distilled spirits.

Already, in his annual address of 1791, the President had to announce that there was discontent in some places with the tax. By 1792 he had to report that there was opposition to the collection of duties; that he had had to issue a proclamation against all unlawful combinations and proceedings tending to obstruct the operation of the excise law; that he had taken measures to prosecute offenders. Two years later he had to issue, not one, but two proclamations (Aug. 7 and Sept. 25, 1794) against actual insurrection. In his annual address of that year he had to report that in four counties of Pennsylvania there had been riots, and societies formed to resist the law; that the United States' marshal, in endeavouring to enforce the law, had been fired upon, detained, and forced to renounce the serving of processes West of the Alleghanies; that the inspector's house had been attacked and burned, and that the militia had had to be called out. We learn from other sources that the insurgents mustered by the thousand; that delegates met to the number of 200, not only from the Western counties of Pennsylvania, where resistance had first begun, but from another Pennsylvanian, and even from one Virginian county. However, by the appointment of commissioners, by conferences, and last, not least, by the marching of 15,000 troops into Western Pennsylvania, the mischief was put down. The insurgents laid down their arms, eighteen were tried for treason, but not convicted; and the tumults subsided, having cost the lives of three men,—one a military officer.

In respect to foreign affairs, what is most to be observed is the breaking out of the French revolutionary war, and the advantages and dangers at once which it presaged to America. So long as the United States retained their neutrality, they were sure to see a large portion of the trade of the world pass into their hands. But neutrals are always sure to excite the jealousy of both contending parties, and to receive knocks eventually from both, more or less. When this takes place, their only resource, short of war, is to cut off their own trade, and lay an embargo on their own shipping. Accordingly, we see Washington proclaiming American neutrality, 1793 (April 22), and the next year a thirty days' embargo is laid on, though, it is true, one mainly directed against the ravages of Algerine corsairs.

But the Continental war not only affected the foreign trade of America—it added to the divisions of parties at home. The American people were at this period divided between those who, looking more to community of origin, leant rather to cultivating the friendship of England, and those who resenting, above all, English misgovernment, and grateful to France for her support during the revolutionary war, preferred her friendship to that of the mother-country. The former party, the Federal, looked chiefly, as respects home-politics, to the strengthening of the Federal authority. The English constitution was avowedly their model, so far as it could be applied to circumstances so novel as that of the young republic; they promoted the establishment of a national bank; they were accused of tending to hereditary monarchy through a central despotism. The other party, then called the Republican party (a name, you must observe, which has entirely changed sides in modern days, and is now applied to a party the true successor of the old Federal one), were full of admiration for the French revolution; but, strange to say, as respects internal politics, they were entirely false to its lead, taking their stand upon the states'-rights doctrine, whereas it is evident that the Convention only saved France through a tremendous concentration of power at the seat of authority; they were also strongly opposed to a national bank. Washington himself, by habit and by the tendency of his mind, sided naturally with the Federalists, of whom, however, Colonel Hamilton, the Secretary to the Treasury, must be considered rather as the head; Jefferson, on the other hand, heading the Republicans. The latter, of course, appealing as it did to the best and the worst passions,—gratitude to France, and vindictiveness towards England,—was the popular party. The lawless raids upon British territory, the buccaneering expeditions by sea, which had disgraced the history of the Constitution, had not entirely ceased; and in 1792 we find Washington recommending measures for preventing "those aggressions by our citizens on the territory of other nations, and other infractions on the law of nations," which, as he said, furnished just subjects for complaint, and endangered peace. Relying apparently upon popular support, Genet, the French republican minister, proceeded openly to organise, from the United States, military operations against England, treating at the same time the Federal authorities in the most overbearing manner. It was his proceedings, more especially, that Washington had in view in his message for 1793, when he urged that decisive measures were required, "when individuals within the United States array themselves in hostility against the powers at war, enter upon military expeditions or enterprises, ... or usurp and exercise judicial authority within the United States." Already he foresaw war in the future. "The United States," he says, "ought not to indulge a persuasion that, contrary to the order of human events, they will for ever keep at a distance those painful appeals to arms with which the history of every other nation abounds. There is a rank due to the United States among nations which will be withheld, if not absolutely lost, by the reputation of weakness."

His last appeal is, however, against domestic divisions. Re-elected once, he declined to serve a third term, and no President of the United States has ventured since to aspire to a longer duration of power than the "Father of his country" (so Washington was termed) was content with. In his "farewell address" (September 17, 1796), he dilated upon the value of the Union. "The unity of government," he said, "which constitutes you one people is also now dear to you. As this is the point in your political fortress against which the batteries of internal and external enemies will be most actively and constantly (though often covertly and insidiously) directed, it is of infinite moment that you should properly estimate the immense value of your national union to your collective and individual happiness—indignantly frowning upon the first dawning of every attempt to alienate any portion of our country from the rest, or to enfeeble the sacred ties which now link together the various parts. To the efficiency and permanency of your union a government for the whole is indispensable. No alliances, however strict, between the parts can be an adequate substitute. The Constitution which at any time exists, until changed by an explicit and deliberate act of the whole people, is sacredly obligatory upon all."

He left his country in a state of growth hitherto unexampled. The exports, which were twenty-six millions of dollars in 1793, had risen to upwards of forty-seven millions in 1795. The first parcel of cotton of American growth had been exported in 1791. The first vessel had cleared from America to the East Indies in 1795, starting from Carolina. Public debt to a large extent had been paid off. Much new territory had been settled; Ohio in particular, 1788. State improvements had generally kept pace with Federal ones. The magnificent American public-school system had taken root, the legislature of Massachusetts, for instance, requiring every town of two hundred families to support a grammar-school (1789).

John Adams, of Massachusetts, the late Vice-President, succeeded Washington in the Presidency (1791). The candidate of the Federal party, he was opposed by Jefferson, who became Vice-President.

Party spirit already ran so high, that, as we find from Jefferson's correspondence,* there was already talk of secession. His words in reference to such a notion—he being the chief of the vanquished party—deserve to be recorded. "If," wrote he to Mr. J. Taylor (1st June, 1798), "on a temporary superiority of the one party the other is to resort to scission of the Union, no Federal government can ever exist. If, to rid ourselves of the present rule of Massachusetts and Connecticut, we break the Union, will the evil stop there? Will our natures be changed? Are we not men still to the South of them, and with all the passions of men? Immediately we shall see a Pennsylvania and a Virginia party arise in the residuary confederacy, and the public mind will be distracted with the same party spirit. What a game, too, will the one party have in their hands by eternally threatening their neighbours that, unless they do so and so, they will join their northern neighbours! If we reduce our union to Virginia and North Carolina, immediately the conflict will be established between the representatives of these two states, and they will end by breaking into their simple units." Prophetic words, which have yet to receive their complete fulfilment.

Three years younger than Washington (born 1735), John Adams, a farmer's son, who had taught in a country school, then practised at the Boston bar, had taken a prominent part in the civil direction of the

* Vol. iii. pp. 400, 401.

War of Independence; had seconded the motion for drawing up a Declaration of Independence; had proceeded as commissioner to Paris, as ambassador to Holland, as first ambassador from the United States to Great Britain, had remained in England from 1785 to 1787, and had published during this period "A Defence of the Constitution and Government of the United States," in 3 vols. 8vo. It would be tedious to dwell on the events of his presidentship in detail. For the most part they do but continue those of his predecessor's term of office. Its history is chiefly filled with a quarrel with the French "Directoire." Presuming on the past services of the French monarchy to the United States, the French republic assumed the most arrogant airs towards the former. The American Minister, Pinckney, was expelled; American vessels were captured. To avoid a rupture, new envoys were sent; they were not acknowledged, and the needy traffickers of the "Directoire" went so far as to demand money as a preliminary to negotiations (1798). The pride of the Americans was roused by this proceeding: "Millions for defence, not a cent for tribute," was the common sentiment. Corps of Artillery and Engineers were added to the permanent establishment; additional troops were raised, and above all, a vigorous impulse was given to the navy, so that a French frigate was taken by an American one (1797). The rulers of the French republic now became more civil; new American envoys were respectfully received, and finally a convention was concluded

(30th September, 1800), which restored friendly relations between the two countries. The additional military forces were disbanded, but the navy remained, and the work of fortifying the coasts and harbours was entered upon; both navy and fortifications, be it observed, being no less necessary against the Americans themselves, than against foreigners, for in his address of 1797 (May 16), Mr. Adams had to record the discreditable fact that the greater part of the cruisers which harassed the American trade, were built, and some equipped, in the United States, while American citizens abroad had equally fitted out or commanded privateers.

The administration of John Adams was marked, like that of Washington, by some resistance to taxation. In Pennsylvania, that old focus of discontent, the valuations and surveys, required for a direct tax laid on in 1798, were opposed, and a military force had to be employed. But order was restored this time without bloodshed; the offenders were brought to trial, and some of them convicted. No new States were admitted during Mr. Adams's term of office, but the territories of Mississippi and Indiana were organised into governments. Population and prosperity still followed their onward course. The second census showed a population of 5,305,482. The shipping of America, which in 1792 had been somewhat over 800,000 tons, had risen to 939,000 in 1800; whilst the war navy numbered forty-two vessels, mounting 950 guns.

But the one event which overshadows Adams's administration is the death of Washington, which took place on the 14th December, 1799, he being then sixty-seven years old. A man perhaps unique in history, who seems to have been moulded by God for the express purpose of showing how one can be great without genius, by the mere might of pure purpose, coupled with common sense and resolute will. Our own great Duke resembles him in many points, but with more promptness and vigour on the one hand, and more narrowness and obstinacy on the other. Each fills his own allotted place in history; the one as the ruler of his nation, the other as the greatest of servants in his own. We probably all of us remember how the whole English people mourned for Wellington. For Washington the American people mourned thirty days. But his place was never more to be filled by one " like-minded."

He did not live to see what, in his last annual address, Mr. Adams was able to record, when he congratulated "the people of the United States on the assembling of Congress at the permanent seat of their Government"—Congress having sat hitherto at Philadelphia, and removing now to the Capitol, at Washington,—and Congress itself "on the prospect of a residence not to be changed." He called upon them to consider the question of the exercise of their powers over the district of Columbia, viewing Washington "as the capital of a great nation." Such words sound strange in our ears just now, when the first great point at stake under Mr. Lincoln's presidency has been the defence of Washington against Southern aggression.

John Adams held the President's chair for a single term of office. Many of his measures,—those for direct taxation and internal duties,—an alien bill,— the increase of the regular army,—the protraction of the Indian war, &c., had made him unpopular. His former competitor, Jefferson, was elected by a majority of one over him (1800)—owing, in fact, his election, for want of a sufficient majority, to the House of Representatives, and elected even thus only at the thirty-sixth ballot. A man, who, perhaps more than any other, has contributed to mould the American mind. Born to an independent fortune, well-educated, he was also quick-minded, impetuous, rhetorical; kind of heart, yet sharp in language; prone to the heats of partizanship, yet capable of retaining the friendship of his political enemies; full of noble impulses and generous theories, yet incapable of carrying out either to their logical and practical conclusions; a slave-owner, professing to abhor slavery, yet who left slaves behind him, even, it is said, of his own blood,—he was unquestionably the most brilliant of American statesmen. He was quicker, however, and more effective with his pen than he was in speech, and except the "Inaugural" (which has always remained customary), he substituted the form of the message for that of address, in all his subsequent communications with Congress,—a practice which has been followed ever since. The Vice-President, during Jefferson's first term of office, was Aaron

Burr,—a somewhat singular personage, of whom we shall presently hear more.

Jefferson's Inaugural Address (4th of March, 1801), whilst it exhibits fully the temper of the man, should also supply many a lesson to his Southern admirers of the present day. "During the contest of opinion through which we have passed," he said, "the animation of discussion and of exertions has sometimes worn an aspect which might impose on strangers unused to think freely, and to speak and write what they think. But this being now decided by the voice of the nation, announced according to the rules of the Constitution, all will of course arrange themselves under the will of the law, and unite in common efforts for the common good. All too will bear in mind this sacred principle, that though the will of the majority is in all cases to prevail, that will, to be rightful, must be reasonable; that the minority possess their equal rights, which equal laws must protect, and to violate which would be oppression. . . . If there would be any among us who would wish to dissolve this Union, or to change its representative form, let them stand undisturbed, as monuments of the safety with which error of opinion may be tolerated, where reason is left free to combat it." After saying that he believed the American government to be "the strongest government on earth," the "only one where every man at the call of the laws would fly to the standard of the law, and would meet invasions of the public order as his own personal concern," he went on to enumerate, among the objects of American policy, as he conceived it, "equal and exact justice to all men . . . peace, commerce, and honest friendship with all nations; entangling alliances with none; the support of the State governments in all their rights, as the most competent administrations for our domestic concerns, and the surest bulwarks against anti-republican tendencies, the preservation of the general government in its whole constitutional vigour, as the sheet-anchor of our peace at home and safety abroad. . . . *absolute acquiescence in the decisions of the majority, the vital principle of republics, from which there is no appeal but to force, the vital principle and immediate parent of despotism.*" . . .

You must consider this address as being the triumphant manifesto of the so-called Republican majority, directed against the Federal party, with its suspected leanings to monarchy. What would the great Virginian leader of 1801 have said if he could have foreseen that sixty years later his beloved Southerners, instead of adhering to that "absolute acquiescence in the decisions of the majority, the vital principle of republics," would wholly set at nought "the voice of the nation, announced according to the rules of the Constitution," and would make the very expression of that voice the ground of seceding from the "general government," the "sheet-anchor," as he termed it, of peace at home? To put such a question is enough to show how the tone of public feeling in the United States has retrograded in the course of a couple of generations.

Jefferson set a bad example, which has been but too well followed of late years, in effecting sweeping removals from office. His plea for doing so was that Adams had filled all offices exclusively with his own partizans, and that he found no subordinates whom he could trust. New brooms sweep clean; and undoubtedly Jefferson seems to have infused at once economy, and a new vigour into the administration, and to have worthily filled his double term of office. Internal taxation was dispensed with ; continual payments out of surplus revenue were made on account of the principal of the debt. Peace was concluded from the first with the Indians, and large cessions of land were repeatedly obtained from the different tribes ; thus, to quote one instance only, the Kaskaskias ceded a tract of country along the course of the Mississippi to, and up, the Ohio river, which is described as " among the most fertile within our limits." The state of Ohio, now one of the most populous in the Union, was admitted in 1802. A more momentous event in the internal history of the Union was the purchase of Louisiana (1803), till then a French colony, though with conflicting claims of Spain over it. The Constitution, evidently, never contemplated the acquisition of foreign territory by purchase, and Jefferson himself, at the first aspect of the plan, recoiled from it as unconstitutional. However, the advantage of securing for the United States the course of the Mississippi was obvious, and for fifteen millions of dollars, payable in fifteen years, this vast territory, with slavery planted in it, was secured. As if to point the way for future extensions of territory, Lewis and Clarke (1804) explored the course of the Missouri to the west, and descended the Columbia to the Pacific, on which the short-lived settlement of Astoria was founded (1811), whilst Lieutenant Pike ascended the Mississippi to its source. Already lawless invaders from America combined to harass and occupy the Spanish coast, so that a proclamation had to be issued by the President against military expeditions to the Spanish territory. Such was, indeed, the ostensible purpose of one of the most singular, and still perhaps doubtful events in American history, Aaron Burr's conspiracy. Colonel Aaron Burr, who had somewhat distinguished himself in the revolutionary war, and had been elected Vice-President during Jefferson's first term of office, obtained a further unenviable notoriety in 1804, by killing, in a duel, Col. Hamilton, the ablest statesman of the Federal party. In 1807, this ex-Vice-President was arrested for conspiracy. His objects were, as Jefferson stated in a special message to Congress, first, to divide the Union by the chain of the Alleghanies; second, to attack Mexico, under pretext of a purchase of land. The scheme was to be entered on by an attempt on New Orleans. His arrest, however, was too hasty; for want of proof of any overt act he was released, and this premature Jeff. Davis sank for the future out of notice. Thus ended the first attempt at secession.

Whilst the area of slave-soil was increased by the purchase of Louisiana, on the other hand, the slave-trade, under the American flag, was put an end to. In his yearly message of 1806, Jefferson congratulated Congress on the approach of the period when the citizens of the Union might be withdrawn "from all further participation in those violations of human rights which have been so long continued on the unoffending inhabitants of Africa, and which the morality, the reputation, and the best interests of our country have long been eager to promote." Legislative measures were taken accordingly, and on the 1st of January, 1808, the American (foreign) slave-trade ceased. Jefferson did not foresee that by the impetus thus given to the internal slave-trade, the States whose soil became gradually exhausted by slave cultivation would become the great breeders of slaves for the others, so that eventually his own Virginia, where he and his contemporaries had so openly denounced slavery, would join in tearing up the Union over which he presided, to join a Confederacy of which, as its Vice-President, Mr. Stephens, has publicly announced, slavery is to be the corner-stone. In the meanwhile, we should not overlook the fact of a rebellion of the coloured people in Virginia itself (1801), when, under the command of one "General Gabriel," but armed only with scythes, they attempted to take the town of Richmond, the capital of the State. They were dispersed by the militia, General Gabriel and their other chiefs tried and hanged; from which time a "public guard" was always kept on foot in the town.

Although peace was one of the professed objects of his administration, Jefferson had to conduct the first foreign war of the United States, and must have been very glad that his predecessor had created to his hand that navy, against the cost of which he and his party had clamoured. The war in question was one with the Barbaresque state of Tripoli. I need not give you its details; there was a naval action or two, a bombardment, a land expedition, a pretender set up, and then discarded, and lastly a peace (1805), which seems to me to have left things much as they were, although we are told it was considered more honourable than any concluded for a century by a Christian power with the Barbaresques.

But a more formidable contest was looming in the distance. The wars of the first French empire were at their height. America was the only maritime nation of the civilized world that was beyond the reach of coercion, or of an influence equivalent to coercion, on the part of the two great belligerents. Her trade was enormously increasing, and she was fast becoming the foremost carrier of the world, whilst her production was increasing in like manner. South Carolina alone, in 1801, exported 14,304,045 dollars' worth, including 8,000,000 lbs. of cotton. American ships were the natural refuge, not only of almost all the peaceful commerce of Europe, but of all seamen,—including, of course, many English,—who preferred peace to war, and sought to escape the English press-gang. Nor was America over-scrupulous in encouraging the transfer of their services to herself. Naturalization as an American citizen was a cheap and easy process; American ships were accused of openly stimulating desertion. We, on the other hand,—using the only efficient means at our command, as an insular nation, rich in ships, but comparatively poor in men, towards crippling our enemy by cutting off his trade,—could not but look askance on this prosperous neutral commerce which was daily developing itself under our eyes. Straining every nerve to multiply our seamen, we could not but look with covetousness on these crews of men, kindred to ourselves in blood, in language, in seamanship, in hardihood, even when not, as they frequently were in great measure, born actually on our shores and trained upon our decks. Hence, among other sore subjects between America and ourselves during the war, the English claim to search for deserters and impress seamen. England claimed this by virtue of a royal prerogative. The Sovereign, she said, has a right to the allegiance of his subjects, especially in time of war; they cannot throw off that allegiance. She claimed, therefore, without violation of a neutral flag, the right to take British seamen from on board any neutral ship. And as the distinction is often difficult to draw between a British seaman and an American one,—and that distinction was far less marked half a century ago than it is now,—and naval officers are not necessarily the best and coolest of judges,—and in time of war especially, they would always be strongly tempted to take an able seaman wherever they found him,—it followed that, by mistakes which I fear were too often willing ones, American sailors were constantly being impressed and compelled to serve on board the British fleet. As early as 1793 (22nd December) we find Washington, always moderate towards England, complaining of her for having violated American rights "by searching vessels and impressing seamen within our acknowledged jurisdiction," and even "by entire crews in the West Indies."* In the short period of nine months, from July, 1796, to 13th April, 1797, Mr. King, the American minister in London, had 271 applications from seamen claiming to be Americans, of whom eighty-six were actually discharged as such, thirty-seven had been detained as British, and no answer had been returned as to the remaining 148. Raw lads just entered on ship board were impressed before landing even, and had to serve for years before they could obtain their freedom. Two nephews of Washington himself were impressed on their return from England. Altogether, it was reckoned that, before the end of the great Continental war, more than 1000 American-born seamen were serving as pressed men on board English ships.

But the event which brought this question home to the feelings of the whole American people, was the unfortunate affair of the "Leopard" and "Chesapeake." On the 22nd June, 1807, the American frigate "Chesapeake," imperfectly armed and equipped, was standing off to sea from Hampton Roads for a cruise in the Mediterranean. The commander of the British brig "Leopard," under orders from Vice-Admiral Berkeley,

---

* Washington's "Correspondence," by Sparks, vol. xi. p. 100.

Commander-in-Chief of the North American station, to search all American vessels for deserters from certain specified frigates, sent to request leave to search the "Chesapeake" accordingly, offering at the same time equal facilities for searching his own ship. The American Commodore, Barron, replied that he had no knowledge of having any English deserters; that particular instructions had been given not to ship any, and that he could not allow his crew to be mustered by any other officer. The "Leopard" now engaged the "Chesapeake," which offered but slight resistance. Three men were killed on board of her, the Commodore, a midshipman, eight seamen and marines slightly, and eight severely wounded, whilst no blood was spilt on the "Leopard;" and Commodore Barron struck his flag. The commander of the "Leopard" boarded this too easy prize, took out four men as deserters, and left her. Of the four men thus taken, who, strange to say, did not belong to any of the frigates specified in the Vice-Admiral's order, one was really an Englishman, and was hanged; one was a Marylander born, another from Massachusetts, a third claimed also to be from Maryland: all the three latter were men of colour; one had been a slave; two had been pressed from an American brig in the Bay of Biscay, one from an English Guineaman (slaver) off Cape Finisterre. There was thus a complication of outrages,—in the original impressment of the men, in the second seizure of them, in the insult offered to a vessel of war.

The British government acted promptly and handsomely in the matter. The news reached London on the 26th of July, and on the 2nd of August, before any formal demand for redress by the American minister, the government disavowed the right to search ships in the national service of any state for deserters, and promised reparation; Vice-Admiral Berkeley was recalled. But, meanwhile, the indignation in America was intense. President Jefferson, by proclamation countersigned by his then Secretary of State and immediate future successor, Mr. Madison, interdicted the American harbours and waters to British armed vessels, dwelling on the fact that "it had been previously ascertained that the seamen demanded were native citizens of the United States;" a point which was again insisted on in Mr. Madison's instructions to Mr. Monroe, then United States' minister in London, and afterwards President, who in turn, with his formal demand upon the British government for restoration of the men, transmitted documents which, he presumed, would satisfy it, "that they were American citizens."* (You will see hereafter why I insist on this detail). Two of the men eventually were restored; one seems to have died.

Ample amends were thus done for this particular outrage. But there can be little doubt that it was one of the chief events which inflamed the minds of the American people against England, and made them ripe for the war which broke out under Jefferson's successor. Yet it was only one in a chain of complications.

* See Appendix to "A legal Review of the case of Dre Scott." Boston, 1857.

The time had come when the two giant combatants on the European battle-field could no longer abide the goings and comings of neutrals. In May, 1806, an English Order in Council had declared a blockade of all ports and rivers from the Elbe to Brest. In November, 1806, Napoleon retorted by his Berlin decree, blockading all the British islands and forbidding all intercourse with them. The British government informed the Americans, that if they should submit to this decree, we should retaliate upon them. By fresh Orders in Council, 11th November, 1807, we placed in a state of blockade the whole of France, and all her dependent powers. Napoleon's answer was by the Milan decree (17th of December), declaring that every vessel searched or visited against her will by a British cruiser, or proceeding to or returning from England, should be a good prize. In self-defence, and indeed before even the news of the decree had reached America, Congress laid a general embargo (recommended by the President) on American trade (22nd of December). Napoleon met this measure by a more open attack, the Bayonne decree (17th of April, 1808), rendering every American vessel found on the ocean liable to seizure and condemnation. There was no alternative but to continue the embargo, and to strengthen the navy. Two hundred gun-boats were already deemed requisite, and in his eighth and last annual message (November 8, 1808), Jefferson was able to state that 103 of these were completed. He had recommended the army and militia to be again increased; the manufacture of arms was improving; military stores had been increased; internal manufactures, fostered by the European war, were growing apace. In a word, Jefferson had come in as a peace-President; he left his country well nigh ready for war.

James Madison (born 1751), third Virginian President out of four who had taken office, was the son of a planter, brought up in strict Presbyterian principles. With Hamilton, he had been one of the chief writers in the "Federalist," (a series of political publications which had greatly contributed to the successful framing and acceptance of the Constitution), but afterwards rather adhered to the decentralising views of Jefferson, and as member of the Virginian Legislature drew up in 1798-9 certain resolutions, with a report, which may be considered to have carried the States-rights' doctrines to their furthest *lawful* extension; indeed this report is considered to have mainly contributed to the triumph of Jefferson in 1800, and Madison became not unnaturally Secretary of State under him. Always in delicate health, though he reached the age of eighty-five, sweet-tempered, and enjoying great personal popularity, yet he succeeded in being always in hot water with foreign powers during his administration, and for a time involved his country in serious difficulties. It is but just to say that he is alleged to have been forced into this course by younger and then hot-tempered men, and particularly by Mr. Clay, of whom we shall hear more hereafter.

Madison's inaugural address (4th March, 1809) recommended his fellow-citizens "to hold the union of the States as the basis of their peace and happiness, to support the Constitution, which is the cement of the Union, as well in its limitations as in its authorities,"—well-balanced counsels, leaning rather to the States-rights' views. The leading feature of his administration consists in the growing difficulties with France and England, ending in open war with the latter. America, whilst taking off her general embargo, forbids all trade and intercourse with France and England (1st March, 1809). Napoleon retorts by a Rambouillet decree, directing all American vessels and cargoes arriving in the ports of France, or of countries occupied by French troops, to be seized and confiscated (23rd March, 1810). America now excludes British and French armed vessels from her waters, but provides that if either country modify its edicts before the 3rd March, 1811, so as no longer to violate neutral commerce, commercial intercourse may be resumed with it (1st May, 1810). A temporary lull takes place, intercourse is renewed with France (2nd November, 1810), with Great Britain (10th November); Great Britain officially disavows the attack on the "Chesapeake," and restores the men taken out (except one who could not be found, 11th November, 1811). But a new mishap like that with the "Chesapeake" again influences the American mind; the English sloop of war "Little Belt" engages the United States' frigate "President;" eleven men are killed and twenty-one wounded.

A general embargo of ninety days is again put on (3rd April, 1812), and in a special message of June 1st, the President shows himself very hostile to England, recapitulates her outrages, and attributes to her a renewed warfare with the Indians on the frontier,—though, at the same time, he cannot but record also that the French, in spite of the revocation of the decrees against America, are continuing to commit outrages on American trade. On the 3rd June, the Committee of Congress on foreign relations recommends war; on the 17th an Act is passed declaring it; on the 19th it is proclaimed.

As we look back upon these times, we cannot but see that it was temper, rather than justice, which dictated to the Americans the choice of the enemy they were to fight; that they had to suffer as much provocation from France as from England, and that of a more faithless character. The British orders in council were stern acts of warfare by a maritime and trading power, endeavouring simply to cut off the trade of her enemy and his dependents. The French decrees were the attempt, by a power without trade and without a navy, to ruin the trade of all Europe, by an appeal to all the privateering rascality of the world, or by the terror of such ruin to force the ships of all the neutral powers to make naval war, as France could not, upon her enemy. This was seen well in those days by many Americans, and a minority in the House of Representatives protested against the war, declaring the French the aggressors, and expressing a confidence that the English orders in council would be repealed after official notice should be received of the repeal of the French decrees. So well-grounded was this hope, that, four days only after the American declaration of war, the French decrees of Berlin and Milan having been officially revoked, the British orders in council were repealed. But it was too late; the war-fever was at its height. At Baltimore the offices of the "Federal Republican" were destroyed by a mob, for having published some strictures on the declaration of war; the editor and others were attacked (27th July) in a house from whence the paper was distributed. The military were called out; the occupants of the house surrendered themselves on a promise of safety, and were lodged in the gaol for this purpose. The next morning the mob broke open the gaol, killed one of the party (a General Lingan), bruised and mangled eleven others, and threw eight of them, whom they supposed to be dead, in a heap in front of the gaol. For this outrage the ringleaders were tried, but escaped punishment. This story may be recommended to those who fancy that the breaking of presses and maltreating of editors, which have unfortunately been of late chronicled of some Northern localities, are either acts novel in themselves, or indigenous to a free soil. Baltimore, I need not remind you, is the chief city of slaveholding Maryland.

I need not give you the details of the war. It was all carried on at sea, on the American continent, or on its inland waters. There was a British invasion of

Michigan territory, and an American invasion of Canada; the American seaboard was harried by the British ships, by landings of troops, which, besides taking and destroying smaller towns, marched to Washington, repelling the Americans on the way,—took the city (which had been deserted by the President and heads of departments), with seven hundred men, under General Ross (24th Aug., 1814), burnt the Capitol, the President's house, the public offices, arsenal, navy-yard, and bridge over the Potomac, and then marched towards Baltimore, again defeating the Americans, but gave up the attempt against the latter city. There were a number of battles, some very gallant ones, lost and won on either side; divers instances also kindred to the Bull's Run one,—surrenders or surprises of whole bodies,—as when, in 1813, the Americans being eleven hundred, the British three hundred, with six hundred Indians, Brigadier-General Winchester, with five hundred men, was taken prisoner at Frenchtown,—panics,—abandonment of forts because the time of the Militia was nearly expired. On land it may be said that the Americans fought rashly and ill at first (surrender of General Hull at Detroit, with two thousand men, 15th August, 1812; surrender of Major-General van Rensselaer, November; surrender of Brigadier-General Winchester, above mentioned, January, 1813), but improved as the war went on (victories of Stony Creek, June 6, 1813; the Thames, 5th October; Chippewa, July 14, 1814,—the last, however, the only pitched battle). On the water, it is beyond doubt that the Americans had, on the whole, the upper hand of us; their navy was newer and better built, their ships larger and better manned. We had so long been accustomed to sweep the seas, that we had become careless. Our best sailing ships were French prizes; few of our commanders took the trouble to exercise their men in gunnery, which the Americans practised assiduously. Lastly, the severities of our impressment system had made our service hateful, even to our own men; and many of the best of them —to say nothing of the many Americans whom we had pressed and trained at once to seamanship and hatred—were serving in the American fleet. The consequence was, that when the few but splendid American ships took the sea,—their frigates a match for our smaller liners, their sloops well nigh for our frigates,—their successes were such that " all the world wondered.". Three of our frigates and two of our sloops were taken in a very short time (1812), whilst a gallant action on the inland seas of the North (September 10, 1813),—the taking of the British squadron on Lake Erie, by Commodore Perry, deserves to be noticed, were it only on account of the pregnant brevity with which the captor announced his success to his superior officer : " We have met the enemy and they are ours. Two ships, two brigs, one schooner, and one sloop."

That the entering into such a conflict on the part of America was one of the rashest acts recorded in history, can hardly be denied. America, says Mr. Alison, rushed into a war with Great Britain, "with an army of six thousand men, and a navy of four frigates," whilst Great Britain had a hundred ships of the line in commission, and in all one thousand vessels of war. This is a little too sharply put, as he shows soon after himself that, besides four frigates and eight sloops in commission, America had four more frigates and four more sloops building, whilst her total military force was 24,000. But there is no doubt that the disparity of force between the antagonists was tremendous, incredible; and it reflects the highest credit on America that she should have done so much with such slender means.

The credit of the British navy was indeed retrieved by the far-famed fight of the "Chesapeake" and "Shannon." Eight months before English sailors had sung:

> And as the war they did provoke,
>   We'll pay them with our cannon;
> The first to do it will be Broke
>   In the gallant ship the "Shannon."

Attached to the North-American station, Broke had destroyed all prizes that he had fallen in with—some twenty-five sail—in order to keep the "Shannon" constantly in a state to meet one of the new American frigates, the loss of some of the English ships having been attributed to their weakening themselves by drafts for prize-crews. In the spring of 1813, he lay off Boston harbour, watching for one of his coveted foes, and at last (1st June) being, as he said, "short of provisions and water," and unable to stay much longer, after various verbal messages, he sent a direct written challenge to the captain of the "Chesapeake." Before, however, the challenge had reached, the "Chesapeake" stood out to sea under a gentle breeze, many a pleasure-boat sailing beside her, as well as a large schooner gunboat, three ensigns flying, and at her fore a large white flag, with the motto "Sailors' rights and free-trade," all trim from harbour, whilst the "Shannon" awaited her, "much in need of paint," under a rusty old Union-Jack. American ingenuity, great even then, had exhausted itself in devising appliances for securing victory to the "Chesapeake." She carried double-headed shot, bars of wrought-iron a foot long, connected by links and folded together by rope-yarns, so as to extend six feet in width; other bars twice that length, three or six of them connected together by a ring, and which should expand into four points as they flew; such projectiles being meant to cut away her opponent's shrouds and facilitate the fall of her masts: her canister-shot contained angular and jagged pieces of iron and copper, broken bolts, copper and other nails; her musket-cartridges two or three buck-shot, that they might be more deadly. On her deck (though unknown, it seems, to Captain Lawrence) stood a cask of unslaked lime, and in the foretop was a bag of it, to blind the eyes of boarders. But "all is not gold that glitters;" and whilst the "Shannon's" crew are men in the highest state of training, both as to seamanship and gunnery, and full of confidence in their commander, as he is himself in them, the "Chesapeake" has a reputation for "unluckiness," a crew disaffected through some keeping back of prize-money, and who had to be pacified by promises at the very last, many foreigners also among them; officers acting for the first time in their respective posts, and a captain, though of undoubted gallantry, yet distrustful of his men and ship.

A challenge-gun is fired by the "Chesapeake." Standing slowly further out from the shore, so as to let the "Chesapeake" overtake her, the "Shannon" (5·50 P.M.) fires in her turn, and hits. An early shot from her strikes the lime-cask on board the "Chesapeake," and flings it into the faces and eyes of her own men. Six minutes of firing elapse, and then, by unskilful manœuvring, the "Chesapeake" falls so as to expose stem and quarter to her foe's broadside; four minutes more (6 P.M.), and the ships fall together. Both commanders are ready to board; Lawrence gives the order, but a negro, whose bugle was to replace the drum, has hid himself for fright, and when found cannot sound a note. Broke bids the ships be lashed together; Stevens, his boatswain, in doing so, has his left arm hacked off, and is mortally wounded, but finishes his work with his right arm before death. Meanwhile Lawrence has fallen wounded; and "seeing that the enemy were flinching from their guns," Broke boards (6·2). There is at first little resistance on deck, but a fire is kept up from the main and mizen-tops till these are stormed by the "Shannon's" men. Presently Broke is stunned, and nearly killed, by one of the Americans, who, after laying down their arms, had taken them up again, but is soon avenged; though his first lieutenant and four or five men are killed by their own comrades, through a mistake in hoisting the wrong flag to the mizen-top —the British flag flying already from the main-top. Some fire of musketry from the enemy's hold is soon silenced, and by 6·5 the "Chesapeake" is taken, and hostilities have ceased. Immediately after Broke's senses fail him, and he is conveyed to his own ship.

That quarter-of-an-hour's fight, though it did but little positive injury to either ship, cost the "Shannon" (with a crew of 306 men and twenty-two boys) in killed twenty-four, including the first lieutenant, and in wounded fifty-nine, including the captain (two moreover being mortally so), and cost the "Chesapeake" (crew 381) forty-seven killed (including the fourth lieutenant and master), and ninety-nine wounded, of whom fourteen mortally, according to the American official account. The two ships were fairly matched, with a slight advantage in favour of the "Chesapeake," which had seventy more men, and a broadside of 52 lbs. more weight than the "Shannon." Wrapped in his ship's colours, the body of the gallant Lawrence was laid upon the quarter-deck till the arrival of the ship at Halifax, where it was followed to the grave by every naval captain in the port; that of Lieutenant Ludlow being equally interred with military honours. The fortunes of the war at sea were more chequered after this.

On land, the last event of mark—but certainly not the least in American opinion—was the so-called battle of New Orleans (8th January, 1815), where General

Jackson, with scarcely any but militia to depend upon, was able, by his skilful arrangements, after an obstinate conflict, to repel the attack of the English, with heavy loss on their side, and scarcely any on his. It is a sign of the growth of a new interest, that he formed a sort of abattis of cotton-bales, which the British balls and bullets failed to penetrate, although a red-hot shot at last set them on fire. Nor is it less remarkable that in this campaign an express appeal was made by General Jackson to the patriotism of the coloured race. In a proclamation dated Mobile, September 14, 1814, addressed "to the free coloured inhabitants of Louisiana," he says:—" Through a mistaken policy you have heretofore been deprived of a participation in the glorious struggle for national rights in which our country is engaged. This no longer shall exist. As sons of freedom, you are now called upon to defend our most inestimable blessing. As Americans, your country looks with confidence to her adopted children for a valorous support. . . . On enrolling yourselves in companies, the major-general commanding will select officers for your government from your white *fellow-citizens*. Your non-commissioned officers will be appointed from among yourselves."*

The war had always been unpopular in the New England states. On the first call of the President on the States for their quotas of militia to man the fortresses on the sea-board, Massachusetts, Connecticut,

---

* Appendix to "A legal Review of the case of Dred Scott," before quoted.

and Rhode Island had refused their contingent (1812), and their opposition had lasted throughout the war, which, in consequence, fell heavily upon them, as they were specially exposed to sea-attacks from the enemy, and had to defend themselves. Not only did this opposition of the north-eastern states come to a head in a celebrated convention of the Federal party at Hartford, when secession doctrines are said to have been broached, but the dissatisfaction with the war at last became nearly general, and peace was concluded at Ghent between Great Britain and the United States (24th December, 1814), to be followed the next year by a convention of commerce (22nd December, 1815). Both parties were to use their best endeavours for abolishing the slave-trade.

Although we undoubtedly provoked the American war by our overbearing conduct towards neutrals, yet it is difficult not to feel that that war is a far worse moral blot in the history of America than any previous proceedings of our own. In the gigantic struggle which was then going on, we were yet, though under Tory colours, the champions of the liberties of Europe, threatened by a despot whose genius was only exceeded by the selfishness of his insatiate ambition. The war commenced at a time when he was engaged on the most audacious and unprovoked of his aggressions, the invasion of Russia; it continued during the whole of that noble year 1813, the true birth-year of nationality, not for Germany alone, but for nearly all Europe, when people after people rose at last as one man on the lawless invader; after having served, while it lasted, as a diversion in favour of the Napoleonic tyranny,—so that one of the leading American cases in international law established the lawful capture of a neutral ship carrying provisions from Ireland to the British forces engaged in liberating the Peninsula (the " Commercen "),—it came to a speedy end after Napoleon's fall, when the whole strength of England might otherwise have been brought to bear upon America. For England, although no brilliant successes marked the war for her, it is sufficient honour that, whilst carrying on with undiminished vigour the Continental war, she should have been able to find ships and men enough to keep at bay the whole forces of the United States;—that in Belfast and Glasgow, in Liverpool and in Plymouth, Englishmen should have slept secure, whilst the whole seaboard, the whole northern frontier of the United States, were in terror or in flames, while Washington was taken and the Capitol burnt down. Her old ships might not have been a match singly for the new American ones; but her adversary had never had such a thing as a fleet to oppose to hers. And after all, she had in the main been beaten by the seamen whom she had trained herself, and even by her own sons. After an engagement between the frigates "Macedonian" and "United States," in which the former was taken, the American Commodore Decatur publicly declared that there was not a man on board his ship who had not served from five to twelve years in a British man-of-war. The whole crew of one gun had served in the "Victory," that of another had been bargemen to Lord Nelson. And what was the result of the war for the Americans?

Jefferson had in 1807 rejected, without even communicating it to the Senate, a treaty concluded with Great Britain by Monroe and Pinckney, on the ground that it contained no renunciation of the right claimed by Great Britain of impressment of Englishmen from on board American ships. "Impressment," Colonel Benton tells us, "with the insults and the outrages connected with it," was the main ground of the war, without which it would not have been declared. Yet "the treaty of peace did not mention or allude to the subject,—the first time, perhaps, in modern history in which a war was terminated by treaty without any stipulation derived from its cause." In fact, as he expressly admits, America could no longer carry on the war: "In less than three years the government, paralysed by the state of the finances, was *forced* to seek peace." The American foreign trade, as you may see in Alison, had been annihilated for the time. Whilst our exports had risen during the war from £38,041,573 to £53,573,234, those of America fell from £22,000,000 to £1,400,000; her imports from £28,000,000 to less than £3,000,000; 1400 of her ships had been taken in two years and a half. In his first annual message (1809) Madison had been able to speak of his having paid off 5,300,000 dollars of debt, whilst he had 9,500,000 dollars in the treasury. In his message of 1815 he had to speak of a debt of 120,000,000 dollars, of which 64,000,000 dollars of war debt, with

17,000,000 dollars unfunded, the value of stocks being proportionately impaired.

The English war was not the only one which marks Madison's tenure of office. Hostilities had broken out again even previously with the Indians (1811) who were worsted on the Wabash at Tippecanoe, by General Harrison, in a somewhat considerable action, where the Americans lost sixty-two killed and 126 wounded. In the war with England, the Indians generally took part with the latter; and in a battle on the Thames (so called), where the English were defeated, it is recorded that Tecumseh, the Shawnee, the greatest Indian chief since a celebrated one of the name of Pontiac, was killed (1813). This was in the north-west; a war with the Creeks in the south-west was raging at the same time, and claiming the services of general officers. Treaties were concluded with several Indian tribes after the war, and latterly large purchases of land from them effected (1816).

A neighbour far less formidable than the Indians, whose possessions were equally tempting to the American land-hunger, was Spain,—invaded at home, scarcely able to maintain a nominal authority abroad. A regular buccaneering establishment had been formed in part of West Florida, claimed indeed by the United States, but in the nominal possession of Spain. Madison put a stop to this, taking possession by proclamation of part of Florida west of the Perdido river (27th of October, 1810). A little later, however, we find an event recorded which is ominous for the future,—a proclamation by the governor of Louisiana against any invasion of Texas (1814).

Last in the list of wars or quasi-wars is to be mentioned that with Algiers, from whence the American consul and American citizens had been banished (1812). When the navy was set free by the peace with England, it was employed to punish these Barbaresques. The war, declared in March, 1815, was short and smart, Commodore Decatur taking two ships of the Algerines, one their principal one, with the admiral on board; and by July peace was concluded, the Algerines renouncing all pretensions to tribute from American ships or citizens.

In spite of all these storms, and of the straits to which the government was reduced, the country was yet growing. Two new States were admitted: Louisiana (1812), Indiana (1816). The third census (of 1810) had shown a population of 7,239,903. Upwards of twenty-two million of newspapers were already in circulation. Manufactures were multiplying. The President called for navigation laws (1815), urged the construction of roads and canals. To the next year belongs the first protective tariff of the United States. Till now import duties had been laid on solely for revenue. Now they were imposed also, after much discussion, with a view to encourage American manufactures. William Lowndes and J. C. Calhoun of South Carolina were prominent advocates of the tariff. A majority of the representatives of South Carolina, about two-fifths of the southern representatives in general, voted in its favour. Lastly, an attempt was made to check the growth of slavery by forming a society to colonise the coast of Africa with emancipated slaves. Hence the republic of " Liberia."

After a double term of office, Madison was succeeded (1817) by James Monroe, his contemporary in age (born 1759), and the fourth Virginian President. He had been a soldier in the revolutionary war, reaching the rank of colonel just before its close, had been senator, twice minister to France, to Spain also, and to Great Britain; governor of his State, and Secretary of State under Madison; he had had a share in the treaty for the cession of Louisiana, and in that treaty with Great Britain which Jefferson refused to lay before the Senate. A cautious, persevering man, watchful of the currents of popular feeling, and obsequious to it, I suspect he must be considered as the earliest specimen in date of the mob-flattering Presidents, a race from which the United States have had much to suffer. John Quincy Adams, who was to become Monroe's successor, as the candidate of the so-called Whig party, was his Secretary of State, whilst John C. Calhoun, the future head of the Southern party, was Secretary at War. This was a period, it may be observed, when the old party distinctions of Federalist and Republican had died out, whilst new parties had formed under new names and upon new bases.

A chain of events, the distant consequences of the great Continental war, which was to exercise a good deal of influence upon the ulterior development of the Union, was now unrolling itself, of which the first link is to be noticed in Monroe's inaugural address (March 5, 1817), I mean the insurrections of the Spanish American colonies against the mother-country. He refers to these risings, and announces certain measures which he has been obliged to take in consequence of them. A premature Walker, "citizen Gregor McGregor, Brigadier-general of the armies of the United Provinces of New Granada and Venezuela," had taken possession of Amelia Island, at the mouth of St. Mary's River, in East Florida, near the boundary of that province (still Spanish) with Georgia. This had been made, the President states, "a channel for the illicit introduction of slaves from Africa into the United States, an asylum for fugitive slaves from the neighbouring states, and a port for smuggling of every kind." A similar establishment, he tells us, had at an earlier period been made at Galveston, in Texas, but within, "as we contend," the Louisiana cession. So the United States authorities took possession of Amelia Island—not intending, they declared, to make a conquest from Spain, but simply to take the island from adventurers whom she was incapable of resisting. Presently the matter became complicated with the war (1818) against the Seminole Indians of Florida, one of the most savage of the Indian tribes, protected by almost impassable swamps and forests. In pursuing them, General Jackson took possession of the towns of Pensacola (May 28, 1818), and St. Mark's, in Florida; whilst at the same time a negotiation was being carried on with Spain for the purchase of the whole territory,

—the United States relinquishing at the same time the claims of Louisiana on Texas. To conciliate Spain, Pensacola and St. Mark's were restored. But the King of Spain refused to ratify the treaty of cession (February 22, 1819), when presented to him, chiefly on the ground of American outrages in Texas. Monroe, in his yearly message of that year, coolly recommended that the treaty should be carried out as if ratified.

Three new states had meanwhile been added to the Union; Mississippi (1817), Illinois (1818), Alabama (1819), while the Arkansas (or, as it was then called, Arkansaw) territory, further part of the Louisiana cession, was organised as a territorial government. Serious debates, however, arose on the question of the admission of Missouri as a state.

The Missouri territory formed the extreme North of the Louisiana cession, running considerably North and West of the Ohio. Now, whilst Louisiana was claimed by France and Spain, slavery was sanctioned by both those countries, as it is still by Spain. But, on the other hand, the greater part of the Missouri territory came within the terms of the Ordinance of 1787, prohibiting slavery to the North-West of the Ohio. When it applied for admission (1819), "The territory must be free," said the North. "It is slave, and should remain so," retorted the South. The debates ran very high. For fear of the increase of power which might arise to the slave-holding interest, Massachusetts now lent (1819) a willing ear to the claims of her Northern population to take rank as a separate state; and Maine was admitted, with the Declaration of Independence preamble to her constitution, as to human equality and the rights of man (1820). To stop further agitation, moreover, a compromise was adopted. A law was passed, enacting that there should be no slavery in any state to be formed in future out of the remainder of the Louisiana territory North of the latitude of 36° 30'; but that, South of that line, states might be admitted either with slavery or without it. Thus was the famous "Missouri Compromise Line" established (1820) ;—an event which may be said to have bisected the history of the United States, as it did its political geography.

LECTURE IV.

FROM THE MISSOURI COMPROMISE TO THE PRESIDENCY OF GENERAL JACKSON (1820—1829) — THE SLAVERY QUESTION AS RESPECTS THE TERRITORIES.

(Monroe, 1817 to 1825 ; John Quincy Adams, 1825 to 1829.)

THE year 1820—the date of the Missouri Compromise—opens what may be termed the second era of the history of the United States. The consolidation of the Union, it may be said, is what the former period of forty-three years exhibits; the preparations for its disruption occupy the latter forty or forty-one. Not, indeed, but what the germs of disruption may be very visible to us now in the former period; not but what many a measure of real consolidation may belong to the latter: but had the history remained a blank for us since 1820, we might have retained a doubt whether any of those germs would ever have sprung up and fructified; whereas the narrative might stop almost at any time henceforth without leaving us in doubt that they had sprung up, and were growing apace into maturity.

The chief results of the former period have been these:—1st. Development of the geographical limits and population of the United States, the original thirteen states having swelled to twenty-three,* which Missouri will presently carry to twenty-four, whilst the Floridas are claimed to have been ceded by Spain, and the American flag has even been hoisted on the Pacific, at the mouth of the Columbia River, in the ill-fated settlement of Astoria, which for us prefigures the now flourishing State of Oregon; the census, on the other hand, giving a population of 9,708,305, more than doubled since 1790—or within a single generation. 2nd. Subjugation of the great bulk of the Indian tribes within the territory of the Union, and restriction of them, by purchases of the lands over which they claimed a title, to ever-narrowing limits. 3rd. Development of the trade of the United States. Thanks to the great Continental wars, the Americans had become for a time the foremost carriers of the world, and the extension of their neutral trade had, as we have seen, been such as seriously to thwart the action of the contending powers, till, wearied and outraged by both, the Americans had at last taken up arms against one of them (England), and carried on a three years' war. Hence, 4th, The creation of a very efficient naval force, which, besides various achievements against the Barbaresques in the Mediterranean, had obtained many signal successes over our own ships in the war of 1812-15, and the rise of the United

---

* New States admitted: Vermont (1791); Kentucky (1792); Tennessee (1796); Ohio (1802); Louisiana (1812); Indiana (1815); Mississippi (1817); Illinois (1818); Alabama (1819); Maine (1820).

States to a very important position among the secondary naval powers of the world; and 5th, The rise, through the frequent interruptions to trade during the Continental wars, and again through the war with England, of domestic manufactures, especially in the North-Eastern states, which already called for protection. 6th and last, The development in the South of the cultivation and export of cotton. In the year 1791, as I told you, the first parcel of cotton of American growth was exported from the United States, the production being 1,000,000 lbs. In the year 1801, the export was 20,911,201 lbs., the production nearly 50,000,000 lbs. In the year 1807, the export was 66,000,000 lbs. already, and the acquisition of Louisiana had given a further enormous impetus to it. A vast increase of value had thus been given to slaves, and a powerful centre created for Southern interests.

Slavery had, until the question of the admission of Missouri into the Union, formed no topic of popular agitation. The two great parties into which the politicians of the United States were originally divided—those of the "Federalists," or their successors the "Whigs," and of the "Republicans," afterwards Democrats—were composed alike of slaveholders and non-slaveholders. Some increase of power had indeed been gained by the slaveholding states, which had succeeded in heading the national movement of expansion in the following manner:—The custom had grown up of admitting a free and a slave state alternately or together. But this had only taken place after the successive admission of the slave states of Kentucky and Tennessee; so that although, of the ten states which had been added to the original thirteen, five were free (Vermont, Ohio, Indiana, Illinois, Maine) and five slave (Kentucky, Tennessee, Louisiana, Mississippi, Alabama), yet the next turn of admission belonged not to the free, as it should have done, but to the slave states; whilst the remainder of the Louisiana purchase, with Florida, already in process of annexation, afforded the prospect of future extensions of slave territory, in direct opposition to the views of Mr. Jefferson, as to the exclusion of slavery from all after-admitted states. Of disunion there had been for years no talk at the South. On the contrary, what talk there had been of it, or tending to it, lately, had been in New England, at the "Hartford Convention." But "the difference between the American Union and a league," we are told by a prominent representative of a slave state, Colonel Benton, "being better understood at that time," the "leading language" with respect to the convention "south of the Potomac was, that no state had a right to withdraw from the Union—that it required the same power to dissolve as to form the Union—and that any attempt to dissolve it, or to obstruct the action of constitutional laws, was treason." The main subject of difference between North and South even at this time, indeed, was not slavery, but the tariff. Headed by politicians from the Border slave states, the North, which had become more and more manufacturing, sought for high import duties; the South, whose agricultural exports were receiving an enormous development, desired a low tariff, to procure supplies and encourage the foreign demand for its productions. But the South itself was divided upon this question; the sugar-growing interest of Louisiana, which found inland the great market for its staple, leading it to side with the North. Thus an avowedly protective tariff, though still a moderate one, had been in force since 1816.

But we have seen how, on the question of the admission of Missouri, an agitation on the subject of slavery had grown up, and had been sought to be stifled by fixing at 36° 40′ N. lat., a line beyond which slavery was not to be permitted in new states to be formed out of the Louisiana territory. It is worth while to consider now the question of the territorial extension of slavery in itself, as respects its bearing upon the history of America.

I shall not insult your consciences by tarrying over the moral side of the slavery question. If the negro be a man (and I shall not insult your understandings by attempting to argue that he is), your hearts know well that no brother-man of whatever colour has the right to buy or to sell him. That deep moral conviction of the utter hatefulness of slavery, embodied in the glorious principle of our law, that the very dust of our English soil gives freedom to the slave, is the only answer which England deigns to give to the blasphemous pleading of the South in favour of the divine right of slavery. That conviction was shared, more or less, by a vast number of our Transatlantic brethren at the North; that principle had been embodied, so far as it could be under the fetters of the Constitution of the United States, in the constitutions or laws of several of the Northern States. In resisting the further extension of slavery, therefore, the North had of course the vantage ground of moral principle; it had equally the text of the Declaration of Independence, the spirit of the Constitution and of the early legislation of the country, the avowed tradition of almost all the Fathers of the Republic. The economical ground on which such resistance was or could be attempted remains to be considered.

The tide of emigration had, up to this period, poured faster Westward on the more Northerly than on the more Southerly parallels. Illinois, for instance, had become a state before Alabama, as, in later time, her next neighbour to the West, Iowa, was to become one with Florida, Alabama's next neighbour to the South-East. And the process of settlement to the North had been, in the main, of the healthiest nature. It was a perpetual flow of labour. The European worker sought the shores of the great Republic in order the better to realise and enjoy the right to live by his toil. If his arrival displaced any of the older settlers, they too moved further West, with precisely the same object—workers in search of work. Why did they not move South as well as West? Why, in 1790, was the population of the free states only a few thousands greater than' that of the slave states (1,968,453 against 1,961,374), and in 1820 more than half-a-million in excess (5,152,372 against 4,502,224), notwithstanding the Louisiana cession, and the addition of its population, or nearly the whole of it, to that of the existing slave states? Why was Virginia foremost in point of population in 1790, and only second in 1820, New York having risen to the first rank in her stead?

The cause lay not in climate, for that of Virginia is temperate, its soil is intersected by healthy mountain ranges, and much of it actually runs further North than part of the free states of Ohio, Indiana, Illinois. The real reason lay in the profound incompatibility between free and slave labour, which all reasoning demonstrates, which all experience confirms. The mere establishment of slavery was, as it were, a wall raised up against the progress of the European labourer. As a general rule, free labour and slave labour cannot work side by side, shoulder to shoulder. Wherever slavery exists, those kinds of labour on which the slave is employed become dishonourable to the freeman; whilst, on the other hand, it is no less true that the mere employment of the freeman upon them is a danger to slavery; since the slave, working with the freeman, insensibly imbibes the habits, the tone of mind, the hopes of the freeman. Nor is this all. The conditions under which the two kinds of labour can be employed are totally opposite. The main incentive to the freeman's labour lies in the hope of bettering himself. The main incentive to the slave's labour lies in the fear of making his condition worse. The freeman lives by his labour, and his greatest punishment is to lose it. The slave lives through the care which by law, or custom, or self-interest, or humanity, his master is obliged to bestow upon him, and labour is to him in itself a punishment, not a boon. Hence, you cannot rule freemen by the lash; I can say, from personal observation in the West Indies in the days of slavery, how difficult it is to rule slaves without it.

Again: This peculiar public opinion, which brands manual labour as dishonourable when practised by slaves—these peculiar conditions of labour, which impose on it for regulators coercion and fear—mould rapidly the character of the freemen themselves in the slave countries, so as to make them averse to the introduction of free labour. As long as the value of slave property does not increase so as to make its owner tender about risking it, as has been the case of late years in many parts of the Southern states (where Irishmen, as Mr. Olmsted shows, have been set to do work too dangerous for negroes[*]), he will not hear of free labour, because he cannot depend upon it, and cannot drive it[†]—*i. e.*, because it has an awkward trick of walking off with itself when ill-treated, instead of standing to be ill-treated still further, under fear of State codes, fugitive slave laws, and Cuban bloodhounds.

Thus, once more, free labour and slave labour

---

[*] See "Journeys and Explorations in the Cotton Kingdom," vol. i. p. 30 and *passim*.

[†] *Ibid.*, p. 83, and *passim*.

cannot co-exist except temporarily, and under peculiar circumstances. There must be a realm of free labour, and a realm of slave labour. "That is just what we want, says the South," and its English sympathisers repeat the lesson, parrot-like, after it; "that is the meaning of Secession. We want nothing more than to be left alone. We should never have seceded if we had been."

Whether the South has wanted nothing more than to be left alone, the future course of this history will show. What I want you now to consider is, whether in America these two realms, brought into close proximity, can exist otherwise than in a state of perpetual warfare, ending in the triumph of the one over the other.

The essential characteristic of slave labour is its wastefulness, untrustworthiness, dishonesty, and consequently dearness. The slave, as a slave, is a liar and a pilferer. To use the words of Jefferson himself, "The man in whose favour no laws of property exist, probably feels himself less bound to respect those made in favour of others." His propensity to waste, to destroy, to do mischief, is carried sometimes to such extraordinary lengths, that a learned Louisiana doctor, named Cartwright, has classed it as a disease, under the solemn title of "Dysæsthesia Æthiopica." His description of the symptoms, though written in perfect good faith, is the most bitter satire on slavery ever penned. Speaking of the individuals afflicted with this disease, he says: "They break, waste, and destroy everything they handle, abuse horses and cattle, tear, burn, or rend their own clothing, and, paying no attention to the rights of property, steal others, to replace what they have destroyed. They slight their work, cut up corn, cane, cotton, and tobacco when hoeing it, as if for pure mischief. They raise disturbances with their overseers, and among their fellow-servants, without cause or motive, and seem to be insensible to pain when subjected to punishment." (O for a good dose of freedom to cure this strange disease!)

Hence, I repeat it, the greater dearness of slave labour as compared with free. Mr. Olmsted, contrasting Virginia with its immediate neighbours among the free states, declares that, taking infants, aged, invalid, and vicious and knavish slaves into account, the ordinary and average cost of a certain task of labour is more than double in Virginia what it is in the free states adjoining. In speaking of Virginia, observe that he is speaking of a state which exports negroes, instead of importing them, as is done further South; where, consequently, slave labour should, in proportion to the demand which there is for it, be superabundant and cheap. Nor must you confound the cost of slave labour with the quantity of it which must be bestowed on a given object. Here the difference is far more marked, and is only lessened by the minimizing through slavery of the labourer's standard of comfort. Mr. Olmsted shows, for instance, on the authority of a Virginia planter, that in harvesting wheat—a light crop of six bushels to the acre—by slave labour, "one quarter of an acre a day was secured for each able hand engaged;" whereas, in New York, he tells us, a gang of fairly working men "would be expected, under ordinary circumstances, to secure a crop of wheat yielding from twenty to thirty bushels to the acre, at the rate of about two acres a day for each man." The same authority adds, "that the ordinary waste in harvesting wheat in Virginia, through the carelessness of the negroes, beyond that which occurs in the hands of ordinary Northern labourers, is equal in value to what a Northern farmer would often consider a satisfactory profit on his crop;" and that, in his "deliberate opinion, four Virginia slaves do not, when engaged in ordinary agricultural operations, accomplish as much, on an average, as one ordinary free farm labourer in New Jersey."

Now observe what results flow from these facts. Four slaves are required to do the work of one freeman; and that work, when done by the slaves, costs twice as much. In other words, for every acre that slave labour brings into cultivation, and which would have been fit for cultivation by freemen, slavery wastes three, compared with freedom, and the produce of that labour only goes half as far towards employing more. In the demand for new territory, therefore, slavery asks for four times the quantity of land that freedom needs for the same quantity of labour, and repeats the demand as often again. Can you wonder that, even before these conclusions were reasoned out by accurate observation, the rough experience of their reality should have induced, on the part of the free states, constant endeavours to stop the encroachments of the South on yet unallotted territory? Do you not see that it is a question of life and death for them not to allow those encroachments?

Slavery, on its side, cannot stop its progress. It does not only cultivate wastefully, it absolutely wastes the land it cultivates, and that with ever-increasing rapidity, as its baleful system developes itself, since, at the present day, as Mr. Olmsted shows, from undoubted Southern authority, half a century or even less, in the newly-settled states, is sufficient to exhaust the most fertile soils as completely as two centuries have done in Virginia and the Carolinas. Hence the remarkable phenomenon which has been going on for some years, of the practical breaking down of that moral wall of slavery of which I spoke, by the immigration of free labourers into the border slave states. Not only, as Mr. Olmsted states, on the authority of the census returns of 1850, is land in the slave states worth less than in the free, so that it will sell in Virginia by the acre at less than one-third of what it will fetch in neighbouring Pennsylvania, and less than one-fifth of what it will fetch in neighbouring New Jersey; but the time comes when the soil is actually no more fit for slavery, whilst perfectly fit for freedom. Thus it is that you will understand the present faithfulness of Western Virginia to the Union. Take the following extract, as to Fairfax, one of the North-Western and earliest settled counties of that state, which Mr. Olmsted quotes from an official "Patent-office Report" for 1852: "In appearance, the country is so changed in many parts, that a traveller who passed over it ten years ago would not now recognise it. Thousands and thousands of acres had been cultivated in tobacco by the former proprietors, would not pay the cost, and were abandoned as worthless, and became covered with a wilderness of pines. These lands have been purchased by Northern emigrants; the large tracts divided and subdivided, and cleared of pines; and neat farm-houses and barns, with smiling fields of grain and grass in the season, elate the delighted gaze. . . . Ten years ago it was a mooted question whether Fairfax lands could be made productive; and if so, would they pay the cost? This problem has been satisfactorily solved by many, and in consequence of this state of things, school-houses and churches have been doubled in number."

Thus you will see why, scourging the land which it occupies beyond its own powers of recovery, slavery must always be ravening for fresh land to scourge in like manner. It is not so much expansive as dispersive, nomadic. The great slave-owner would fain have never a neighbour to his plantation. A true dog-in-the-manger, he buys up land which he cannot cultivate, for the sole purpose of keeping off squatters. He would raise, if he could, a wall of fire round his negroes, not only that they might not run away, but that they might never come in contact with rascally white traders to sell to them spirits, and comforts, and luxuries of all sorts which they should not have, and buy from them all manner of things which they take—that they might never come in contact with the slaves of other masters, to give them or tell them of examples which they ought not to imitate or to quote,—above all, that they might never come in contact with free blacks, as the most pestilent of all examples. Estranging thus man from man even in the slave-owning class, slavery is encamped on the soil, not rooted in it. All travellers dwell on the absence throughout the South, except in a few cities, of all the usual evidences of the stability of a nation—public buildings, noble monuments, comfortable hotels, solidly built and cheerful homes. Am I stating here anything that is not admitted by slave-owners themselves? Listen to Mr. T. R. R. Cobb of Georgia, in the "Historical Sketch of Slavery" prefixed to his "Inquiry into the Law of Negro-Slavery in the United States of America" (Philadelphia and Savannah, 1858).

"In a slaveholding state, the greatest evidence of wealth in the planter is the number of his slaves. The most desirable property for a remunerative income is slaves. The best property to leave to his children, and from which they will part with the greatest reluctance, is slaves. Hence the planter invests his surplus income in slaves. The natural result is, that lands are a secondary consideration. No surplus is left for their improvement. The homestead is valued only so long as the adjacent lands are profitable for cultivation. The planter himself having no local attachments, his

I

children inherit none. On the contrary, he encourages in them a disposition to seek new lands. His valuable property (his slaves) are easily removed to fresh lands; much more easily than to bring the fertilising materials to the old. The result is that they, as a class, are never settled. *Such a population is almost nomadic. It is useless to seek to excite patriotic emotions in behalf of the land of birth when self-interest speaks so loudly.* On the other hand, where no slavery exists, and the planter's surplus cannot be invested in labourers, it is appropriated to the improvement or extension of his farm, the beautifying of the homestead. . . . The result is, the withdrawal of all investments for the improvement of the lands; another deleterious effect of slavery to the state" (pp. ccxv. ccxvi.).

In short, the slave-owner is nearly as homeless as the slave. By a strange Nemesis, his own condition grows closely to approximate, only upon a larger scale, to that of those petty African tribes whom travellers describe to us clearing, tilling, wasting the soil around one settlement, and then shifting to another, their dwellings as fragile and comfortless as their cultivation is careless. But let the slave-owner cling to the soil as much as he please, when he has wrung by the labour of his slaves all the available profit out of his land, his only resource is, first to sell the slaves themselves; and, when they are all sold off, then the land itself to a freeman. The present condition of the slave-breeding states is what all the slave-states must come to. Human flesh is the last crop which the soil exhausted by slavery can bear.

After that is worked off, slavery itself must become extinct upon it. So that, by simply forbidding slavery to move on, you actually doom it to destruction.

Freedom and slavery, then, at the time of the Missouri Compromise, were pressing, and still press in like manner onward towards the unoccupied or less occupied lands of the west,—Freedom cultivating, enriching, settling; Slavery cultivating, wasting, abandoning. In order to avert as long as possible the clash which must come when either found no more land to occupy, it was necessary that they should move on parallel lines. But in the track of slavery lay the country occupied by the Spanish race; this slavery must either turn or conquer. But the attempt to turn it forced slavery within the limits of freedom; hence the encroachment on Missouri, a country perfectly adapted by soil and climate for white labour. Blocked out, then, necessarily to the Northwards by the Missouri Compromise Line, slavery could henceforth only for its extension use the alternative of conquest; hence will arise the appropriation of Texas, the Mexican war, and, later still, the piratical enterprises against Cuba, Nicaragua, Honduras, and the other republics of Central America. Thus, for the United States, the extension of slavery meant necessarily either the robbing freemen of their destined homes, or foreign war.

We see now, perhaps, both how plausible might seem the expedient of fixing geographical limits to slavery, and yet how necessarily temporary that expedient must be—how costly—how sure to fail. The agitation on the subject of slavery was not stopped, even temporarily, by the Missouri Compromise itself. The question of the actual admission of Missouri yet remained. Her constitution not only sanctioned slavery, but contained a then unusual provision, suggested, Colonel Benton tells us, by himself, which forbade the State legislature to interfere with it, whilst it authorized the same body to prohibit the immigration of free people of colour into the state. Cruel as was the former clause, it was the latter only that was seriously objected to. It was alleged by the North, and apparently admitted by Congress, that such a provision violated the article of the Constitution which secures equal rights in all states to the citizens of any one; and the clause was at last only passed with a proviso that no citizen of the United States should thereby be excluded from any of his privileges under the Constitution of the United States. It is impossible, I think, for any Englishman to doubt that the objection of the North was well founded. Yet the day was to come when the highest judicial authority in the United States was to pronounce the free coloured men incapable of any but local rights of citizenship.

The Missouri Compromise was devised by Clay, of slaveholding Kentucky. It was supported by a cabinet of which he and Calhoun, of slaveholding South Carolina, were members, under a president from slaveholding Virginia. It was, as Colonel Benton terms it, a Southern measure. Taken in conjunction with the Florida treaty, it extinguished slave soil, except in Florida and Arkansas. Yet he tells us expressly that "there was not a ripple of discontent on the surface of the public mind"—*i. e.*, the slaveholding or pro-slavery mind—at the measure; "no talk then about dissolving the Union if every citizen was not allowed to go with all his 'property,' that is, all his slaves, to all the territory acquired by the common blood and treasure of all the Union." The North only complained of the violation of the ordinance of 1787,—of the departure from the spirit of the founders of the republic. The South already insulted their Northern neighbours. John Randolph, of Virginia—the only name connected with the Revolutionary war which deserves to be recollected as that of a partisan of slavery—hot-tempered, warmhearted John Randolph, who boasted all his life of being a slave-owner, yet emancipated his slaves at his death— John Randolph, during the discussions on the Missouri question, used these memorable words:—"We do not govern them" (the people of the free states) "by our black slaves, but by their own white slaves. We know what we are doing. We have conquered you once, and we can and we will conquer you again. Ay, sir, we will drive you to the wall, and when we have you there once more, we mean to keep you there, and nail you down like bad money." For forty years those vaunting words remained true.

Yet already slavery was bearing its bitter fruits. The slaves, who at the time of the Revolutionary war had generally refused to rise against their masters, felt now far more heavily the weight of their chains. The year after the admission of Missouri, a conspiracy of negroes at Charleston called for severe measures: seventy-two were convicted, thirty-five executed, while the remainder were banished. Judge Lynch was not yet sole and supreme in such matters. Nor had the time come when, as now, the protection of slavery was to be alleged to require the reopening of the slave-trade. Monroe's administration is, on the contrary, signalized by stringent measures against the latter. First of all the nations, the United States declared the slave-trade piracy, and punishable with death (1820). In the following year we find President Monroe, in his annual message, announcing that the slave-trade under the United States' flag was suppressed (1821). Instructions are given to all accredited ministers of the United States at foreign courts to propose that the trade be declared piracy, as well as that privateering (then very rife in the American seas, under colour of the wars between Spain and her revolted colonies, and covering much barefaced piracy) be suppressed (1823). Special negotiations are opened with England on the subject of the slave-trade. England offers a mutual right of search, the only *bonâ-fide* guarantee of success. America refuses, holding to her declaration of piracy, and arguing strongly, through the pen of J. Q. Adams, the Secretary of State, against the right of search in general. Eventually a convention is concluded (1824). Meanwhile, the lawless occupation of Florida under the unratified treaty with Spain had been carried out (10th and 17th July, 1821). The treaty was eventually ratified by Mexico.

Monroe's administration saw a new policy inaugurated towards the Indians. Washington's system of a regulated trade with them had failed, chiefly through the inevitable carelessness, misconduct, or corruption of the agents employed. It was put aside, and all the United States' trading establishments were closed (1822). In the message announcing this event (December 3rd), the President now puts forth the doctrine that it is "essential to the growth and prosperity of the territory, as well as to the interests of the Union," to remove or concentrate the Indians of Florida. Two years later (1824) he goes further, and suggests a general transportation of the Indians to a territory between the then limits of the United States, the Rocky Mountains and Mexico. In other words, after all the land has been got from the Indians that they could possibly spare without starving themselves, the time is come when they are to be turned out of what they have retained, because the white man wants it. They are to leave their homes and the graves of their ancestors for a far country which they know not, and where inevitably the same process will have to be repeated. It is ominous for them that the same message which suggests their general removal recommends also the creation of a military post at the mouth of the Columbia River; so that they may already see themselves in prospect hemmed in on both sides within their future home by a double tide of American immigration from East and West. Nor is it less significant that the same year sees also a convention signed between Russia and the United States (April 5th, 1824), providing that there shall be no settlement of the United States on the Northern coast of America or its islands North of 54° 40″ North latitude, nor any Russian South of the same parallel. In other words, the United States are already deliberately laying hands on the Pacific seaboard, which they had but felt along hitherto.

Graver still is the enunciation by Monroe of what has since been termed, by his name, the "Monroe doctrine" of "America for the Americans." Speaking of the late revolutions in the Spanish colonies—all claiming the example of the United States as their authority—and referring to rumours of intervention by European Powers to restore the Spanish dominion, he declared that he should consider any attempt on the part of European Powers "to extend their system to any portion of this hemisphere as dangerous to our peace and safety." It is not a little singular that the first act of open defiance to this threat on the part of a European Power has been one by the very country whose influence seemed then reduced to the lowest ebb—Spain, whose annexation of the Eastern part of St. Domingo, America, through her secession crisis, finds herself powerless to resist. I regret the event, which seems to me fraught with peril to the independence of the neighbouring republic of Hayti, now at last progressing under the only really great chief (Geffrard) she has had since the days of Toussaint l'Ouverture. But the fact remains, nevertheless, as one of the great lessons of contemporary history.

As respects internal questions, beyond that of slavery, the most important that were agitated were those of the tariff and of internal improvements. The Virginian President was strong in favour of protection to the national manufactures, and is found insisting on it from year to year in his messages (1821, 1822, 1823). Clay, the great Kentuckian, led the Protectionists, supported by the votes of his own slaveholding state, those of slaveholding Delaware, and other scattered votes from the South; Calhoun even, though perhaps now wavering, had been, as we have seen, till 1816 at least, in favour of protection; New England, on the contrary, was for free-trade, and Webster led the free-traders, his own Massachusetts men being strong in the cause. The lapse of a few years was to show a complete interversion of the parts, and the change may be said to date from 1824.

The question of internal improvements turned upon this—how far the Constitution allowed the Federal Government to take them in hand, and, above all, whether it empowered the Federal Government to do so at all, when within the limits of a single state. Colonel Benton tells us that at this period the leading statesmen, J. Quincy Adams, Clay, Calhoun, were in favour of a liberal exercise of the Federal power. But the President brought the matter to an issue by refusing to sanction a bill for the preservation and repair of a particular road called the Cumberland-road, as requiring, in order to be legal, an amendment of the constitution (May 24, 1822). To facilitate matters, an Act was passed (1824) authorising the survey of roads and canals of national importance in a commercial point of view, or for transporting the mail. Among the measures thus introduced, we may notice one of Benton's for a trade-road to New Mexico (1824-5).

After fulfilling his double term of office, Monroe was succeeded by John Quincy Adams, of Massachusetts, son of John Adams (1825). The Adamses were not lucky. J. Q. Adams (who, for want of a sufficient majority among the Presidential electors, was chosen as Jefferson had been, by the House of Representatives) entered upon his office with a majority in the Senate, and a strong minority in the House of Representatives against him, and was only allowed to complete a single term of office. Calhoun was Vice-President under him, Clay Secretary of State. The events of his four years' Presidency were but few. A man of high purpose and of a cultivated mind, we find the President urgently recommending, besides material improvements, such as roads and canals, all means of intellectual advancement—a Federal university, a Federal observatory, a naval academy. He foresees that it is the destiny and duty of the United States to become, "in regular process of time, and by no petty advances, a great naval power" (1826), and supports arrangements for preserving the live-oak timber of the country (1828). He notices the impatience of direct taxation shown by his people, and points out the danger of relying exclusively on indirect, through the extraordinary fluctuations in a revenue consisting largely of import and tonnage dues. You will observe that this was the period of the great commercial crisis of 1824-5, of which, as J. Q. Adams showed, the United States felt severely the effects. With less of justice, whilst advocating protection at home, he found bitter fault with our English legislation for excluding grain, timber, live-stock, rice, the produce of America.

It was now that the tariff question became, in American political language, sectional, Webster turning round with the North in favour of protection, Calhoun with the South supporting low import duties. Benton thus explains the change: " In the colonial state, the Southern were the rich part of the colonies, and expected to do well in a state of independence. . . . But in the first half century after independence this expectation was reversed. Northern towns had become great cities, Southern states had decayed or become stationary, and Charleston, the principal port of the South, was less considerable than before the revolution. The North became a money-lender to the South, and Southern citizens made pilgrimages to Northern cities to raise money upon the hypothecation of their patrimonial estates. And this in the face of a Southern export since the revolution, to the value of eight hundred millions of dollars." He goes on to say that this was attributed to the levying of revenue on one section of the country to spend it on another, and specially to a protective tariff; but observes justly, that the latter had only been in force since 1816, whilst the change had been continuous. The real economic lesson to be learnt from the facts was, that slavery was slowly wasting the South, and that for the benefit primarily of the slave-breeding or border slave-states, ultimately of Northern freedom, as it has continued to do till this day.

The slow spoiling of the Indians, followed by their removal, was still going on. The great means to this end had lain in the advantage taken by the Americans of the division of authority between the Central Government and the states. Repeatedly had the United States treated with the Indian tribes as with independent powers. The several states, on the other hand, insisted on subjecting to their own state jurisdictions the Indians residing within their limits; and when the Central Government at last interfered, it was simply to take the Indians out of the way. Thus, the first year of J. Q. Adams's Presidency (1815) saw a treaty with the Creeks, for their emigration from Georgia to beyond the Mississippi, which was at once carried out by a portion of them, and cessions of land from the Kansas Indians, from the Great and Little Osages. Among those who remained behind, however, a remarkable movement was taking place, exactly analogous to the present "native-king" movement in New Zealand. The most intelligent of the Indian tribes, seeing their own race gradually wasting away, the white race constantly gaining upon them, had reflected upon the causes of the process, and seeing the value to the white man of his habits of organization and settled forms of government, had modelled for themselves republican polities after the fashion of the United States. Foremost on this path were the Cherokees, of whom upwards of 13,000 formed quite a settled and civilized community. This was going too far. American statesmen till now had lamented the want of civilization among the Indians, as that which rendered them unfit neighbours for the white man. To have them civilized, and thereby stripping the white man of so convenient a plea for their removal, was a worse evil still. The President's last message of 1828 indicates, not I think dishonestly, this conflict of feelings. He frankly admits past shortcomings as towards the Indians: "We have been far more successful," he says, " in the acquisition of their lands than in imparting to them the principles, or inspiring them with the spirit of civilization." But he is visibly jealous of their efforts for self-government: "When we have had the rare good fortune of teaching them the arts of civilization and the doctrines of Christianity, we have *unexpectedly* found them forming in the midst of ourselves communities claiming to be independent of ours, and rivals of sovereignty within the territories of the states of our Union." There is a curious simplicity about the use of the word "unexpectedly." The states, I believe, in many if not most instances, exclude the Indians from the rights of citizenship; yet the Indians are instructed in "the arts of civilization, and the doctrines of Christianity,"—in other words, fitted and trained to be citizens. When they once come to feel their own fitness, what can they do but form communities of their own, when they cannot enter others? Yet this is treated by the very highest authority, by a truly benevolent man, as an "unexpected" result! The only inference to be drawn from such language is, that the attempts at civilizing the Indians were not meant to be serious ones, since the logical consequences of them were not foreseen. I need hardly add that the Indian polities were disallowed, and that such dangerous savages, who could really practise civilization, had to be inexorably turned out. So important was it deemed to conciliate the Cherokees, that twelve thousand square miles of the Arkansas territory were ceded to them (1828), and Benton observes that this measure, although it curtailed the extent of slave soil, was a Southern measure, negotiated by Calhoun, and voted for by nineteen approving senators from the slave-holding states, against four dissenting.

One or two remarkable diplomatic transactions belong to J. Q. Adams's Presidency. A convention for joint occupation was entered into with Great Britain, as to the territory on the North-West coast (6th August, 1827); a correspondence (9th June, 1826 to 2nd October, 1828) was carried on with the same power, to obtain the delivering up of fugitive slaves seeking shelter in Canada. So far were English officials from having reached the level of English convictions on the subject of slavery, that they are reported to have treated as "mania" the state of public feeling respecting it, and were ready to lay the matter before Parliament, as they " could not conceive that any people would wish to see their numbers increased by such subjects" as the fugitive negroes. Nothing, however, thank God! was done in the matter. But the treating of such a point under a Northern President shows how dull Northern feeling was yet upon the point.

Again, there was obtained from Mexico (12th January, 1828) a boundary treaty, ratifying the old one with Spain, which Monroe had thrust upon the latter power unratified, for the cession of Florida; the United States on their part, as before mentioned, ceding all their claim to the territory lying West and South of the boundary agreed upon, including all Texas. One clause of the treaty is remarkable:—" The *inhabitants* of the territories which his Catholic Majesty cedes to the United States by this treaty shall be incorporated in the Union of the United States, as soon as may be consistent with the principles of the federal constitution, and admitted to the enjoyment of all the privileges, rights, and immunities of the *citizens of the United States*." Does not this pledge eventual emancipation and admission to citizenship of the whole slave and coloured population?

Among other miscellaneous events of Adams's Presidency we may mention a contract, not indeed carried out, for the cutting of the American isthmus by a canal *vid* Nicaragua, the first presage of the present Panama Railway, and organised system of inter-oceanic communication. Nor should we forget the visit (1824-5) of General Lafayette, Washington's old companion in arms, to America, who arrived indeed during Monroe's Presidency, though he took his departure under Adams. His progress throughout the states was a triumphal procession; money was voted by Congress for his reception, and private persons almost everywhere refused payment for any expenses on his account.

This was followed, the next year, by a still more affecting event, and one which must have marked painfully for John Quincy Adams the term of his Presidentship. Old John Adams, his father, now eighty-five years of age, had withdrawn from public affairs after his ejection from the Presidency, carrying on, however, for a long time, an active correspondence upon political matters, especially with his old opponent Jefferson, till at last, for some years, he became extremely feeble. On the morning of the 4th July, 1826, the fiftieth anniversary of the Declaration of Independence, as the bells were ringing, and the nation's ceremonial joy was sounding forth in honour of the day, feeble old John Adams was asked if he knew the meaning of all this: "O yes," he replied, "it is the glorious 4th of July—God bless it! God bless you all!" "It is a great and glorious day," he said, some time after; then paused, and said, "Jefferson yet survives!" These were his last words. He became alarmingly ill at noon, and died at 6 o'clock, at his residence at Quincy. Jefferson did not survive; he died that self-same day, at his own residence at Monticello. The Federalist President and the Republican one passed out of life together. They were taken away in time from the evil that should be.

John Quincy Adams, as I have said, held his Presidentship but for a single term. He was probably too lofty-minded for the new generation of American politicians. Although only the son of one of the old revolutionary statesmen, he may be considered to belong to their dynasty, and closes it not unworthily. Yet probably he left office in time. It is at least doubtful whether he had the strong will and clear head to grapple with difficulties which were even now looming over the country. For these the man was at hand.

LECTURE V.

FROM THE PRESIDENCY OF GENERAL JACKSON TO THE END OF THAT OF MR. VAN BUREN (1829—1841)—THE DEMOCRATIC PARTY IN POWER—SOUTH CAROLINA NULLIFICATION—THE SLAVERY QUESTION AS RESPECTS THE TARIFF AND CONSUMPTION—THE UNITED STATES' BANK.

(Jackson, 1829—37 ; Van Buren, 1837—41).

THE so-called "Democratic Party" had carried its candidates at the Presidential election of 1828; Andrew Jackson, of Tennessee, became President, Calhoun was Vice-President, both slaveholders, both receiving a large vote (75) from the free states.

The displacement of power was in itself a remarkable one. For from this period, or rather from the actual exit from office of Mr. Adams in 1829, to that of Mr. Buchanan in 1861, a period of thirty-two years, the nomination of the executive was to lie, with but two exceptions, in the hands of the same party ; and, thanks to the early deaths of the two whig Presidents who mark the exceptions, and the weakness of the one and the popularity-hunting of the other Vice-President who filled their places, its tenure of power may be said to have been practically continuous. Fortunately for itself, it put forward its best men first.

Andrew Jackson—described as a tall gaunt man, sallow, with iron-grey hair and hawk-like grey eyes

—was the son of an Irish emigrant, a linendraper's son, who had gone over to America in 1765, and settled in South Carolina, where his third son, Andrew, was born (1767). He was at first meant for a clergyman, and studied theology, but, in the War of Independence, joined the ranks, a boy of thirteen, and served till the end of the war. He seems till this time to have been a rather dissipated young scapegrace, but suddenly reformed himself, began studying the law in 1784, and already in 1787—a youth of twenty consequently—was appointed solicitor for what is now the State of Tennessee. We find him then in succession serving as a private against the Indians; acting as a member of the convention for establishing a constitution for Tennessee; when the state is constituted, elected a member of its House of Representatives, then of its Senate; then appointed Judge of the Supreme Court for the State (having been made a Major-General of the State's forces just previously); then resigning, and living on his farm at Nashville till the breaking out of the war with England in 1812. Here he greatly distinguished himself, amongst other exploits, by a campaign against the Creeks and victory over them (1813-14), by the taking of Pensacola (1814), and by the repulse of the British from New Orleans (8th January, 1815). By this time a Major-General in the United States' service, he next conducted the Seminole war in 1818, acting throughout in the most independent manner, disregarding the orders of the Federal Government, seizing Spanish towns, and shooting, not only Indian prisoners of war, but two Englishmen who were found acting with them. Notwithstanding these irregularities, his conduct was sanctioned in Congress; he was appointed Commissioner to treat with the Spaniards for the transfer of Florida, became its first Governor (1821), and was a candidate for the Presidentship at the election of 1824, obtaining the largest number of votes (101), but not an actual majority, so that, as before mentioned, John Quincy Adams was chosen by the House. His return at his second candidateship was a triumphant one.

I have no natural sympathy with Jackson. He was a slaveholder, and some of his hardest words were put forth against abolitionist doctrines. He had shown himself reckless of human life, bold and unscrupulous as a politician. Yet, for all this, I cannot help thinking that, as a President, he has been singularly underrated, chiefly, I believe, through the influence of that brilliant thinker, but unsound judge of men, Tocqueville. Next to Washington, he seems to me to stand out in the list of Presidents as the one strong man, fit to ride any storm, to cope with any emergency.

Jackson entered office as a supporter of the States' Rights' doctrine, selecting Martin Van Buren as his Secretary of State. In his "inaugural" (March 4, 1829) he expressed his hope that he would be found " animated by a proper respect for the sovereign members of our Union, taking care not to confound the powers they have reserved to themselves with those they have granted to the confederacy." Amongst other measures he constantly recommended were (1829, 1830, 1831) the removal of "all intermediate agency in the election of President and Vice-President;" the representation in Congress of the district of Columbia (1830, 1831); a limiting of the Presidential term of office to four years, and a general limitation of official appointments to that period (1829, 1831). But he, nevertheless, accepted a renewal of his own term of office for a second period.

Three great questions—three great contests—chiefly occupy Jackson's administration, that of Internal Improvements; of the Tariff, with its offshoot, Nullification; and of the Bank.

Following Monroe's example, Jackson resolutely set his face against cumbering the action of the Federal Government with bills for local improvements. He vetoed (27th May, 1829) a bill for a federal subscription of stock in a road company, called the Maysville Road, on the ground of the road lying exclusively within a single state, and not being of national interest, nor authorised by the state itself. If the construction of roads and canals was to be by the Federal Government, he argued, let there be an amendment of the Constitution. For himself, he feared "a scramble for appropriations." Later experience, even confined within the limits which were thus fixed, has shown how well grounded was this fear. There is probably no country in the world which has seen such jobbing for public works, such trafficking in legislation for internal improvements, as the United States. Again, in his annual message of that year, we find him declining to ratify appropriation bills for lighthouses, light-boats, &c., for improving harbours and directing surveys, and for a subscription of stock in a canal company (Louisville and Portland). He does not object to direct appropriations for lighting purposes, but disapproves of subscriptions to the stock of private associations. Let it be observed that in thus refusing to sanction state improvements out of Federal moneys, Jackson went directly contrary to the interest of his own section, the poorer and more thinly peopled South.

Such a course was, of course, far from palatable to the whole crew of speculators, with capital or without. Jackson cut at the very roots of their influence by seeking to restrain within the narrowest limits the revenue of the country. Perhaps over-careless of the navy, he recommended the reducing of ship-building, whilst materials only should be accumulated. The public income was overflowing, both from a too high tariff and from the sale of public lands. At first (1829) he recommended that any surplus should be apportioned among the states, according to their ratio of representation, though he afterwards modified his views on this point. He wished also to abandon the raising of public revenue by the sale of public lands (1832). On the other hand, he recommended a reduction of import duties, especially on articles of consumption. He was willing still to encourage domestic manufactures, but only whilst directed to national ends, and as tending to increase the value of agricultural productions. The chief object of a tariff, he insisted, should be revenue, although it might be so adjusted as to encourage manufactures for the general good. On this point, his views are clearly those now adopted amongst ourselves, and which experience has sanctioned; although he stopped short, and I think wisely, of the doctrines of our extreme free-traders.

High duties were now energetically opposed by the Southern states. Already in 1820 South Carolina had petitioned against the tariff as unconstitutional, oppressive, and unjust. Georgia, Virginia, North Carolina, Alabama, Mississippi, had since protested against it. In spite of this opposition, the tariff had been modified in a Protectionist sense in 1824 and 1828. The "Nullification" doctrine, precursor of that of Secession, was now put forth. It was but an exaggeration of the States' Rights' theories. According to this doctrine, each state, retaining its sovereignty, had the right to interpret the laws of Congress, and to suspend their execution when it should deem them unconstitutional or unjust. The right of Secession was already assumed in such a doctrine, and indeed openly claimed.

The President—a Southerner, a Democrat in politics, an avowed opponent of high protective duties—seemed almost a natural ally to the Nullificationists. It was sought to commit him openly in their favour. He was invited (April 13th, 1830) to a banquet in honour of Jefferson's birthday. After twenty-four set toasts had been given, all, Benton tells us, savouring of nullification, the President was called upon to give one. He gave it, short and telling: "Our Federal Union: it *must* be preserved." Nothing daunted, Calhoun (now the avowed leader of the South, and holding, as you will recollect, the next highest office in the state after the President) gave, "The Union: *next* to our liberty, the most dear. May we all remember that it can only be preserved by respecting the rights of the states, and distributing equally the benefit and burthen of the Union." The strong man and the headstrong one had both spoken out. There was a moral gulf between them. In another year (1831) there was open rupture. A break-up of the cabinet followed. Livingston, of Louisiana, an eminent jurist, became Secretary of State; Cass, then of Ohio, better known afterwards as General Cass, Secretary at War. The President nominated Van Buren for the English mission.

And now comes the disgraceful part of the story, not for the President, but for the whole crew of so-called statesmen below him. Calhoun, the Nullificationist, ought to have been evidently considered, by whoever was attached to the Constitution, as the common enemy. His doctrines as to low duties seemed naturally to separate him from Protectionists such as Clay and Webster. Yet these, the heads of the so-called Whig party, boasting to be Constitutional, united with Calhoun to oppose the President. This coalition carried the Senate (whose consent, you will recollect, is needed for the appointment of foreign ministers) against him, and Van Buren's nomination was disallowed. The next year, Clay is found making a great Protection speech, and so irritating still further the South, whose dissatisfaction he admitted. Observe always, that this Protectionism of which the South so complained, was not forced upon it by the North alone, or even mainly, since Clay, the Protectionist leader, was from Kentucky, and was supported by senators from other border slave-states, such as Delaware and Maryland.

South Carolina this time set herself in open opposition to the Federal authority. In 1832, she named a national convention, authorized to take extraordinary measures. On the 24th of November, this convention published an ordinance, founded on an elaborate report of a committee, which nullified the Federal tariff, and forbade the levying of duties under it, and the appealing to Federal tribunals. The ordinance was to take effect from February in the ensuing year, unless Congress in the meanwhile should modify the tariff. Before it was officially communicated to the Federal authority, Jackson sent his fourth annual message of December 4th, 1832, in which he only stated that there was opposition to the revenue laws in one quarter. But on the 11th of December, 1832, he sent forth a proclamation concerning the Nullification ordinance, the reasoning of which, as well as of the later documents emanating from him on the same subject, is singularly apposite to present circumstances. The ordinance, he said, was founded "on the strange position that any one state may not only declare an act of Congress void, but prohibit its execution. . . . Reasoning on this subject is superfluous, when our solemn compact in express terms declares that the laws of the United States, the Constitution, and treaties made under it, are the supreme law of the land; and, for greater caution, adds, 'that the judges in every state shall be bound thereby, anything in the constitution or laws of any state to the contrary notwithstanding.' And it may be asserted. without fear of refutation, that no Federative Government could exist without a similar provision . . . If this doctrine had been established at an earlier day, the Union would have been dissolved in its infancy. . . Before the Declaration of Independence, we were known in our aggregate character as the United Colonies of America. That decisive and important step was taken jointly. We declared ourselves a nation by a joint, not by several acts; and when the terms of our Confederation were reduced to form, it was in that of a solemn league of several states, by which they agreed that they would collectively form one nation for the purpose of conducting some certain domestic concerns and all foreign relations. In the instrument forming the Union is found an article which declares that any state shall abide by the determination of Congress on all questions which by that Confederation should be submitted to them. Under the Confederation, then, no state could legally annul a decision of Congress, or refuse to submit to its execution; but no provision was made to enforce these decisions. . . We could scarcely be called a nation. We had neither prosperity at home, nor consideration abroad. This state of things could not be endured, and our present happy Constitution was formed . . . . for important objects that are announced in the preamble. The most important of these objects—that which was placed first in rank—on which all the others rest, is, '*to form a more perfect Union.*' Now, is it possible that, even if there were no express provision giving supremacy to the Constitution and laws of the United States over those of the states, it can be conceived that an instrument, made for the purpose of '*forming a more perfect Union*' than that of the Confederation, could be so constructed by the assembled wisdom of our country, as to substitute for the Confederation a form of government dependent for its exercise on the local interest, the party spirit of a state, or of a prevailing faction in a state? Every man of plain, unsophisticated understanding, who hears the question, will give such an answer as will preserve the Union."

Powerful and conclusive reasoning, which Jackson's admirer, Mr. Jefferson Davis, would have done well to lay to heart. But what follows is even more to the point:—

" The right to secede is deduced from the nature of the Constitution, which they say is a compact between sovereign states, which have preserved their whole sovereignty, and therefore are subject to no superior. . . . . But each state, having expressly parted with so many powers as to constitute jointly with the other states a single nation, *cannot from that period possess any right to secede, because such secession does not break a league, but destroys the unity of a nation,* and any injury to that unity is not a breach which would result from the contravention of a compact, but it is an offence against the whole nation. To say that each state may at pleasure secede from the Union, is to say that the United States are not a nation. . . Secession, like any other revolutionary act, may be morally justified by the extremity of oppression; but *to call it a constitutional right is confusing the meaning of terms, and can only be done through gross error, or to deceive* those who are willing to assert a right, but would pause before they made a revolution, or incurred the penalties consequent on a failure. Because the Union was formed by compact, it is said, the parties to that compact may, when they feel themselves aggrieved, depart from it. But *it is precisely because it is a compact that they cannot.* . . . . An attempt by force of arms to destroy a government is an offence, by whatever means the constitutional compact may have been formed, and such government has the right, by the law of self-defence, to pass acts for punishing the offender, unless that right is modified, restrained, or resumed by the constitutional act. In our system, although it is modified in the case of treason, yet authority is expressly given to pass all laws necessary to carry its powers into effect, and under this grant provision has been made for punishing acts which obstruct the due administration of the laws."

Returning to the States' Rights' doctrine, of which

he now, perhaps, only sees the full danger, he proceeds :—

"The states severally have not retained their entire sovereignty. . . . The right to make treaties, declare war, levy taxes, exercise exclusive judicial and legislative powers, were all of them functions of sovereign power. The states then, for all these important purposes, were no longer sovereign. The allegiance of their citizens was transferred in the first instance to the government of the United States. They became American citizens, and owed obedience to the constitution of the United States, and to laws made in conformity with the powers it vested in Congress. . . . How then can that state be said to be sovereign and independent, whose citizens owe obedience to laws not made by it, and whose magistrates are sworn to disregard its laws when they come in conflict with those passed by another? What shows conclusively that the states cannot be said to have reserved an undivided sovereignty is, that they expressly ceded the right to punish treason, not treason against their separate power, but treason against the United States. Treason is an offence against sovereignty, and sovereignty must reside with the power to punish it."

After repeating his arguments from the original unity of the American polity, its maintenance under the confederation, the more perfect form introduced by the Constitution, and showing that it is by a logical fallacy that "compact" is used as synonymous with "league," he continues :—

"So obvious are the reasons which forbid this secession, that it is necessary only to allude to them. The Union was formed for the benefit of all. It was produced by mutual sacrifices of interests and opinions. Can these sacrifices be recalled?" After referring, as instances of such sacrifices, to the surrender of territories claimed by the particular states, the duties paid by inland states &c., "No one," he declares, "believes that any right exists in a single state to involve the others in these and countless other evils, contrary to the engagements solemnly made. *Every one must see that the other states in self-defence must oppose at all hazards.*"

This was but the first of several admirable state-papers on the same subject. I quote from them at some length, because they cover, it will be seen, the whole ground occupied by President Lincoln and the North in the present movement, and utterly convict the Southerners out of the mouth of one of their own slave-owning Presidents. Jackson's manful resistance to Nullification is indeed all the more admirable, on account of the imperfect means of coercion which were at his command. The army was in a very bad condition. Out of 6000 men, Benton tells us, the desertions in 1831 were 1450, in spite of an increase of pay: a state of things to which the resolute unanimity of the North at the present day to check Secession offers a most remarkable contrast.

South Carolina took up the challenge thrown down by the President. Not only was the "Nullification ordinance" officially communicated to the Federal authority, but the Governor retorted to President Jackson's proclamation by one of his own, openly defying the Federal authority. He announced his readiness to accept the services of volunteers. Jackson now sent to Congress his so-called "Nullification message" (16th January, 1833). After stating what South Carolina had done, he said: "If these measures cannot be defeated and overcome by the powers conferred by the Constitution on the Federal Government, the Constitution must be considered as incompetent to its own defence, the supremacy of the laws is at an end, and the rights and liberties of the citizens can no longer receive protection from the Government of the Union. *The right of the people of a single state to absolve themselves at will, and without the consent of the other states, from the most solemn obligations*, and hazard the liberties and life of the millions composing this Union, *cannot be acknowledged*. Without adverting to the particular theories to which the Federal compact has given rise, and without inquiring whether it be merely federal, or social, or national, it is sufficient that it must be admitted to be a compact, and to possess the obligations implied in a compact. To this compact the people of South Carolina had freely and voluntarily given their assent, and to the whole and every part of it they are upon every principle of good faith inviolably bound. However it may be alleged that a violation of the compact by the measures of the Government can affect the obligations of the parties, it cannot even be pretended that such violation can be predicated of those measures, until all the constitutional remedies shall have been fully tried. If the Federal Government exercise powers not warranted by the Constitution, and immediately affecting individuals, it will scarcely be denied that the proper remedy is a recourse to the judiciary. . . . And it is equally clear that, if there be any case in which a state as such is affected by the law beyond the scope of judicial power, the remedy consists in appeals to the people, either to effect a change in the representation, or to procure reform by an amendment in the Constitution." " The duty of the Government," he declared, " seems to be plain. It inculcates a recognition of that state as a member of the Union, and subject to its authority a vindication of the just powers of the Constitution, the preservation of the integrity of the Union, and the execution of the laws by all constitutional means. In all cases similar to the present, *the duties of the Government become the measure of its powers*, and whenever it fails to exert a power necessary and proper to the discharge of the duties prescribed by the Constitution, it violates the public trusts not less than it would in transcending its proper limits. We are called upon to decide whether these laws possess any force, and that Union the means of self-preservation. The decision of this question by an enlightened and patriotic people cannot be doubtful."

Jackson at this time spoke with singular authority. He had been re-elected President by a triumphant

CLAY'S COMPROMISE TARIFF.   145

majority, his opponent, Clay, only receiving forty-nine votes out of two hundred and eighty-eight—South Carolina throwing away hers. As a further indorsement of the President's policy, Van Buren, whose appointment as Minister to England the Senate had refused to sanction, was elected Vice-President.

In his second "Inaugural" (March 4, 1833), Jackson went further, and prefigured the evils of successful secession:

" Divided into twenty-four, or even a smaller number of separate communities, we shall see our internal trade burdened with numberless restraints and exactions, communications between distant parts and sections obstructed or cut off, our sons made soldiers to deluge with blood the fields they now till in peace, the mass of our people borne down and impoverished by taxes to support armies and navies, and military leaders, at the head of their victorious legions, becoming our lawgivers and judges. The loss of liberty, of all good government, of peace, plenty, and happiness, must inevitably follow a dissolution of the Union."

But already, Clay, Jackson's late opponent for the Presidency—Clay, the father of compromises—had patched up the feud for a time. In conjunction with Calhoun, he had devised a new tariff bill, reducing duties, and providing that they should be prospectively and annually lowered till 1842; after which time they should only be maintained for revenue purposes. The bill was hurried through Congress in four days, by immense majorities. The plan of course failed, like

L

all similar attempts to fetter future legislation. A so-called "force bill" was passed at the same time with the new tariff, for facilitating the collection of the revenue—an empty parade of resolution, which South Carolina met simply with contempt. The same convention which had nullified the old tariff bill met again, accepted the new one, and nullified the "force bill" at the same time. More audacious yet, Calhoun had brought forward in the Senate a series of "nullification resolutions." These declared, amongst other positions, that the people of the several states were "united as parties to a constitutional compact, to which the people of each state acceded as a separate sovereign community, each binding itself by its own particular ratification, and that the Union of which the said compact is the bond, is a union between the states ratifying the same. . . . That the assertions that the people of these United States, taken collectively as individuals, are now or have ever been united on the principle of the social compact, and as such are now formed into one nation or people, or that they ever have been so united in any one stage of their political existence," are "not only without foundation in truth," but "contrary to the most certain and plain historical facts, and the clearest deductions of reason."

It would have been difficult to fly more completely in the face of the constitutional doctrines enunciated by the President. According to Calhoun, there really is no such thing as an American people. There are Georgians and New Yorkers, Pennsylvanians and

South Carolinians, but nothing else. Daniel Webster, who, to his credit be it said, though opposed to the general policy of the President, supported him manfully throughout on the Nullification question, brought forward a series of counter-resolutions, declaring " 1. That the Constitution of the United States is not a league, confederacy, or compact between the people of the several states in their sovereign capacities, but a government proper, founded on the adoption of the people, and creating direct relations between itself and individuals. 2. That no state authority has power to dissolve these relations; that nothing can dissolve them but revolution ; and that consequently there can be no such thing as secession without revolution. 3. That there is a supreme law, consisting of the Constitution of the United States, Acts of Congress passed in pursuance of it, and treaties, and that, in cases not capable of assuming the character of a suit in law or equity, Congress must judge of and finally interpret this supreme law ; . . . and in cases capable of assuming and actually assuming the character of a suit, the Supreme Court of the United States is the final interpreter. 4. That an attempt by a state to abrogate, annul, or nullify an Act of Congress, or to arrest its operation within her limits, on the ground that in her opinion such law is unconstitutional, is a direct usurpation on the just powers of the general government, and on the equal rights of other states—a plain violation of the Constitution, and a proceeding essentially revolutionary in its character and tendency."

Neither of these sets of resolutions came to any practical end. It is useful, however, to record them, as instances of the two opposite views then and now prevailing in the country,—but then, indeed, only taking the shape of paper formulas and set orations; now of hostile armies and all the stern realities of war. Nor let us forget that beyond the tariff lay another question, now foremost, that of slavery. In the tariff discussion, Calhoun spoke of the contest as one "between power and liberty; . . . in which the weaker section, *with its peculiar labour*, productions, and situation, has at stake all that is dear to freemen."

The President had not failed the nation, but Congress had failed the President. The new tariff was in fact a surrender on the part of the Federal authority. To use the words of Benton, the Missourian, "A compromise with a state in arms is a capitulation to that state." South Carolina remained as it were in possession of the field at the battle, and effected her retreat not only without loss, but defiantly, ready to recommence the conflict on any opportunity. But the large amount of popular support given to Jackson had made Calhoun feel that the field itself was not a safe one. He declared this year, Benton tells us, that the Southern slave states could never be united to the Northern ones on the tariff question, alleging that the sugar interests of Louisiana, which bound her to the North, would keep her aloof. The basis of Southern union, he said, must henceforth be shifted to the slavery question. Much of the subsequent history of the Union is a mere comment upon this saying.

I do not mean henceforth to dwell much on the fluctuations of the American tariff. No doubt the planters of South Carolina were substantially right at the time in contending that the tariff was too high. No doubt there are circumstances when the rate of a duty becomes of itself a vital question in a nation's history: when, for instance, that nation is yet so young as to be struggling for the means of production; or, when it is old, and the springs of production are so heavily weighted, that they are ready to snap under an extra pennyworth of fiscal burthen. But while those springs have yet all their elasticity, in a rapidly growing country, capable, in fact, of producing in superabundance all it needs, or all that is requisite to purchase what it needs, I believe that tariff questions are far from having that importance which English merchants imagine, and Southerners, with their sympathisers, try to persuade us they have in the United States. The insistance with which this point is urged at present, as a plea for secession, may, however, justify us in stopping for a moment to look into it.

The South and its advocates are never tired of exhibiting the enormous and ever-increasing production of the Southern States, and how it furnishes all the staple exports of the country, contributes six-sevenths of the whole freight of American shipping, and actually supplies Boston itself with one-third of all its flour and five-sevenths of all its corn.* And then they accuse Northern tariffs of the strange fact which they have to allege on the other side, that the South is dependent upon the North for five-sixths of the tonnage requisite to transport her produce, and for nearly all the capital by means of which she raises it; doing "little of her own transportation, banking, insurance, brokerage," but paying "liberally on those accounts" to Northern capital.

But the South, blinded by attachment to its "peculiar institution," has never yet had the courage to recognise the simple truth, that production and consumption are interdependent, and that it is as ruinous to produce without consuming as to consume without producing; or simply, to force production out of proportion to consumption, as to force consumption out of proportion to production.

The cause of the anomaly which it complains of lies really in this: Slavery is for ever contracting the purchasing power of the South, stinting its consumption. What demand for foreign produce is there in a country where, not a certain number of ill-paid workers, but so to speak, the whole of the labouring class, from year's end to year's end, from birth to death, consume on an average but Indian corn, salt, and generally salt meat for food; most of the corn, and a portion of the meat, when it is bacon or salt pork, being grown at home; and, say two suits per annum of the coarsest

* See Dr. Lemprière's "American Crisis considered;" *passim*.

clothing, with a warm blanket? Now 15 to 30 dollars a year, or say from 3*l*. 15*s*. to 7*l*. 10*s*., Mr. Olmsted shows from official documents, and the statements of slave-owners, is the cost of clothing and boarding a first-class slave-labourer. Take the larger estimate. Multiply 30 dollars by 4,000,000, for the total number of slaves, and you will have 120,000,000 dollars* for the amount of slave consumption. We are told that the South sends North yearly over 460,000,000 dollars, to say nothing of its direct trade with foreign countries. Supposing the whole consumption of the slave came from the North, the difference between the two figures is enormous. Whence comes it? Does it represent the superabundant consumption of the white man in the cotton Eldorado? Is the slave-owner to be found habitually rolling in wealth, his every want supplied, every luxury within his reach?

Quite the contrary. In restricting the consumption of his slave he has in fact restricted his own. Listen to Mr. Olmsted: "I went on my way into the so-called cotton states . . . and for every mile of road-side upon which I saw any evidence of cotton production, I am sure that I saw a hundred of forest or waste land, with only now and then an acre or two of poor corn, half smothered in weeds; for every rich man's house, I am sure that I passed a dozen shabby and half-furnished

---

* Of course there are slaves employed in mechanical arts, &c., who consume far more. On the other hand, it is beyond question that vast numbers consume far less than even the lower figure, which is that of South Carolina.

cottages, and at least a hundred cabins, mere hovels, such as none but a poor farmer would house his cattle in at the North. And I think that, for every man of refinement and education with whom I came in contact, there were a score or two superior only in the virtue of silence, and in the manner of self-complacency, to the sort of people we should expect to find paying a large price for a place from which a sight could be got at a gallows on an execution day at the North, and a much larger number of what poor men at the North would themselves describe as poor men ; not that they were destitute of certain things which are cheap at the South, fuel for instance, but that they were almost wholly destitute of things the possession of which at the North would indicate that a man had begun to accumulate capital. . . . The proportion of the free men who live as well in any respect as our working classes at the North, on an average, is small, and the citizens of the cotton states, as a whole, are poor. They work little, and that little badly ; they earn little, they sell little; they buy little, and they have little, very little, of the common comforts and consolations of civilised life."

Do you wonder at this ? Think for a moment of the effect of demand in creating, and (until it becomes excessive) cheapening supply. Would you expect to get a bottle of beer, or a coat, or a book, or a pianoforte, as cheap in a place where no one else should want one within five, ten, twenty, a hundred miles, as here in London, where there is a constant demand for all such articles? Would you make sure of getting it at all? Would you care much to get it if no one else cared for it? Now such, more or less, except in the great towns,* is the condition to which slavery reduces the white population itself, the very slave-owners. By stinting the consumption of the labouring class, they have simply stinted their own. By limiting the demand for every article which, but for slavery, would be within the reach of the labouring class, they have limited or cut off the supply to themselves, not only of such articles, but of all other articles which, even without slavery, might not have been within the labourer's reach. By underpaying their native labour, they have condemned themselves to overpay the produce of all other. The profits which they extract from their slaves (and those of a good cotton plantation are no doubt enormous), so far as they are not simply drunk or gambled away, are wasted to a great extent in struggling to overcome the dearth of supply which they themselves, by slavery, create; these profits are largely spent, by all who are rich enough to afford the change, on annual excursions to reach that supply in the North;

---

* In Mobile, the great seaport of Alabama, with a population of 40,000 souls, Mr. Olmsted could find no working hatter. With abundance of timber in the neighbourhood, it is found cheaper to send thence for furniture to New York. Even as respects agricultural products, Mr. Olmsted mentions having bought Ohio maize at two dollars a bushel in a slave district which boasts of growing 100 bushels of it to the acre; whilst amidst rich grazing ground in Eastern Texas, the only butter to be had came in firkins from New York.

or, finally, they are sunk in the price of slaves. This is the last result of the stunting and dwarfing of consumption through slavery which we have to contemplate.

Wherever slavery is considered as perpetual, or simply as deserving to be perpetuated, its natural tendency must be, as a rule (subject, of course, to many exceptions), to reduce the labour of the slave to the lowest functions; since the qualifying him for any higher one, by developing his intelligence, must develop also his thirst for freedom and his means of acquiring it. Slavery, in short, must, in the main, be agricultural. The articles of exchange which it will supply to the slave-owner will simply be raw produce. The only force which it will apply to production will, in general, be brute human force (if the two epithets can be conjoined). Machinery for saving labour can only be introduced with the greatest caution. It runs at all times the risk of being destroyed by the slave, through sheer carelessness and stupidity. If it can be confided to slaves, it runs the risk of destroying slavery.

Hence, on the one hand, under the slave system, an ever-increasing development in the production of the raw material; on the other, and as necessarily consequent thereupon, a constant rise in the value of the slave. You remember how Mr. Cobb describes the slaves as affording " the greatest evidence of wealth in the planter," "the most desirable property for a remunerative income," "the best property to leave to his children." The labour of the slave, in short, becomes the one key to comfort (such as it may be had), enjoyment, respectability, wealth, station, honour, political power. It comes thus to be worth almost any price that can be asked for it. It grows to be the very sink of profit. "Let a man be absent from almost any part of the North twenty years," says Mr. Olmsted, "and he is struck, on his return, by what we call the 'improvements' which have been made; better buildings, churches, school-houses, mills, railroads, &c. . . . But where will the returning traveller see the accumulated cotton profits of twenty years in Mississippi? Ask the cotton-planter for them, and he will point, in reply, not to dwellings, libraries, churches, school-houses, mills, railroads, or anything of the kind, he will point to his negroes—to almost nothing else. Negroes such as stood for 500 dollars once, now represent 1000 dollars." In a word, under American slavery, everything turns in a vicious circle. Men produce more and more, to enjoy less and less, and to pay dearer and dearer for that labour which alone procures them any means of enjoyment at all.

It is slavery, I repeat it, and not a Northern tariff, that hampers Southern consumption. The Southerner pays 20 cents a pound for "crackers" in Texas, worth 6 cents in New York, or sends to New York for furniture from the very borders of the Alabama forest, not because there is a high import duty upon either, but because, for the sake of his "peculiar institution," he chooses to live at some six hundred miles from that intelligent labour which might otherwise produce either at his very door. In short, as Mr. Olmsted says, " The whole slave population of the South consumes almost nothing imported (nor would it, while slave, under any circumstances). The majority of the white population habitually makes use of no foreign production except chicory, which, ground with peas, they call coffee." And I believe it perfect insanity on the part of our English commercial class to imagine that they will be able to drive a profitable trade under secession, with a slave-holding Southern Confederacy.

We must not, however, forget that we are not arrived in our history at Secession, but only at its half-way house, Nullification; and that, at the period of which we are treating, slave-holding Tennessee was yet, through its tough old citizen, the President, the mainstay of the Union. We have seen him fighting through one great struggle: we have now to witness him in another.

What indeed had added to Jackson's difficulties in respect to South Carolina Nullification was the position he had taken up in reference to the " Bank of the United States." It is difficult for us here to understand how the question of the renewal of a bank charter could be one of first-rate importance, not only in a political, but in a social point of view. In a country, however, where the very principle of sovereignty is continually in question, as between the central power and the states; where the exercise of the supreme executive authority is uncertain beyond four years, and limited by custom to eight as its utmost term; where most judicial offices are elective, and there is no established church: in such a country we can easily see, on reflection, that the more or less permanent existence of a corporation invested to a great extent with the control of the circulating medium, is not unlikely to become, in the long run, a serious danger to the due working of the state machine. Shareholders are a more fixed body than a people voting by universal suffrage; they are bound together by a fixed money interest which does not bind the crowd. If they, or the directors whom they have chosen, once see that political power is a useful acquisition for the purpose of their money interest, they are likely to acquire it, and when acquired, to use it steadily for that purpose. Such was the danger; on the other hand, that very element of fixity which created the danger, constituted at the same time a recommendation for a National Bank in the eyes of the more conservative portion of the nation, that which feared above all the dissolvent, centrifugal force, so to speak, of local interests and local passions. The clamour of the various provincial banks, impatient not only of all control, but of any superior, seemed of itself further to recommend such an institution. Tocqueville, for instance, declared that it was sufficient to go through the United States to appreciate the advantages of the Bank, whose notes were received at par on the very limits of the wilderness. He admits that it may have meddled in politics to hinder Jackson's election. But he treats Jackson as acting only in a spirit of personal rancour; speaks of the fury with which the papers sold to the provincial banks attacked their great rival. The President's only strength against it, he thinks, consisted in the support of "the secret instincts of the majority," jealous of any central power, of any shape of aristocracy.

A shallower criticism on a grave political question was, I believe, never put forth. I believe the *selfish* "instincts of the majority" are everywhere for a widely extended circulation, and the high nominal wages which abundance of paper money is sure to promote.* They are, above all, for a circulating medium everywhere the same, and which never troubles the working man with calculations of discount and exchanges. So far as the Bank of the United States secured these points, its influence over the masses must have been enormous. If, as we shall see, those masses supported the President in his struggle against it, even through much distress and stagnation of trade, such conduct must have been due to instincts of a far higher character—loyalty to the man of their choice, implicit trust in his judgment. If his popularity weathered the severe trial of a contracted circulation and a return to specie payments—about the most severe ordeal, as all history, including our own, sufficiently shows, that a statesman's popularity can go through—

* See ante, p. 20.

we may rest assured that something else than revenge or paid fury is necessary to explain such a phenomenon.

The renewal of the United States' Bank Charter, although it might have been made before this period an occasion of party strife, yet had not become till now a set ground of party division. Although a National Bank had been opposed in its creation by the old Republican party, such an institution had yet been chartered in 1816 by that party, Webster leading the Federalist opposition against it. But in 1832, the same Webster led the new Whig party in support of its re-charter, whilst the President and the so-called Democratic party were opposed to it; the President vetoing the bill for its renewal, as explained in his celebrated "Bank veto message" (10th July, 1832). You will see at once the boldness of the stroke, when you recollect that his proclamation against South Carolina Nullification is dated December 11. In other words, he braved a Whig majority in both Houses of Congress, on the very eve of engaging what may be called the extreme wing of the Democratic.

His re-election, as we have seen, took place at the end of 1832. The Bank moved heaven and earth against him. Jackson replied by selling out the stock held by the United States in the Bank, and in his message of 1833 (December 8) complained of it as converted into a "permanent electioneering engine." His next step—as I conceive, a perfectly right one—was to withdraw from it the public deposits, hitherto intrusted to its keeping, but which, by its interference in politics, it had plainly forfeited all claim to retain. Not only did the blindness of party spirit in the Senate not sanction this simple proceeding, but its whole influence was employed to screen the Bank. According to its charter, the Federal authority had the right of appointing five public directors, named by the President, confirmed by the Senate. Seven directors constituted a board, and it was the most obvious, necessary intention of the charter, that the public directors should share in the actual control of the Bank's affairs. Instead of this, many of the most important money transactions of the Bank—loans, discounts, and the like—were carried on exclusively by an "exchange committee," chosen, not by the board of directors, but by the president of the Bank. Not only had the public directors no vote as such in this committee, but not one had been put upon it since the beginning of the year. When the time came for their re-appointment, Jackson named four who had already served, and had made the report on which the order for removal of deposits had been founded. The Senate rejected these nominations, and Clay brought forward resolutions, which were carried in the Senate by a majority of twenty-six out of forty-six, directly condemning the act of removal (28th March, 1834). The President protested (April 15). He was supported by the House of Representatives, which attempted to investigate the proceedings of the Bank by means of a committee. 'The Bank set this committee at defiance. The House, stung for a moment by this audacious proceeding, passed a resolution to arrest and bring to its bar the officers of the contumacious corporation, but the resolution was not acted upon. The senate, in turn, determined upon an investigation, which simply whitewashed the Bank. Nor was this all.

There had been a number of international claims, sometimes reciprocal, for seizures of property during the great continental war, which the United States had adjusted from time to time by treaties and conventions which I have not deemed it necessary to recal. There was, amongst others, a claim of some considerable amount against France. This was finally settled by a convention with Louis Philippe's Government, and a bill drawn for the amount. But the treaty was disallowed by the French Legislature, and the bill protested. Hereupon the Bank of the United States, the medium of the transaction, actually seized the dividends on the public stock, of which it had yet the management, to cover its damages on the protested bill. In his sixth annual message, Jackson called attention at once to the differences with France—announcing that he should insist on a prompt execution of the treaty—and to the unwarrantable proceedings of the Bank. The Senate refused, nevertheless, to sanction an appropriation for defence against France. To dispose of this part of the matter, I will add that there was an actual rupture of diplomatic relations with France, and a special message of the President (January 15, 1836) on the subject; but by the end of that year he was able to announce that diplomatic relations were resumed (December 6).

Meanwhile, the Bank, besides the most insolent attacks on the President in its reports, had been doing its best to organise public distress, in order to force a renewal of its charter (1833-4). The course now followed, it may be said in self-defence, by the President, was to effect a return to a metallic circulation. The country was actually prospering, the distress, to a great extent at least, fictitious. A report of one of the President's most efficient subordinates, Roger Taney (now Chief Justice of the Supreme Court, and who has attained to a lamentable notoriety by the so-called "Dred Scott" judgment), showed this conclusively, exhibiting an increase of revenue, and the revival of a gold currency. The President proposed Taney as Secretary of the Treasury. The Senate rejected the nomination. To facilitate the diffusion of metallic money, which the President now insisted on in each yearly message (1835, 1836), the establishment of branch mints was recommended at New Orleans, and in the *then* gold regions of Georgia and North Carolina. The measure was carried, but against the opposition of Clay. A more serious step yet, and one which shows at least how far Jackson was ready to imperil his popularity for what he deemed a needful end, was his famous "specie circular" (1836), forbidding the sale of public lands except for hard cash. At the close of the last session of his Presidentship, a bill for rescinding this circular was sent up to the President, but he returned it without further acting upon it, and it fell through.

Here we take leave for the present of the Bank struggle, which we shall see continued under Jackson's successor, Van Buren. How triumphantly Jackson's policy was justified by the subsequent conduct of the Bank, facts will show. In the meanwhile, I will simply point out that, if the removal of the public deposits from the Bank of the United States to approved state banks might serve to strengthen Jackson's popularity with the interests connected with those bodies, yet his advocacy of specie payments must have done far more to alienate them. The placing of the deposits with them was an act of necessity; they could no longer be left in the hands of a body in open opposition to the executive; they must be placed somewhere. We need not of course suppose that they were placed with other smaller institutions equally uncompromising in their hostility to the executive. Jackson, as I have said before, was not over troubled with scruples as to the choice of means toward an end. What I am concerned to show you is, that his end was a thoroughly right one,—that the very existence of the Union was at stake in this conflict with a great central money-power, freely interfering in politics, openly defying the executive, the House of Representatives, supported in all its irregularities by a majority of the Senate. Badgered and thwarted on all sides, at every step, the President had in effect won the day. He had hindered the re-chartering of the

Bank as a national institution. He had rescued the public purse from its grasp, and shown how its agency could be dispensed with. Time would do the rest. If he was not able to do more, it was simply that, in this case, as in that of Nullification, Congress had failed the President.

I have been anxious to do justice to Jackson on these three great questions, as I have now to turn to a side of his policy which is in the highest degree distasteful to me, that relating to slavery, and, as connected with slavery, to the Texas admission question.

Behind Nullification, as I have stated, lay Slavery. The agitation on this subject, as Benton clearly shows, arose not from the North, but from the South. He quotes a letter from Madison to Clay in June, 1833, in which the veteran statesman writes: "It is painful to see the unceasing efforts to alarm the South by imputations against the North of unconstitutional designs on the subject of slavery." Writing to another correspondent in reference to Nullification more particularly, the ex-President says, in words which distinctly foretell the present crisis: "It is not probable that this offspring of the discontents of South Carolina will ever approach success in a majority of the states. But a susceptibility of the contagion in the Southern States is visible, and the danger not to be concealed, that the sympathy arising from known causes"—*i.e.*, a common slaveholding interest—" and the inculcated impression of a permanent incompatibility of interests between the

South and the North, may put it in the power of popular leaders, aspiring to the highest stations, to unite the South, on some critical occasion, in a course that will end in creating a new theatre of great though inferior interest. In pursuing this course, the first and most obvious step is Nullification, the next Secession, and the last a final separation." Calhoun had established a paper in Washington, the "United States Telegraph," which was incessant in denouncing the North. The first struggle took place through the presentation of a temperately-worded memorial from the quaker body for the abolition of slavery and the slave-trade in the district of Columbia,—placed, as you will recollect, by the Constitution, under the direct jurisdiction of the Federal Legislature, and where slaves continue to this day to be bought and sold. Calhoun opposed the very reception of such documents. He took up what his brother slaveholder, Benton, terms "the new and extreme ground, entirely contrary to the Constitution itself, and to the whole doctrine of Congress upon it," of declaring that Congress had no right to meddle with slavery in the district, but only the people of the district itself. He was ahead yet of his party. Senators from slaveholding North Carolina and Georgia condemned his doctrine. Hill, of New Hampshire, declared that, though he abhorred the Abolitionists, he must protest against the excitement kept up in Congress against the North. Of all Abolitionist publications, he said, not one had contributed so much to this excitement as one paper published in the city,—

referring to Calhoun's "Telegraph." The Senate voted for the reception of the petition. The House of Representatives, on the other hand, voted that Congress ought not to interfere with slavery in the district. Siding yet more decidedly with the South, the President, in his message of the year (December 2, 1835), called attention "to the painful excitement produced in the South by attempts to inculcate through the mails inflammatory appeals addressed to the passions of the slaves, in prints and in various sorts of publications calculated to stimulate them to insurrection, and to produce all the horrors of a servile war." He suggested "the propriety of passing such a law as will prohibit, under severe penalties, the circulation in the Southern States, through the mail, of incendiary publications, intended to instigate the slaves to insurrection." A bill, however, for this purpose, was rejected in Congress.

The national feeling was at this time not only clearly opposed to abolition, but by no means sensitive on the subject of any moderate extension of slavery. In the border slave states, indeed, the old traditional feeling of hostility to slavery was not yet extinct. Thus, the question of gradually abolishing slavery in Virginia was actually discussed at great length in its legislature, in the sessions of 1831 and 1832, whilst, of thirty-six anti-slavery societies existing in the United States, twenty-eight were composed of slave-owners. But in the North, a little later, a poor printer, William Lloyd Garrison, who set up a paper called the "Liberator"

(1835), claiming equality of rights between black and white, was seized, dragged with a halter round his neck through Boston streets by a yelling mob, and flung into gaol. George Thompson, the English abolitionist lecturer, who visited America a year or two after, was equally, several times, most roughly handled by Northern mobs. The very Missouri Compromise line was altered, by the addition to that state of a triangle between the then existing line and the Missouri river, equal in area to the states of Rhode Island or Delaware, and containing space for seven counties. There were three great difficulties in the matter, as Benton, who carried through the measure, himself informs us. 1st, It made still larger a state already one of the largest in the Union; 2, It required the removal of two Indian tribes (the Sacs and Foxes), from a possession which had just been assigned to them in perpetuity (!); 3, It altered the Missouri Compromise line in reference to slave territory, converting free into slave soil. Yet he was supported in carrying the measure, he tells us, by the "magnanimous" assistance of the Northern members.

The North was not to be quite so yielding on the subject of Texas—a name of ominous import in American history.

Texas was a province of Mexico, which republic had declared itself free in 1820, and had been speedily recognised by the United States, who had, as you may recollect, obtained from it the ratification of the old Spanish treaty of 1819, by which Florida was ceded to the

United States, and the latter, in turn, gave up all claims to Texas. Perfect amity prevailed between the two republics.'

But Mexico, three years after her own political emancipation, emancipated her slaves (1823), and the act was confirmed by her several provinces, by Texas among the rest. This became at once an eyesore and a real danger for the Southern states. We have seen that there had been repeated lawless expeditions to Texas carried out, or attempted, from the beginning of the century. The country was avowedly coveted; thinly peopled, and by an indolent race, it whetted such covetousness ever more and more. American adventurers crossed the border. They had slaves, or they wished to have them, or, still worse, they lost them there. The example might easily prove contagious. The country itself must be annexed. General Jackson offered to purchase it from Mexico. The offer was refused. He repeated it yearly for several years. At last, in December, 1835, a band of about ninety men, all but two of whom are said to have been Americans, declared the independence of Texas. The standard once raised, fresh adventurers flocked to it, bold, desperate men. The President of Mexico marched against the rebels. He was defeated at San Jacinto (April, 1836) by 800 men, of whom fifteen-sixteenths were Americans. Texas was lost henceforth to Mexico.

Memorials now began to pour in upon Congress for acknowledging the independence of Texas. Calhoun advocated not only immediate recognition, but the simultaneous admission of Texas as a state, on the ground that the "Southern states, owning a slave population, were deeply interested in preventing that country from having the power to annoy them." The President, in his message of the year (December 6, 1836), referred in terms of sympathy with Texas to its struggle with Mexico, and to the "known desire of the Texians to form part of our system." The great difficulty was, simply, that America was at peace with Mexico, and that the recognition of Texas would be an evident breach of friendship with that country. The committee of Congress on foreign relations reported, however, in favour of the recognition of Texas, as soon as satisfactory information could be obtained that its civil government was capable of performing the duties and fulfilling the obligations of a civilised power. In a special message (December 21) the President stated that he was disposed to concur with the resolutions passed to this effect, but he thought it expedient to wait till after the then threatened attack of Mexico upon Texas should have taken place. So matters stood for the present.

Closely connected with the slavery question is that of the treatment of the Indian tribes. From Jackson's antecedents we shall be prepared not to find him very delicate in the handling of this matter. In his first year of office he distinctly refused to sanction the formation of the Indian governments in Georgia and Alabama for the settled tribes, and recommended establishing all the tribes in a district to be set apart west of the Mississippi (December 8, 1829). The work once begun, was vigorously prosecuted. In his second annual message he was able to announce that two important tribes of Indians, the Choctaws and Chickasaws, had accepted the offer of removal, and expressed his opinion that it was the duty of government to extinguish as soon as possible the Indian title within the states (December 7, 1830). The civilised Cherokees refused to move. They had to be coerced (1836). An English traveller, Mr. Featherstonhaugh was an eyewitness to this cruel break-up of a harmless and most interesting community. The small guarantee of permanency which they could hope for in their new abodes was sufficiently shown by the instance of the Sac and Fox Indians in Illinois, who, after a short war (1832), known as "Black Hawk's war," were, as we have seen, removed on such a guarantee, and then turned out of the guaranteed territory, simply to square a corner of Missouri. The Creeks resorted to arms in vain (1836). Only the Seminoles of Florida remained indomitable, and, under a gallant chief named Osceola, maintained a war with success. By the commencement of the session of 1836-7, under Jackson's successor, Benton tells us, the final removal of the Indian tribes was almost completed, and by these measures—always, he declares, supported by the North, even when coercion had to be resorted to—the area of slave population was almost doubled in the slave states. He tries hard on this occasion to prove that the Indians were fairly dealt with by the United States. The Creeks, he says, received

22,000,000 dollars for 25,000,000 acres, or 7,000,000 more than were paid for Louisiana, and 17,000,000 more than for Florida. The Choctaws received 23,000,000 for 20,000,000 acres, the Cherokees 15,000,000 for 11,000,000, not to speak of advantages in kind, such as blacksmith's shops, cows, calves, horse-gear, &c. Let his figures go for what they may be worth.

In spite of the struggle with the Bank of the United States, Jackson's administration was eminently prosperous. The national debt was practically extinguished. There was a constantly-overflowing surplus, which, as we have seen, Jackson originally proposed distributing among the states; latterly, however (December 6th, 1836), he expressed his disapproval of the plan, admitting a partial change in his views. The states of Arkansas (1836) and Michigan (1837)—one slave, the other free—were admitted; the former with a constitution declaring slavery perpetual, though giving the slave the practically-illusory privilege of a trial by jury. Both states had inaugurated the till then revolutionary practice of forming constitutions for themselves without a previous act of Congress. Economy was practised, and, with the exception of Mexico, the demeanour of the United States towards foreign powers was not unworthy of a great nation. A treaty was entered into with Great Britain, by which the United States recovered the direct trade with our West India colonies (1829); and the President spoke of the negotiation as characterised "by the most frank and friendly spirit on the part of Great Britain" (December 7th, 1830); and whilst the government established in France by the revolution of 1830 was promptly recognised, Jackson yet, as we have seen, showed a thoroughly bold front to France on the question of indemnity—in both instances rising superior to the traditional policy of the party which he represented.

Jackson's Presidency saw gathered to their fathers almost all the survivors of the generation of public men which had figured prominently in the War of Independence: Monroe, who, like Adams and Jefferson, but five years later, died on the anniversary of the Declaration of Independence (4th July, 1831); Charles Carroll, the last-surviving signer of the Declaration (1832); hot-headed John Randolph (1833); Madison, lastly, who fell short by six days of reaching the national anniversary (28th June, 1836). Nay, the President himself ran the risk of swelling the list, as there was an attempt made to assassinate him (30th January, 1835).

The seal of national approval was emphatically stamped upon Jackson's policy by the election of his ablest lieutenant, Van Buren, as his successor (1836). Yet he continued to be thwarted by Congress to the last. To the final session of his Presidency belongs, as already mentioned, the abortive bill for rescission of his specie circular, whilst the government saw also the rejection of an appropriation demanded for purposes of fortification.

Jackson took leave of his countrymen in a farewell

address, which is only second in importance to that of Washington:—

"At every hazard, and at every sacrifice," he told his countrymen, "this Union must be preserved." After referring to the systematic efforts made to excite the South against the North and the North against the South, and indicating the ultimate result of such efforts in a division of the Union, he proceeded:—" The first line of separation would not last for a single generation; new fragments would be torn off, new leaders would spring up, and this great and glorious republic would soon be broken into a multitude of petty states, without commerce, without credit, jealous of one another, armed for mutual aggressions, loaded with taxes to pay armies and leaders, seeking aid against each other from foreign powers, insulted and trampled upon by the nations of Europe, until, harassed with conflicts, and troubled and debased in spirit, they would be ready to submit to the absolute domination of any military adventurer, and surrender their liberty for the sake of repose. It is impossible to think on the consequences that would inevitably follow the destruction of this government, and not feel indignant when we hear cold calculations about the value of the Union, and have so constantly before us a line of conduct so well fitted to weaken its ties. . . . But in order to maintain the Union unimpaired, it is absolutely necessary that the laws passed by the constituted authorities should be faithfully executed in every part of the country. . . . Until the law shall be declared void by the courts or repealed by

Congress, no individual or combination of individuals can be justified in forcibly resisting its execution. It is impossible that any government can continue to exist upon any other principles. It would cease to be a government, and be unworthy of the name, if it had not the power to enforce the execution of its own laws within its own sphere of action. It is true that cases may be imagined disclosing such a settled purpose of usurpation and oppression on the part of the government as would justify an appeal to arms. . . . If such a struggle is once begun, and the citizens of one section of the country arrayed in arms against those of another in doubtful conflict, let the battle result as it may, there will be an end of the Union, and with it an end of the hopes of freedom. The victory of the injured would not secure to them the blessings of liberty; it would avenge their wrongs, but they would themselves share in the common ruin. But the Constitution cannot be maintained, nor the Union preserved, in opposition to public feeling, by the mere exertion of the coercive powers confided to the general government. The foundations must be laid in the affections of the people, in the security it gives to life, liberty, character, and property, in every part of the country, and in the fraternal attachment which the citizens of the several states bear to one another, as members of one political family." After reprobating all efforts on the part of the people of certain states "to cast odium upon the institutions" of other states, and "all measures calculated to disturb their rights of property, or to put in jeopardy their peace and internal tranquillity," he declared that the legitimate authority of the general government was "abundantly sufficient for all the purposes for which it was created," and that "every friend of our free institutions should be always prepared to maintain unimpaired and in full vigour the rights and sovereignty of the states, and to confine the action of the general government strictly to the sphere of its appropriate duties." There had been, he considered, an abuse of the taxing powers of the general government; the tariff was oppressive "on the agricultural and labouring classes of society;" too much revenue was raised; extravagant schemes of internal improvement were entertained. Corporations and wealthy individuals engaged in large manufacturing establishments, he observed, desired a high tariff to increase their gains. Making a last onslaught on his old enemy the Bank, he pointed out, as a serious evil of the present system of banking, that it enabled one class of society, and that by no means a numerous one, by its control over the currency, to act injuriously upon the interests of all the others, and to exercise more than its just proportion of influence in political affairs. "The agricultural, the mechanical, and the labouring population," he said, "have little or no share in the direction of the great moneyed corporations, and, from the habits and the nature of their pursuits, they are incapable of forming extensive combinations to act together with united force." And he warned his countrymen that "unless you become more watchful in your states, and check the spirit of monopoly and thirst for exclusive privileges, you will in the end find that the most important powers of government have been given or bartered away, and the control over your dearest interests has passed into the hands of these corporations."

How far Jackson's words have yet to be realized, we are now called upon to witness. To the South they are more especially ominous. It remains to be seen whether his language is not to prove itself prophetic in a deeper sense than he used it himself; whether it is not for want of its foundations being laid "in the security it gives to life, liberty, character, and property, in every part of the country," as respects four or five millions of coloured people, that the present fabric of American government is breaking up.

Andrew Jackson was not a great man. To use the expression of a clever Irish priest (Father Kenyon) respecting O'Connell, he possessed "many of the elements of greatness, but alloyed below the standard." Such as he was, however, he seems to me the one statesman whom the Democratic party has produced. And, however ill-seconded or thwarted by his Congress, I believe him to have been literally the second founder of the Republic. To him, and to no other, I believe, is it owing that the United States have lasted for nearly a generation after him.

Whilst Jackson withdrew to his farm at "the Hermitage," near Nashville (where he died in 1845), Martin Van Buren, of New York, succeeded at once to his chair, and to his policy. I find it difficult to form to myself a judgment respecting Van Buren. He seems to me to have been a man of unquestionable ability, but whose character has remained undeveloped. On one point he evinced a clearer insight than his predecessor. The first among American Presidents, he showed a full appreciation of the weight of the slavery question, when, in his "Inaugural" (4th March, 1837), he spoke of it as "perhaps the greatest of the most prominent sources of discord and disorder" supposed to lurk in the political condition of his country. Not that, practically, he went for the present one step further than Jackson. He emphatically ratified a pledge given by him prior to his election, that he "must go into the Presidential chair the inflexible and uncompromising opponent of every attempt on the part of Congress to abolish slavery in the district of Columbia against the wishes of the slaveholding states, and also with a determination equally decided to resist the slightest interference with it in the states where it exists." And he predicted that all attempts at agitating the question would always fail. As to the Constitution, he took the Democratic view of it, as "limited to national objects," and "leaving to the people and to the states all power not explicitly parted with."

Van Buren's administration so completely continues Jackson's, both as respects the questions which occupy it and the policy followed, as to seem almost undistinguishable from the latter. It opened with a striking act of reparation to Jackson, in the passing (16th March, 1837), by the Senate, of "the Expunging Resolution,"

—*i. e.*, a resolution for expunging from its journals the censure passed upon Jackson a couple of years before. The Bank question occupies nearly the whole of Van Buren's administration, which lasted but a single term. The financial crisis, which had been coming on during the close of Jackson's term of office, came to a head in the first year of Van Buren. The banks generally suspended specie payments, while Nicholas Biddle, the president of the late Bank of the United States, revived since 1836 as the "Pennsylvania Bank of the United States," represented the crisis as a consequence of the refusal of the late President to allow the re-chartering of his bank as a national one—the fact being that it was mainly caused by his own gambling speculations, of which the best known in this country is, that by which he endeavoured to monopolise the whole cotton crop of the United States, in order to sell it at his own price to England and France. The Federal Government, however, were taken by surprise. Van Buren addressed a special message (Sept. 4th) to Congress, stating that he had directed a refusal by the Treasury of anything but gold and silver, and intimating an opinion against the system pursued by Jackson of deposits with selected banks. But whilst taking only gold and silver, the government were able at first to pay but in depreciated paper, so that the army and the public services were disgusted. To avert such mischief in future, by the establishment of an "Independent Treasury," and a system of hard money payments, or, as it was termed, a "divorce of Bank and State," became henceforth the leading object, and was the crowning achievement of Van Buren's administration.

In his first annual message (Dec. 4, 1837) he showed how the late Bank had been continued for two years, from the 4th of March, 1836, for final liquidation, a new institution being incorporated to discharge its debts and settle its affairs. The two years were now nearly at an end; but, instead of its affairs being wound up, there were $10\frac{1}{2}$ million dollars of notes still outstanding, and these were being still re-issued. An act had to be passed against this abuse in the following session (1838). In a few months, however, the general crisis was at an end, specie payments were resumed in New York by the 10th of May, and by the Pennsylvania Bank of the United States on the 13th of August; the government meanwhile refusing to deposit public moneys with or to receive the notes of any banks which would not redeem their notes in specie.

The existence, however, of the famous bank was now drawing to a close, though it behaved itself to the last with its usual audacity. On the 1st of January, 1839, it published its assets at over 66 million dollars, its liabilities at over 33. On the 30th of March Nicholas Biddle resigned the presidency of it, on the ground that its affairs were in great prosperity, and that it no longer needed his services. On the 9th of October it suspended payments once more, yet, on the 1st of January, 1840, still boldly returned its assets at 74 millions, its liabilities at 36. The final exposure of the gigantic swindle did not indeed take place till after Van Buren's term of office. But his doctrine of the "divorce between Bank and State" now prevailed, and a "Sub-Treasury Department" was created for the purpose of keeping the public moneys. Probably to humour national prejudices, Van Buren did not put this measure on the ground of the unsafeness of American speculation, but upon its subserviency to English. After Biddle's attempt to create in England a famine of cotton, the President still declared (Dec. 2, 1839) that the American banking system subjected the country "to the money power of Great Britain." "The want which presses upon a large portion of the people and the states," he said, "is an enormous debt, foreign and domestic. The foreign debt of our states, corporations, and men of business, can scarcely be less than 200 million dollars." In his message of the next year (Dec. 5, 1840), he reverted to the subject, dwelling on the heavy debts of the states; on which more than 12 million dollars annually went to the subjects of the European governments. And although he had previously (1839) urged that "the faith of the states, corporations, and individuals already pledged be kept with the most punctilious regard," yet, in dwelling on the burthen of the debt, in urging its extinction, he must evidently, to many of his more unscrupulous hearers, have seemed to suggest or sanction those short cuts to this end (in the shape of "repudiation") which were taken about this time, or a little later, by too many of the states (wealthy Pennsylvania herself suspending payments); the guilt, indeed, being equally shared by the North and the South, free-soil Michigan giving hands to slave-soil Mississippi, destined one day to give a President to a "Southern Confederacy." Repudiation in Mississippi, with which the name of Mr. Jefferson Davis is disgracefully connected, dates from 1837.

The deterioration of American commercial morality, which had become evident in the Bank struggle of Jackson and Van Buren, which exhibited itself so glaringly in state "repudiation," came out perhaps still more incontrovertibly in a smaller matter. A collector at New York had abstracted very large sums of public money. The law, as it stood, was insufficient. Van Buren asked Congress to devise a severer system for the safe keeping and disbursement of public moneys. The "Sub-Treasury" Act partly answered this suggestion. But Congress refused to punish the use of public money for private purposes as a crime (1838-9).

The relations with the Indian tribes continued much on the same footing as under Jackson. In his message of 1838, Van Buren was able to tell the Congress that, since the 4th of March, 1829, the Indian title to 116,349,897 acres had been acquired for 72,560,056 dollars in permanent annuities, lands, reservations, expenses of removal and subsistence, merchandise, mechanical and agricultural establishments, and implements. Only 2000 Seminoles in Florida remained obstinately attached to their forests and their swamps. A seven years' war with these was on foot since the treacherous cutting to pieces, in December, 1835, of 109 out of a party of 113 Americans; when the wounded were slaughtered by " a squad of about 40 negroes, fugitives from the Southern States, more savage than the savage" (Benton); the four who escaped only doing so by feigning insensibility, whilst these bloody avengers of the black man's wrongs went about " cutting throats and splitting skulls whereever they saw a sign of life." More disgraceful yet, because the act of a civilized man, was the seizure of the chief Osceola by General Jessup, when presenting himself with a flag of truce (1837), and the sending him prisoner to Fort Moultrie, where he died the next year. Peace was signed in 1839; but Van Buren had to inform Congress that year that, after entering into solemn engagements, the Indians, without provocation, had renewed their treachery and murder; and the war dragged on till 1842.

The slavery question, more and more complicated with that of the admission of Texas, was growing daily in importance. The South took to holding conventions, first at Augusta in Georgia, then at Charleston in South Carolina, by which an address to the Southern and South-Western States was issued, setting forth the gradual decay of the South; how, in 1760, the foreign imports into Virginia were 850,000*l*. sterling; into South Carolina, 555,000*l*.; into New York, 189,000*l*.; into Pennsylvania, 490,000*l*.; into all the North-East, only 561,000*l*.; whilst in 1821 the imports into New York were 23,000,000 dollars, into South Carolina only 3,000,000 dollars; in 1832 they had more than doubled for New York, standing at 57,000,000 dollars, whilst in Virginia they had fallen to 500,000 dollars, in South Carolina to 1,250,000 dollars. Instead of concluding for the extinction of their domestic curse, the wise men of the South, of course, only concluded, more or less explicitly, for a separation of interests, and differential duties, on Northern vessels in Southern ports.

A memorial from Vermont against the admission of Texas (which was indeed declined in August, 1837), together with other petitions on the subject of slavery, gave occasion to the South to take a further step in advance. " Until this time," Benton observes, "every memorial and petition as to slavery had been disposed of according to the wishes of the senators from the slaveholding states." But the South could not brook that any one should have the audacity to petition or memorialise on the subject. Calhoun proposed a series of resolutions, the fifth of which bore "That the intermeddling of any state or states, or their citizens, to abolish slavery in the district [of Columbia], or in any of the territories, on the ground, or under the pretext that it is immoral or sinful, or the passage of any act or measure of Congress with this view, would be a direct and dangerous attempt on the institutions of all the slaveholding states." He now declared himself opposed to the Missouri Compromise. Somewhat modified by Clay, the resolution passed (1837-8). But the heats of party continued to rise. The next year, the killing of a representative from free Maine, in a rifle duel with one from slaveholding Kentucky, led to the passing of an Anti-duelling Act for the district of Columbia. The slavery agitation continued through a motion by Slade, of Vermont, in the House of Representatives, as to petitions. When he read in his speech the memorial of Franklin against slavery, the opinion of Madison against it, the Southern members were about to retire from the hall. A resolution was passed, " that all petitions, memorials, and papers touching the abolition of slavery, or the buying, selling, or transferring of slaves in any state, district, or territory in the United States, be laid on the table without being debated, printed, read, or referred, and that no further action whatever be had thereon." So the representatives of the people tried to thrust away the unwelcome subject from them.

It came back, however, in another shape, through the cases which occurred of the liberation of slaves belonging to American citizens in British colonial parts, when ships were driven there by stress of weather, and the colonial authorities detained the slaves. Some redress, it would seem, was obtained in the two first cases. The Senate passed resolutions condemning the practice. Such a course was not calculated to improve relations between America and England, already much embittered by the part taken by American sympathisers in the Canadian insurrection, and their incursions across the border to abet it (1837-8). A party of them actually took possession of and fortified Navy Island, a British island in the Niagara river. Hence, on our part, the well-known incident of the seizure, on the American side of the river, of the "Caroline," a vessel used to carry munitions to the American sympathisers on Navy Island, and its destruction, and the many stormy discussions and long diplomatic correspondence which followed it. The excitement on the subject came to a head in 1840, by the arrest in the United States, and the commitment for murder and arson, of a Mr. McLeod, as having taken part in the affair. But such excitement went down again as rapidly, when it turned out that he was not present.

Van Buren seems, on the whole, to have behaved honourably in his foreign policy. He disavowed these lawless proceedings; declined, as we have seen, to admit Texas (though recognising it by a convention to settle American claims for the capture of two vessels by the Texans, 11th April, 1838, and afterwards by a boundary treaty, 25th April, 1838); treated with Mexico. He fell from power, probably from being too good for his party, which, however, fell for awhile with him. The Whig candidate, his former opponent, was elected in December, 1840.

It may be mentioned here, at once, that under Van Buren's administration the designs of the American slave power on Texas were, in fact, aided by the mistaken policy of Great Britain, in acknowledging Texan independence (Treaty of Commerce, 13th November, 1840). France did the same.

LECTURE VI.

FROM THE CLOSE OF VAN BUREN'S ADMINISTRATION TO THE FUGITIVE SLAVE LAW (1841—1850)—THE ERA OF MEDIOCRE PRESIDENTS—THE NATURE AND RULE OF THE SLAVE POWER—THE ADMISSION OF TEXAS—THE MEXICAN WAR—CALIFORNIA.

(Harrison, 1841; Tyler, 1841—5; Polk, 1845—9; Taylor, 1849; Fillmore.)

IF the Missouri Compromise forms an era in the history of the United States, the exit of Van Buren from office forms one in that of the Presidents of the republic. During a period of fifty-two years, from Washington to Van Buren inclusively (1789-1841), the Presidential chair had been held by eight Presidents, all of them, if not always of first-rate ability, yet without exception able men, fit to be the first officers of a great country, which, in five instances out of eight, had confirmed its choice by a re-election, thus giving an eight years' tenure of office to these five, or an average one of six and a half for the whole number. During the ensuing period of twenty years (1841-61), the same chair will be held by seven Presidents, all of whom, except probably one who was prematurely cut off, gave evidence of being altogether inferior to their great office, and who held, none of them, that office for more than a single term of four years—the average period of holding, owing to the premature deaths of two, being even below that figure, or not quite three years.

We enter, in short, upon the era of mediocre Presidents, which is at the same time an era of unvarying instability of rule. During this period the foremost politicians of the day—the Clays, Websters, Calhouns,—kept out of, or spurning the President's chair, reach no higher than the desk of the Secretary of State. The government thus becomes a sort of ugly copy of constitutional monarchy, except that the second-rate personages who fill the highest place have not the good sense of an ordinary constitutional sovereign in Europe, in shielding themselves behind their cabinets, and are invested by the Constitution with too much power to be harmless. Hence, instead of a simple change of ministry and of policy, as would happen in Europe, when they are checked by the legislative body, they are found frequently spending nearly their whole term of office in unseemly wranglings with one or both Houses of Congress.

But this period of mediocre Presidents, and instability of rule, is emphatically one of the ascendency of the slave-power. No doubt the history of the United States hitherto ever has been one of almost unbroken *Southern* ascendency; since the only three Northern Presidents (the two Adamses, Van Buren) are precisely those who have held office for a single term only, and one of them (Van Buren), the candidate of the Democratic party, came into power pledged to support the abdication by Congress of its jurisdiction as to slavery, over precisely that portion of American soil which is most directly subject to it—viz., the district of Columbia.* But Southern ascendency has not till now meant the ascendency of the slave-power. So long as lasted the revolutionary dynasty of the great Virginians —slave-holders opposed to slavery, and longing for its extinction—and again, during what may be called the Jacksonian era, of Southerners who yet held the Union as sovereignly paramount to any Southern interest— that ascendency had, on the whole, been used for the general good. Henceforth, on the contrary, although, of the seven Presidents who held office during the period, only three are directly elected by the Southern party, two of whom are men from the free states, yet the ascendency of the slave-power is really interrupted only during one term of Presidential office (that of Taylor and Fillmore), giving even then a President from the slave states. By means of the Virginian, Tyler, shifted from the Vice-Presidency to the Presidency, through the early death of General Harrison, it will establish itself even after a defeat at the Presi-

* Reckoning at a somewhat later period (1845), Mr. Palfrey shows that at that time the slave states had named, as against the free, 17 Judges of the Supreme Court to 10, 14 Attorneys-General to 5, 61 Presidents of the Senate to 16, 21 Speakers of the House of Representatives to 11, and 80 Foreign Ministers to 54; thus showing that, over and above the Presidential chair, of which they had secured the possession during four-fifths of the time, they had kept in their hands the bulk of all the high offices in the state.

dential election; and its most audacious encroachments will take place under the rule of its Northern instruments. Let us now consider for a moment the nature of this slave-power.

We have seen how slavery starves the consumption of the slaveholding states, and by the exhaustive effect of its special cultures, unsettles and disperses the population, leaving no money to be invested in public buildings and institutions. Now, in most countries, now-a-days, education is to a great extent a matter of demand and supply. The cases are few where, as in Iceland, a high traditional standard of intellectual attainments is kept up, chiefly by their own exertions, amongst a thinly scattered peasantry. Least of all is this the case in America. We should expect, therefore, to find that education is deficient among the Southern population. This is fully admitted by the South itself: "A slaveholding state," says Mr. Cobb, "can never be densely populated. . . . Another result of a sparse population is, that a perfect system of thorough common-school education is almost an impossibility. *Extensive plantations occupied by slaves only*, independent of the exhausting crops cultivated and annually adding to barren fields, *render a perfect system of common schools impossible*" ("Historical Sketch of Slavery," pp. ccxiv., ccxv.). Let us test this statement by a few details.

Virginia claims still to stand "pre-eminent" among her sister states "in intellect and fitness to command." In the year 1838, Governor Campbell told her legislature that, of 4614 men who had applied to him for marriage licences, 1047 could not write their names. Mr. Howison, the historian of Virginia, as quoted by Mr. Olmsted, writing ten years later (1848), speaks of " the horrible cloud of ignorance that rests on Virginia ;" and reckons that there are in the state 166,000 youth between seven and sixteen years of age, of whom 126,000 attend no school at all, and receive no education but what can be imparted by poor and ignorant parents; making, with 449,087 slaves and 48,852 free negroes, "with few exceptions, wholly uneducated," and amongst whom a " necessary" policy " discourages further extension of knowledge, 683,000 "rational beings" (according to " the most favourable estimate") " destitute of the merest rudiments of knowledge."

This, then, represents the very summit of intellectual cultivation among the slaveholding states. I will not weary you with details of yet greater ignorance in other slave states, as North Carolina, South Carolina, Georgia, Mississippi. Perhaps you will think that Louisiana can hardly be surpassed, where "the state superintendent lately recommended that two out of three of the *directors* of common schools, &c., should be required to know how to read and write; and mentioned that in one parish, instead of the signature, the *mark* of twelve different directors was affixed to a teacher's certificate. Yet I fear that worse results still might be traced further West. In short, whatever may be said of the degraded condition of the free coloured men of the North, the proportion of children among them attending school (22,043 upon 196,016) is greater than amongst the whites of the South—more than one-ninth, against less than one-tenth; whilst in Massachusetts the proportion of school attendance among the coloured people has actually reached one-sixth, or to the level of Prussia.* As towards the North, the proportion of persons unable to read was, in 1850, one in twelve South of the Ohio, one in fifty-three beyond that river, the total number of school children 581,861, as against 2,769,901. What is true of schools, is of course true to a great extent of places of worship. All religious denominations whatsoever in America treat the South and South-West as the blackest spots in the field of their ministrations. Throughout South Carolina the number of churches is one to every twenty-five square miles; in Georgia, one to every thirty-two.

The supremacy of the slaveholding states is, therefore, so far as it is exercised by the whites at large, distinctly that of a population steeped in ever-increasing ignorance, intellectual and religious. I shall not insult you by seeking to prove that it is also that of a population in which the moral sense is, on one whole side of man's nature, wholly perverted. None of you can imagine, what Southern planters and their sympathisers have the effrontery, or at best the insanity, to assert, that a man is better fitted to rule his white fellowmen in a Christian country, because he is accus-

* From an article by M. Elisée Reclus in the "Deux Mondes," for Jan. 1, 1861.

tomed to make his black fellowmen work under the fear of the lash; to appropriate to himself the whole fruit of their labour, beyond a certain coarse minimum of food and clothing; to deny them all means of intellectual development, under penalties to the teacher; to buy and sell them according to his need or caprice. None of you can imagine that a social system in which nearly half the population have "no recognised marriage relation in law"—cannot give evidence against the other half—are "entirely deprived" of the right of property—in which the worst outrage to a woman's honour, committed by a master on his own slave, goes absolutely unpunished (see Mr. Cobb's work *passim*), —will ever be a fit school for the governors of a free country, unless those governors are themselves men who hate that system.*

---

* The moral importance of the slavery question in the United States is, I believe, grossly degraded, when that question is made to turn, as Southerners invariably try to make it do, upon the physical well-being of the negroes. No man of ordinary sense and ordinary powers of observation, who has witnessed amongst ourselves the cruelties practised upon animals by their masters, and has felt how just are laws for the prevention of such cruelties, can surrender himself to the shallow fallacy, that men must treat their slaves kindly, simply because they are their property. But, without quoting any of the many recent well-proved and harrowing instances of exceptional cruelty to which American slavery gives rise, it will be sufficient to refer to the conviction which Mr. Olmsted says he has "not been able to resist," that "in those districts where cotton is now grown most profitably to the planter, the oppression and deterioration of the negro race is much more lamentable than is generally supposed." Eighteen hours a day he shows us to be the period of labour of the slave during the grinding season on a Louisiana sugar estate.

But it so happens that the supremacy of the slave-states was, in reality, not that of the Southern whites in general, but that of the slave-holding ones. It was distinctly one of the slave-power as such. Through the state governments, primarily. In South Carolina, as Mr. Palfrey shows, in 1840, out of 259,084 white inhabitants, less than one-fifth, or 49,503, inhabiting the five counties which are the principal seats of the slave-holding interest, elected twenty-three out of forty-five senators in the State Senate. The ten districts where slaves were most numerous, having 77,939 white inhabitants, elected twenty-eight senators and sixty-four representatives, whilst the remaining seventeen, where there were fewest slaves, but numbering 181,145 whites, elected only seventeen senators and sixty representatives; and the thirteen whose proportions were lowest in the scale, had 134,353 white inhabitants, or more than one-half of the whole, but only thirteen senators,—a number equalled by two slave-holding

The excessive labour of the slave on the great plantations is everywhere admitted to him by all disinterested persons. A free white in Alabama says: "These rich men are always bidding for the overseer who will make the most cotton. If they make plenty of cotton, the owners never ask how many niggers they kill." *The legal limit of a slave's day's work in South Carolina is fifteen hours.* And Mr. Olmsted says: "I was accustomed to rise early and work late, resting during the heat of the day, while in the cotton district, but I always found the negroes in the field when I first looked out, and generally had to wait for the negroes to come from the field to have my horse fed when I stopped for the night." The general source of fallacy on this subject lies in judging the condition of the field-hand from that of the petted house-servant.

districts of only 26,795 white population. And the legislature so elected appointed in turn all the judges, the governors, the senators of the state in Congress, and the presidential electors. In Virginia, the eastern or slave-holding districts, numbering a white minority of 401,000, and a slave majority of 413,000, elected nineteen senators and seventy-eight burgesses, as against thirteen senators and fifty-six burgesses, elected by the Western districts, with a majority of 495,000 whites, and only 63,000 slaves. So Mr. Olmsted, in the west of North Carolina, shows us a white man, owning hundreds of acres, declaring that the people about him hate "the Eastern people," because "they vote on the slave-basis;" and some of the "nigger counties," with not more than four or five hundred "white folks," have "just as much power in our legislature as any of our mountain counties, where there'll be some thousand voters." And it is reckoned that the whole number of slave-owners does not exceed 350,000,—who yet, through laws specially framed for the protection of their slave-property,—through the ever-increasing ignorance and degradation of the poorer whites, have managed and do manage to this day to rule not only their 4,000,000 of slaves, but more than 6,000,000 of white fellow-citizens at the South, and through them again enjoyed, as we are about to see, nearly twenty unbroken years of ascendency over the North. It is during this period that the United States will succeed in showing themselves to the world as the type of the grasping and shameless bully, careless of the ordinary decencies of international intercourse; only tolerated in the comity of nations because of the amount of force which they are supposed to wield, and of the recklessness with which they are known to be capable of wielding it. Let us bear this in mind, I entreat you, at a time when all the sins of the self-ejected slave-power are visited by public opinion on the at last enfranchised North, and the crafty Southerners are only too glad to throw such a burthen on their opponents.

But how, will you ask, could these things be? If the free states are wealthier, more densely peopled, more energetic, more intelligent and better informed, more moral and religious than the South, how could they bear such a yoke for twenty years? Of course it was through some superior qualities on the part of the South, through some deficiencies on their own part.

The superiority of the South in some respects is not to be denied. The tendency of the slave-system being to divide the white population into a slave-owning oligarchy, and an ignorant and helpless mass of slaveless freemen, the slave-owner is from childhood trained, not simply to political action, but to the exercise of political power,—trained to rule, not only over the coloured, but over a large portion of the white population. He thus reaches Congress, even though he be but a bad specimen of his own class, with an aptitude for office which even men of superior abilities from the North have wholly to acquire. Again, the struggle of competition which the Northerner has to carry on by his own hands, the Southern slave-owner carries on by those of his slaves. He has thus always, if he chooses to avail himself of it, an amount of leisure which his Northern neighbour has not; he has time to make himself, to all outward intent and purpose, a gentleman, whilst the other remains a "Yankee." Lifted up thus on the shoulders of the crowd, the Southern oligarch seems pointed out by his habits, his education, his manners, as the born statesman of the Union. And though really devoid in modern days of all the higher elements of statesmanship, he has been enabled to palm off his sham-statesmanship upon his country as real, through the ignorance, short-sightedness, infatuation, indolence, cowardice, selfishness, of the North. Let us examine the bearing of two or three of these influences.

Ignorance of the North.—There is very little real intercourse between North and South, except through the summer visits of rich Southern families to the North, and the placing of their children for education there. Beyond a certain number of travellers, the only Northerners who frequent the South, as a general rule, are those who go to make money out of it, and finding it a good milch cow, don't much trouble themselves how it lives, or, if they know, care still less to talk about it. Otherwise—except through Southern members of Congress, who themselves often don't go much beyond Washington—the North chiefly knows the South in the *élite* of its population; the best bred, best educated, most agreeable samples of its dominant class. They are taken as types of the whole population; they know themselves, probably, but the best side of the slavery system; it is a point of honour with them to conceal the worst. A large portion of the North was thus, and to a great extent no doubt is still, ignorant of the real state of things at the South, and of the condition of the mass of its population, both white and black. They accepted Southern ascendency as a traditional principle of the policy of the Southern states, not seeing that it was turned henceforth solely to the purposes of the slave-power, not knowing the nature of that power, and the results to which it must lead.

Short-sightedness.—A large portion of the North saw, and still see, only the immediate danger to the Union of the agitation of slavery, not the ultimate ruin of the Union by slavery. They felt that their generation was lesser and less wise than that of their fathers, who yet had accepted slavery, introduced a recognition of it into the Constitution, hushed up as far as possible all divisions on the subject. As between slavery-abolition and nationality, they preferred the latter, and therefore they were willing to leave the government of the nation in the hands of those who, if abolition were pressed, would break up the nation. Primarily, they were no doubt right. Nationality is a greater and a holier thing than even the restoration to their just rights of a portion of the nation itself. If I were an American, and had to choose to-morrow between the permanent preservation of the Union and immediate abolition, I would choose the former. But I would choose it only in case abolition of slavery remained yet possible—legally within reach. If the question lay between the Union and *perpetual* slavery on the one side, and division of the Union with abolition of slavery on the other, I could not hesitate to choose the latter. Why? Because the perpetuation of slavery is fatal to nationality; because the very existence of slavery is at all times a danger to it. The Union might perish through the agitation of the slavery question, just as a man may die of fever from the cleaning out of a cesspool; but it is the cesspool that kills him, and that would have killed him or some one else in time, if left wholly unstirred.

Selfishness.—This, no doubt, is the main influence which explains Southern ascendency. Intoxicated with enormous material prosperity; given up to the worship of the " almighty dollar;" its religious bodies all dependent upon the breath of popular favour and the power of the purse, the North had no longer the courage to face the moral aspects of the slavery question. The South was its best customer; an ever-increasing portion of the ever-increasing profits upon cotton, to say nothing of other staples, was constantly flowing into its banks. The interest of the South was that of the money-power of the North. If the South wanted political power, why grudge it, while the money-power remained intact? Add now to this all the baser feelings and passions still of all the white "loafers" and "rowdies," for whom it is a pride to feel that they have inferiors to trample on, and who sympathise with the slave-power by natural affinity; as well as all that large interest, composed of the greediest of the greedy, of the most desperate among the reckless, which is connected in the North, directly or indirectly, with the slave-trade, and you will have some idea of that element of Northern selfishness and wickedness which formed a natural ally to the slave-power.

And this wickedness of the worst men found the most useful of allies in the *indolence* of the best. When it was seen that, thanks to the support of the South, the emptiest and most vicious Northern demagogues might obtain the control of public affairs, the well-educated, the refined, the high-minded, withdrew from them often in disgust. Hence the frequent surprise of foreigners whose stay at the North was somewhat prolonged, at gradually coming into contact with a class of persons superior to all who held office or were prominent with the public, but who studiously eschewed political action. Half a generation from the period we are now observing will have to pass away before this indolence is felt to be a crime; for it may be said that the class of which I am speaking only reappeared in public affairs about the time of the Fremont and Buchanan contest (1856).

Nor is this all. It is a far easier thing not to accept a yoke than to shake it off. The North did not feel the actual transition from mere Southern ascendency to the ascendency of the slave-power. When that had taken place, it found the South in possession of a formidable vantage-ground. Thanks to the slave-representation principle, it occupied naturally a very strong position in Congress, especially in the Senate, where the slave-states balanced the majority—where slave-owners (such as Mr. Douglas, of Illinois, Mr. Bright, of Indiana) might actually sit for free states. Hence the aid of a very few Northern allies was sufficient to ensure the dominion of the slave-power. Furthermore, there are, Mr. Palfrey tells us, 30,000 offices in the United States; for the principal of which the President nominates, subject to confirmation by the Senate; whilst for others the principal officers name their subordinates. Thus, the President and the Senate being together generally in the interest of the slave-power, it could practically dispose of the whole resources of the administration.

Let us, lastly, bear in mind that this supremacy of the slave-power was essentially anti-national. You will not have forgotten what Mr. Cobb says of the uselessness of seeking "to excite patriotic emotions in behalf of the land of birth when self-interest speaks so loudly" as in the slave-owner. The truth of that statement is surely fully proved by what took place during the first term of office of the period which is about to occupy us. If there was a politician, if there were a party, whom a patriotic American should have put aside for all purposes of national representation—should have spurned, above all things, from office, it was the politician, it was the party, who in the Nullification struggle had put forward doctrines, had done acts, wholly subversive of the Union, had openly professed the interests of the Union to be only subordinate to those of one of its sections. Yet the spokesman of this anti-national party, the leader of these destructives, was, as we shall see, under Mr. Tyler, made Secretary of State. From this period, indeed, the history of the United States is little more than the track of a ship, with wreckers at her helm, steered recklessly on to the breakers on which she is to split.

I do not purpose to speak in the same detail of the series of mediocre Presidents, as of that of the abler men who preceded them. You will recollect that the democratic party and Van Buren were ejected from office at the elections of 1840. . The successful candidate, General Harrison, of Ohio, was an old celebrity of the Indian and English wars, born in 1773, and the son of a well-known Virginian, Benjamin Harrison, one of the signers of the Declaration of Independence. Although elected by the Whigs, his pompously worded address seemed mainly destined to flatter the opposite party. But it is needless to affix a meaning to it. He took office on the 4th of March, 1841, and on the 6th of April he was dead.

This event gave the Presidential chair to the Vice-President, John Tyler of Virginia. Observe, that the government was not thereby shifted from party to party, as it would have been in the early days of the republic. Now, the same majority elected both President and Vice-President, and Tyler nominally represented the second-best Whig candidate tó Harrison. His Cabinet was at first Whig, but soon quarrelled with him through a presumed gross breach of public duty on the President's part—the proceedings of a Cabinet meeting having been divulged through a newspaper, the *New York Herald*, reputed the Presidential organ. Mr. Tyler's whole administration consists mainly of wranglings with Congress. He vetoes their acts; they reject his measures, pass resolutions against him; he protests like another Jackson, but alas! never to see the obnoxious resolutions expunged. Clay, the great Kentuckian, withdraws for a time from public life in disgust (1842); Webster clings awhile to office, but at last quits it himself, before the growing unpopularity of the President. An unscrupulous Southern Cabinet then takes office, with Virginian Abel P. Upshur at its head, soon to be succeeded, through, perhaps, the most singular event that ever broke up an administration, by one yet more unscrupulous than itself.

The ship Princeton carried a monster gun, firing a ball of 225 lbs. The President and all his Cabinet, with many others, were invited to witness its performances (February 18, 1843). It burst, and killed both Upshur the Secretary of State and the Secretary of the Navy, besides other influential personages. The Cabinet was reconstructed, and Calhoun became Secretary of State. In the course of the correspondence relating to Texas, to which I shall presently advert, he is soon found writing for submission to Lord Aberdeen what Colonel Benton truly calls a " strange despatch,"

—"an argument in favour of slavery-propagandism, supported by comparative statements taken from the United States' census, between the numbers of deaf, dumb, blind, idiotic, insane, criminal and paupers among the free and the slave negroes, and thence deducing a conclusion in favour of slavery." The victory of the slave-power is complete. It has succeeded in identifying itself, as towards foreign powers, with the nation.

To President Tyler's rule belongs the final break-up of the United States' Bank. In 1841 that establishment made a last attempt at resuming specie payments. So little confidence, however, did it inspire, that six millions of dollars were drawn from it in twenty days. So it suspended payments again, for the third time in four years, early in February. The shareholders appointed a committee of investigation into its affairs. The gigantic swindle was now at last unmasked. Sixty-two millions and a quarter of dollars had been sheerly sunk, of which fifty-six millions and three-quarters in Philadelphia alone. From 1830 to 1836— the period of the great struggle with Jackson and Van Buren—thirty millions of dollars had been expended in loans not of a commercial nature, made virtually by Biddle himself to members of Congress, journalists, &c. The famous "Exchange Committee," from which, while the Bank was yet a national institution, the official directors had been so sedulously kept aloof, was simply a device to enable the president of the Bank and his friends to play at ducks and drakes with its assets. "The funds of the Bank were almost entirely at their disposition . . . They exercised the power of making loans and settlements to full as great an extent as the Board" (of Directors) "itself. *They kept no minutes of their proceedings, no book in which the loans made and business done were entered, but their decisions and directions were given verbally to the officers, to be by them carried into execution.*" As to the officers, "there really existed no check whatever" upon them. Such was the institution which had been able to command against the President a majority of the Senate, which all the so-called leading statesmen—Clay, Webster, Calhoun—maddened, it would seem, by jealousy of a military *parvenu*, had combined to support,—which a de Tocqueville, blinded by the prejudices of his Whig friends, has honoured with a favourable notice in a work of European reputation.

In connection with the great moral triumph for General Jackson which the downfall of the United States' Bank must be considered to have afforded, I may mention at once a somewhat remarkable compliment which was paid him by Congress a little later. During the war with England, he had been fined for a contempt of Court in not producing the body of an American citizen whom he had arrested whilst New Orleans was under martial law, in obedience to a *habeas corpus*. He had paid the fine, protesting against the injustice of doing so, and had refused to be refunded the amount by any private citizens. A proposal to refund him out of the Treasury was now made in Congress, and carried. It is somewhat remarkable that the Chief Justice of the United States at this period, Roger Taney, an old Treasury secretary of Jackson's, is the same who, in the present secession crisis, has endeavoured to enforce a *habeas corpus* against an arrest under military law, authorised by President Lincoln.

But to return to the United States' Bank:—Little as the tale of its break-up redounds to the credit of American honour, the sequel to it does still less. The gang of swindlers who had managed it were tried, and discharged. Whereupon Benton philosophically observes: "It has been found difficult in the United States to punish great offenders; much more so than in England or France." Nicholas Biddle died unmolested in 1844. A bankruptcy law was indeed passed about this period, which Benton styles "properly a law for the abolition of debts at the will of the debtor." But, although sanctioned by President Tyler, it appears to have been so outrageous as to have required repeal within his own term of office.

A great movement, which belongs to the period of Tyler's administration, was that of American emigration to the mouth of the Columbia River. In 1842, upwards of 1000 emigrants, chiefly from Missouri, descended its course to the Pacific; 2000 more followed them the next year (1843), and a bill was brought in by a Missouri senator to favour the emigration by a line of stockades and by land-grants, which, though it passed, was not acted upon till the following session. In 1842 had taken place the first exploring expedition of Fremont

—a dashing young officer of French descent, who had not passed through West Point, the military Academy, and whose fame as a discoverer was not looked upon with favour by his more scientific and stay-at-home brother-officers. A somewhat considerable American settlement thus grew up at the mouth of the Columbia. Two years after, Fremont made a second exploring expedition, from which most important results followed, and which was spiced with romance at the outset. Young Fremont, you should know, had made a runaway match with Miss Jessie Benton, the daughter of the rich and influential Missouri senator, Colonel Benton. Much incensed at first, Colonel Benton allowed himself to be appeased by the young man's success as an explorer, and warmly patronised him from henceforth. Almost immediately after Fremont's departure on this second expedition, despatches arrived for him from government, which contained, in fact, a countermand of the expedition. Mrs. Fremont took upon herself to detain the despatches; her husband proceeded, explored California, and, as we shall presently see, was eventually the means of giving it to his country.

Tyler's administration is marked, as respects its foreign policy, by two remarkable events. One is the Ashburton Treaty. The relations between America and England had been for several years, as we have seen, in an uncomfortable position; and President Tyler was far from having the firmness of his predecessor to check the lawlessness of his countrymen. The matter of the "Caroline" remained pending. A new case of the liberation of American slaves (that of the "Creole") took place at Nassau. England complained of the prosecution of the slave-trade under the American flag. There were various unsettled boundaries. The English ministry determined to put a stop to contention as far as possible, and nominated for Commissioner Lord Ashburton, a man who for many years had been intimately connected with America, of great abilities, great authority, and very conciliatory manners. Hence the Ashburton Treaty (10th August, 1842), which settled the North-Eastern boundary at least, and provided for the mutual extradition of offenders, and for the maintenance of an African squadron by America for the suppression of the slave-trade. It is under the extradition clause in this treaty that the fugitive slave Anderson was claimed before the Courts of Canada by the United States authorities. In connection with the really auspicious event of the Ashburton Treaty, let me mention at once that the Florida war also came to an end.

The other leading event in foreign policy was the vote of Congress for the admission of Texas. It soon became evident that the President was likely to pander to the Southern feeling on this point. Already in his second annual message he indicated the possibility of a war with Mexico. At a time when Texas and Mexico, being alike tired of a long, bloody, and yet indecisive war, had concluded an armistice, and were treating for peace under the mediation of England and France, Mr. Upshur reopened the negotiations for the admission of Texas, on express pro-slavery grounds; declaring that "the establishment in the very midst of our slaveholding states of an independent government, forbidding the existence of slavery, and by a people born for the most part among us, reared in our habits, and speaking our language, could not fail to produce the most unhappy effects upon both parties." He complained at the same time of English intrigues, and accused her of hostile abolitionism. Lord Aberdeen replied (February 26, 1843) by a despatch which is a model of really noble diplomacy. England, he said, had recognised Texan independence; she was, therefore, desirous that Mexico should do so. As to slavery, "it must be and is well known, both to the United States and to the whole world, that Great Britain desires, and is constantly exerting herself to procure the general abolition of slavery throughout the world. But the means which she has adopted, and will continue to adopt, for this humane and virtuous purpose are open and undisguised. She will do nothing secretly or underhand. She desires that her motives may be generally understood, and her acts seen by all. With regard to Texas, we avow that we wish to see slavery abolished there, as elsewhere." But England had never sought to stir up disaffection in the slave-states of the Union. "Much as we should wish to see those states placed on the firm and solid footing which we conscientiously believe is to be attained by general freedom alone . . . the governments of the slaveholding states may rest assured, that, although we shall not desist from those open and honest efforts which we have constantly made for procuring the abolition of slavery throughout the world, we shall neither openly nor secretly resort to any measures which can tend to desturb their internal tranquillity, or thereby to affect the prosperity of the American Union." It was this despatch, directed to Mr. Upshur, but which only arrived after his death, to which Mr. Calhoun replied in the pro-slavery one before referred to (April 13, 1843). "It may be asserted," he declared in it, "that what is called slavery is in reality a political institution, essential to the peace, safety, and prosperity of those states of the Union in which it exists."

On Calhoun's entering the Cabinet, after the Princeton disaster (1844), Southern efforts for the annexation of Texas became most vigorous. That *de facto* republic was in anything but a prosperous condition. It had contracted a huge debt, which it was perfectly unable to pay, and was ready to resort to any expedient to live. There was, indeed, within it a small abolitionist party, who were anxious, not for its annexation to the United States, but for its independence as a free-soil republic. But the great annexationist majority were almost all pro-slavery men, and felt themselves strong in the sympathies of the American Cabinet.

Meetings were held in South Carolina to promote a convention of the Southern States, for the purpose of uniting the South with Texas, if the latter were not admitted, and inviting the President to convene Congress for arranging the terms of the dissolution of

P

the Union, should the rejection of Texas be persevered in. "Texas or Disunion" became a common 4th of July toast this year (1844). However, Virginian Richmond, and Tennesseean Nashville, both repudiated the honour of the proposed Southern convention; and the annexation treaty, concluded by the President (April 12, 1844), which provided that the Texan debt of 10,000,000 dollars should be taken up by the United States, was rejected by the senate, by a majority of two to one (June 8, 1844). Colonel Benton now introduced a bill for opening negotiations with Mexico, as well as Texas, with a view to adjusting boundaries and peaceably annexing the latter.

The accident of Tyler's administration was now nearly worked out. In spite of his bids for popularity, Mr. Polk, of Tennessee, had been elected, by a majority of 170 to 105 given to Clay, who had vainly tried to save himself by trimming on the Texas question—representing 1,536,196 votes against 1,297,912. Yet Mr. Tyler only continued to bid the more recklessly for popular favour. His last message amounted to an act of open defiance to Mexico, recommending as it did the admission of Texas under a simple act of Congress. His acts had gone even further than his words. It was the encouragement from Washington, and the actual lending to General Houston, the President of Texas, of detachments of the American army and navy, which had re-opened the war. At last the annexationist party carried the day. Both Houses of Congress came to a joint resolution (March 1, 1845), consenting that "the Republic of Texas may be erected into a new state." South of lat. 36° 30′, "commonly called the Missouri Compromise line," any states to be formed out of Texan territory were to be admitted with or without slavery, as the people of the state asking for admission might desire; North of that line, slavery was to be prohibited. The President instantly adopted the resolution and sent it off to Texas, waiving all negotiation with Mexico. Texan stock rose from nothing to par. Before passing on to his successor, let me mention here, as an instance of the ignorance and prejudice towards England of the slave-power Presidents, that in his last message (February 19, 1845), Mr. Tyler had insinuated that England only pursued the slave trade in order to introduce the captured Africans as apprentices in her West Indian colonies, and work them as slaves. Sir Robert Peel replied (March 19, 1845), in a noble speech, in which he showed that the apprenticeship system had long ceased, and declared that if the United States would appoint a commission to verify the state of the negroes under the British flag, England would offer every facility to its investigations.

President Tyler was at least only an accidental mediocrity in the list of American Presidents. President Polk was, so to speak, the first of a series of normally evolved ones. The Democratic convention that put him forward knew perfectly well that he was only a second-rate man. "That convention," Benton tells us, "is an era in our political history, to be looked back upon as a starting-point in a course of usurpation which has taken the choice of President out of the hands of the people, and vested it in the hands of a self-constituted and irresponsible assemblage." Calhoun was at least high-spirited enough to repel the dictation of such a body. He refused to be put in nomination. All that need be said of Mr. Polk is, that he was a Southerner, and had sat in Congress. In the formation of his cabinet, three names deserve to be noticed. His foreign secretary was James Buchanan; R. J. Walker, of Mississippi, whose name will recur in the story of Kansas, was Secretary of the Treasury; Bancroft the historian, Secretary of the Navy.

Mr. Polk's "Inaugural" (1845) was the longest ever yet delivered. In tone it was quite worthy of Ex-President Tyler. Mr. Polk coolly denied the right of Mexico to take offence at anything that had been done, and reiterated old complaints against her. But where he outshone all rivalry was upon the question of the Oregon boundary. The Ashburton treaty had only fixed the North-Eastern boundary of the United States with Great Britain. But the North-Western boundary remained unsettled. So long as the shores of the Northern Pacific were only haunted by a few whalers, and the waters of the inland country were only trapped and its forests hunted for the furs of beavers and other wild creatures, this was of little moment. But immigration from the American side had now been steadily pouring in for years to the seaboard, whilst something also was trickling in from the English. The convention before noticed for the joint occupation of the mouths of the Columbia river, hitherto in force, no longer suited the altered state of things, and negotiations were pending to fix the frontier line. In his "Inaugural" (1845), President Polk actually asserted the right of the United States to the disputed Oregon territory up to a given latitude. "It was certainly an unusual thing," observes Benton, "perhaps unprecedented in diplomacy, that while negotiations were depending . . . one of the parties should authoritatively declare its right to the whole matter in dispute, and show itself ready to maintain it by arms." But it so happened that the line thus claimed by the President (54° 40' N. L.) was egregiously wrong in point of geography. It had never been an American line in any sense whatever. It was a northern British line, adopted in a convention with Russia to limit her operations. Colonel Benton shows, in the most conclusive manner, that the territory thus laid claim to by an ignorant President, clamorously supported by an organised party in the United States, and every inch of which they declared to belong to America, had been, five-and-twenty years before, by "geography and history, called New Caledonia, and treated as a British possession." The joint occupation of the Columbia territory was put an end to. England now took up again as a boundary the forty-ninth parallel of latitude, which she had once repelled. Discussion had now cleared the question of its mists, and Mr. Polk's blunder was apparent. Not liking to eat his words, he contrived to throw the responsibility of decision on the Senate which adopted the proposed boundary line of 49° N. A new treaty of Washington (January 15, 1846) fixed this basis, but laid the foundation for fresh difficulties by running the boundary "to the middle of the channel separating the continent from Vancouver Island, and thence South through the middle of the said channel and the straits of Fuca." Benton observes with great truth on this matter that "Great Britain is to the United States now what Spain was for centuries to her, the raw head and bloody bones which inspires terror and rage . . . We have periodical returns of complaints against her, each to perish when it has served its turn, and to be succeeded by another evanescent as itself."

Let us now return to Mexico and Texas, the question of which you will see becomes ultimately mixed up with that of Oregon. On the 22nd of December, 1845 (anniversary of the landing of the Pilgrim Fathers at Plymouth), the admission of Texas was finally carried, in spite of the opposition of the free states, the South thus winning its first great victory in a pitched battle. In the interval between two Congresses (1845), the leading Whigs, who till now had opposed the admission of Texas, had abandoned their opposition. The South had skilfully baited its hook with the prospect of a high protective tariff, Clay's especial hobby and Webster's, and seems to have caught its fish. "Let it be known and proclaimed as a certain truth," had written R. J. Walker of Mississippi, not yet in office, "and as a result which can never hereafter be changed or recalled, that upon the refusal of re-annexation now and in all time to come, the tariff as a practical measure falls wholly and for ever." The protectionists of the North, let me say at once, derived but little advantage by thus selling back Texas into slavery. When the high tariff of 1842 was repealed, the two senators from Texas voted against it.

Mexico and the United States were now virtually in a state of war, but no actual collision had taken place. In his first annual message, Mr. Polk dwelt upon the war, throwing the blame of it of course still upon Mexico. But the sought-for collision had yet to be brought on. The Eastern boundary of Mexico was on the river Nueces. After a number of *innuendos*, intended to incite General Taylor, then in command of the American forces on the frontier, to invade the Mexican territory, which the straightforward soldier refused to understand, he was at last explicitly directed to advance (January 13, 1846). Thus, although some fruitless diplomacy, which must indeed have been most offensive to Mexico, was yet attempted at the capital of the latter by Mr. Slidell (perhaps only as a blind for military operations), March 1-17, 1845, to use the words of Colonel Benton, "The actual collision of arms was brought on by the further advance of the American troops to the left bank of the Rio Grande, then and always in the possession of Mexico, and erecting field-works on the bank of the river, and pointing cannon at the town of Matamoras on the opposite side, the seat of a Mexican population, and the head-quarters of their army of observation. It was under these circumstances that the Mexican troops crossed the river and commenced the attack." But it was all that was needed. On the 11th of May, 1846, the President sent a message to Congress, informing it that a state of war existed by the act of Mexico herself, and asking Congress to recognise it. So entirely was the country carried away by the war-fever, that there were only two votes in the Senate and fourteen in the House given against it (13th May). Calhoun —some remnant of Southern honour still lingering apparently in him—spoke against the war, but gave no vote.

Still the President and his cabinet were half frightened at their own audacity. They were afraid of seeing Mexico go to pieces under the blows of their soldiers. They would rather have negotiated her away bit by bit than have conquered her by force. There was an ex-President of Mexico now in exile, named Santa Anna, a dashing, unscrupulous adventurer, not devoid of personal courage nor yet of some sort of patriotism, and certainly not of capacity for intrigue, but incapable alike as a general and a statesman. Under what conventions or what understanding with the American cabinet does not appear, but provided at all events with an American passport, and through the midst of the American fleet, Santa Anna landed at Vera Cruz, and on the 4th of August the President sent to Congress a confidential message, informing them that negotiations were pending, and asking for money. But the Mexican had outwitted them. Instead of selling his country, he defended it. In a series of battles, however (Buena Vista, Cerro Gordo, Contreras, Chirubusco, Chapultepec), the Mexicans were utterly defeated by Generals Taylor and Scott, and their capital, the city of Mexico, was occupied by the American troops. Gallantly as the Americans seem to have fought, their luck was greater than their valour. The whole vast territory of New Mexico fell, without the firing of a cartridge or the spilling of a drop of blood, into the hands of Colonel Doniphan, detached with a single militia regiment by General Kearney, who annexed it by proclamation, 22nd August, 1846. The acquisition of California was hardly less fortuitous, if the term may be used. Fremont, now a captain, had started on his third exploring expedition in 1845. He found the American settlers in the valley of the Sacramento in danger, it would seem, alike from Mexico and from Great Britain, through the Oregon boundary question, to which I have referred. He organised them for defence, and declared them an independent republic, under a "bear-flag," the grizzly bear being the most dangerous of the wild beasts of the country. Meanwhile Commodore Sloat, of the American navy, cruising off the Pacific coast with a squadron, heard of Captain Fremont's being engaged in fighting the Mexicans, and nothing doubting but that he was acting under orders from his Government, took possession of the town of Monterey for the United States. The Californians, in their turn, being informed of his proceedings, and feeling sure henceforth of support from Washington, hauled down their "bear-flag," and hoisted at once the "stars and stripes." So California was won for the United States (proclamation of annexation by Commodore Sloat, 6th July, 1846). We all know how soon (June, 1848) the hardy Anglo-Saxon settlers found out the treasures of the Californian soil, which the lazy Mexicans had trodden under foot unnoticed for centuries, and what a mighty new community thus took root on the seaboard of the North Pacific.

The Mexican war is estimated by Mr. Palfrey to have cost 25,000 lives and 200,000,000 of dollars to each belligerent. At this cost the United States acquired in a year from their neighbouring republic a territory of 850,000 square miles—four times the size of France, five times that of Spain. And now the question arose—For whom was the victory won, for Freedom or for Slavery? Was the free soil of Mexico to remain free soil, as before, or was it, or any part of it, to be handed over to the Southern slave-owners? An attempt was made, by means of a proviso termed, from the name of its proposer, "the Wilmot proviso," to exclude slavery from all territory acquired or to be acquired from Mexico. This was carried in the House of Representatives by a vote of eighty-three to sixty-four, all the representatives from the free states, nine excepted, voting in favour of it. It would have been carried in the Senate, but for a northern senator, Mr. Davis, of Massachusetts, speaking against time till the hour of adjournment. The next year, the present Vice-President of the United States, Mr. Hamlin, of Maine, embodied the proviso in an amendment to the bill relating to the new acquisitions. The House of Representatives again adopted the amendment by a vote of 115 to 106, but it was rejected in the Senate by thirty-one to twenty-one.

Mr. Calhoun now took up higher pro-slavery ground than ever. You remember that the Constitution expressly recognised the right of legislation of the Congress over the territories. That right had been deliberately exercised, in relation to slavery, in the memorable instances of the Missouri Compromise line, and of the extension of that line to Texas. Mr. Calhoun had been a member of the administration which had concurred in the Missouri Compromise. He now came forward with a series of resolutions, denying the right of Congress to legislate on slavery for the territories. These resolutions were—1st. That the territories of the United States belong to the several states comprising the Union, and are held by them as their joint and common property. 2ndly. That Congress, as the joint agent and representative of the states of this Union, has no right to make any law or do any act whatever that shall, directly or by its effects, make any discrimination between the states of this Union by which any of those states shall be deprived of its full and equal right in a territory of the United States acquired or to be acquired. 3rdly. That the enactment of a law which should, directly or by its effects, deprive the citizens of any of the states of this Union from emigrating with their property into any of the territories of the United States, will make such discrimination, and would therefore be a violation of the Constitution and the rights of the states from which such citizens emigrated, and in derogation of that perfect equality which belongs to them as citizens of the Union, and would tend directly to subvert the Union itself, &c. The drift of which string of propositions is, simply, that the United States at large, with their ever-increasing free population, were to acquire no territory but for the benefit of the slaveholders. Nor did Mr. Calhoun stop here. He wrote a letter stating expressly that it was the duty of the Southern states "to ourselves, to the Union, and our political institutions, to *force* the issue"—*i. e.*, on the slavery question—"on the North;" assigning as a ground for so doing that we are "now stronger relatively than we shall be hereafter, politically and morally." In other words, advantage was to be taken of a special opportunity to fix slavery for ever on the increasing free populations of the North. Referring to a late act of the legislature of Pennsylvania for the repeal of what was called the " Slave Sojournment Law," intended to secure to slave-owners the services of their slaves whilst in the state, as well as to recent attempts in the North to obstruct the recovery of fugitive slaves, he declared that there was only "one remedy short of disunion;" this was, to retaliate against the North, by refusing to fulfil the stipulations of the Constitution in favour of the non-slaveholding states, such as the right of their ships to enter into and depart from Southern ports. This he proposed to restrict to sea-going vessels, so as to detach the North-Western states from the North-Eastern. And he recommended the holding of a convention of the Gulf states (*i. e.*, those bordering on the Gulf of Mexico) on the subject.

The land-hunger of the South now outstripped even the ambition of conquest of Mr. Polk. A plan was set on foot for the absorption of the whole of Mexico. Mr. Clay spoke against it. In his annual message of 1847—sent in whilst the city of Mexico was still in the hands of American troops—Mr. Polk, in turn, declared that he had no intention of permanently conquering the whole Mexican country. And in the treaty of peace of Guadalupe Hidalgo, which was concluded in the following year (2nd February, 1848), it was deemed sufficient to strip off from Mexico the provinces of New Mexico and Upper California, the lower course of the Rio Grande from its mouth to El Paso being fixed as the boundary of Texas. For these acquisitions the United States were to pay 15,000,000 dollars, in five instalments; assuming, moreover, on themselves all those claims of American citizens upon Mexico which had given the original colour to those complaints upon which the war had been nominally grounded.

The literature of America owes a weighty debt to the Mexican war. Mr. Lowell's "Biglow Papers," published, I believe, in 1847,—written at least in the teeth of the popular enthusiasm for the war,—not only gave to the world a new model of political satire, but represent the first successful effort to bring what had seemed the hitherto sectarian fanaticism of the abolitionist to a level of broad, genial human interest. In Mr. Whittier, abolitionism had already its poet, and no mean one; but his influence was restricted to a narrow circle. An incalculable service was rendered, I believe, to the cause of human freedom on the day when Mr. Lowell held up to the ridicule of all ages the slave-power and its Northern allies. We may disagree entirely from the extreme peace-views of Hosea Biglow; probably by this time no one feels better than Mr. Lowell that war, even civil war, may be necessary and right. But, apart from any question of opinion, it is impossible to mistake the weight that is given to the book by the *righteousness* of its humour, and the bursts of deep feeling which flash across its cutting satire.

The question of the ceded territory from Mexico settled, that of a territorial government for Oregon now came on. In framing it, the Missouri Compromise line was proposed to be extended to the Pacific, so as to force slavery on California, which rejected it. The proposal was rejected. Calhoun was furious. "The great strife between the North and the South," said he, "is ended. The North is determined to exclude the property of the slaveholder, and, of course, the slaveholder himself, from its territories. . . . . The effect of this determination of the North is to convert all the Southern population into slaves. . . . . The separation of the North and the South is completed. The South has now a most solemn obligation to perform. . . . . She is bound to come to a decision not to permit this to go on any further, but to show that, dearly as she prizes the Union, there are questions which she regards as of greater importance than the Union." On returning to South Carolina, he denounced Colonel Benton, and General Houston, senator from Texas, who had supported the Oregon bill, as traitors to the South. In another speech—in which he took up the extraordinary ground that, by the mere ratification of the treaty, the Mexican laws became extinct in the territory thereby acquired—he declared, that if the Union were to perish, the historian would "devote his first chapter to the ordinance of 1787," his next "to the Missouri Compromise, and the next to the present agitation. Whether there will be another beyond," he added, "I know not. It will depend on what we may do." Thus openly and haughtily was secession threatened and predicted by the South, twelve or thirteen years before it was carried out. As minor features of the slavery agitation at this period, I may mention that in 1847-8 there were renewed attempts, which failed as before, to prohibit the slave-trade and abolish slavery in the district of Columbia, and that in the spring of 1848 there was a riot at Washington against the "National Era," a paper opposed to the extension of the slave-power. The final results of the contest were—1st. That a territorial government was formed for Oregon (August 13th, 1848), excluding slavery from that territory, but leaving California and New Mexico as they were. 2ndly. That the pro-slavery party took up the policy of opposing any act of Congress excluding slavery from any of the territories. 3rdly. That on the other side there sprang up in Massachusetts a "free-soil" party, on the exactly opposite ground of resisting any extension of slave-territory. 4thly. That California, in a convention of its inhabitants, excluded slavery from its limits. It may be added, that in 1849 the House of Representatives abandoned the spirit of the Wilmot proviso.

Among miscellaneous events of Mr. Polk's Presidency, may be mentioned the holding of a court-martial on Colonel Fremont, for having—Benton tells us—as Governor of California, bought an island in St. Francisco Bay; for flagrant defiance, say others, of a superior officer. He was found guilty, and resigned, and then undertook a fourth exploring expedition, which proved a disastrous one, the party having suffered the most frightful hardships in the snow, through the failure of a guide. Not long after, however, the object of all these explorations—viz., a short and safe passage through the Rocky Mountains—was discovered.

Somewhat before this (23rd February, 1848) had occurred the death of ex-President John Quincy Adams, who, though he did not take part in the War of Independence, may be considered as the last representative of the Fathers of the American Republic. After filling the highest dignity in the republic, he had been rejected as a senator by his own state, and had sat since 1831 as a simple member of the House of Representatives; and in that house he met with his death-stroke. He was struck the day before, he died the day after, the anniversary of the birth of Washington. The strife of parties had not yet become so rancorous but that its din fell hushed for a moment before the death of the noble old man of eighty. Although an avowed abolitionist, his character stood so high, his life had been so pure, that even members from slave-holding states, such as McDowell, of Virginia, and Benton, of Missouri, joined in the eulogies which were bestowed upon his memory.

Note also the admission of Florida (slave) and Iowa and Wisconsin (free) as states in 1845, 1846, and 1848; and an event which was to bear still more important consequences, the exodus of the Mormons (1845) from Nauvoo, in Illinois, to the valley of the Great Salt Lake, beyond the Rocky Mountains, under the guidance of Brigham Young. I shall not have leisure in these lectures to dwell upon the curious page of contemporary history which is furnished by these Mussulmen of modern days. It must suffice me to say, that after the murder of the first prophet of these "Latter-day Saints," Joseph Smith, Brigham Young, then "President of the Twelve Apostles," had been appointed successor to Smith (1844); and that, whatever may be the morality of the man, it argues no small intellectual power in him that he should have retained his dominion over his followers for now nearly twenty years.

And now Mr. Polk's popularity-hunting was to come to its fruitless conclusion. Like Mr. Tyler, he failed to achieve a second term of office. At the Presidential election of 1848, three candidates were put forward: General Cass, by the Democrats; General Taylor, by the Whigs; and Van Buren by the new party of the Free-soilers, whose motto was "Free soil, free speech, free labour, free men." Let me dispose of this last at once, by saying that it did not muster strong enough to give one single electoral vote to its candidate; and yet in it lay the germ of the great Republican party which has now given its President to the Union, and on whose firmness and wisdom (the latter not very visible as yet) the existence of that Union itself now depends. The day was won by General Taylor, of Mississippi, a Virginian by birth, the hero of the Mexican war, and who had the great qualification in the eyes of the South of being a slave-holder,—having made an opportune purchase of eighty slaves shortly before the election. If you are familiar with the "Biglow Papers," you will easily recognise in the candidateship of "Birdofredum Sawin" a caricature of those of the military heroes of the Mexican war. Sawin, however, was unluckily not elected, whereas General Taylor beat his older rival by 163 votes against 129. Mr. Clayton, of Delaware, was his Secretary of State. The cabinet had just been enlarged by the addition of a "Secretary of the Interior."

In the last session of Mr. Polk's administration, an insidious attempt at extending slavery was made, strange to say, by a member from the young free state of Wisconsin, Mr. Walker (but prompted by Mr. Calhoun), through a motion for the extension of the Constitution—*i. e.* of the slave representation and restoration of fugitives' principles—to the territories. The character of the attempt was, however, unmasked, and it was opposed by Mr. Webster. In the discussion, Mr. Calhoun avowed his intent to be, to carry slavery into the territories under the Constitution. By tagging a provision to this effect to an Appropriation bill, the South almost broke up the government. Nightly secret meetings of the slave-state members were held to concert their policy, and eventually a manifesto, signed by forty-two members from the slave-states, was issued, directed to the South, and declaring that emancipation, when it came, could only be escaped " by fleeing the homes of ourselves and ancestors, and abandoning our country to our former slaves, to become the permanent abode of disorder, anarchy, poverty, misrule, and wretchedness." A cowardly piece of.bathos, to say no more.

Military Presidents in the United States seem of late years to have held but a short term of office. General Harrison had kept his seat for little more than a month. General Zachary Taylor was destined to hold his but little more than sixteen (4th of March, 1849, —9th of July, 1850). His short administration was, however, not an uneventful one. In his " Inaugural," —the soldierlike brevity and force of which contrasted favourably with the length and looseness of Mr. Polk's,—he insisted strongly on the value of the Union. "In my judgment," he said, "its dissolution would be the greatest of calamities, and to avert this should be the study of every American. Upon its preservation must depend our own life, and that of countless generations to come. Whatever dangers may threaten it, I shall stand by it, and maintain it in its integrity to the full extent of the obligations imposed, and the power conferred upon me by the Constitution." He recommended the admission of California as a state, *i. e.* without slavery, and leaving New Mexico and Utah (the Mormon territory) to settle the slavery question for themselves. With reference to a claim which was now being urged by Texas over the whole of New Mexico, and which was, no doubt, put forward by the slave-interest, mainly to fix slavery throughout that province, he recommended the boundaries of Texas and New Mexico to be settled by the political or judicial authority of the United States. He announced the suppression of a piratical expedition against Cuba, which was now, Texas being won, the proximate object of Southern cupidity.

Mr. Clay had now returned to public life, having been sent up as senator to the thirty-first Congress. With that mania for compromises which distinguished him, he brought forward a set of resolutions, bearing, 1st, That California should be admitted as a state, without reference to slavery; 2nd, That territorial governments should in future be formed without any restriction or condition as to slavery; 3rd, That the Western boundary of Texas should be fixed at the Rio Grande, so as to exclude New Mexico; 4th, That the Texan debt should be assumed by the Union, Texas in return giving up its claims on New Mexico; 5th, That it was inexpedient to abolish slavery in the district of Columbia without the consent of the people and compensation to the owners; 6th, That it was expedient to prohibit the importation of slaves into the district; 7th, That more effectual provision should be made for the recovery of fugitive slaves; 8th, That Congress should be declared to have no power to prohibit or obstruct the slave-trade between the states. These resolutions, embodied in what was called "Clay's omnibus bill," gave rise to a new slavery discussion. In his speech, which sounds as the last echo of the old spirit of the great Virginian fathers of the Republic, Clay declared " that no earthly power could induce him to vote for a special measure for the introduction of slavery where it had not before existed, either South or North" of the Missouri Compromise line. But, he added, that if the citizens of any territory chose to establish slavery, this would be "their work, not ours."

Calhoun's life was itself now at its close. His last speech was read in the senate by Mr. Mason of Virginia. He declared in it that he had always believed that the agitation of the subject of slavery would end in disunion. He noted the snapping asunder through it of the religious tie in the Methodist Episcopal* and the Baptist Churches; it was giving way in the Pres-

---

* It is not a little singular that a late advocate of Southern views in England, Dr. Lempriere, instances this church as one of which the disruption was *not* mainly caused by the slavery question. My readers must choose between the authority of Dr. Lempriere and that of Mr. Calhoun.

byterian; the Episcopal Church only retained it unbroken. As the only issue, he recommended an amendment to the Constitution, which it seems was to consist in the election of two Presidents, one from the free, the other from the slave-states, the assent of each of which would be necessary to all acts of Congress.

Mr. Calhoun died shortly after the reading of this speech (31st March). He was speedily followed by ex-President Polk (June), and by President Taylor. The soldier who had weathered the hardships of a Mexican war was not proof against the heat and fatigue of a 4th of July. On the 10th July, 1850, Mr. Millard Fillmore, of New York, the Vice-President, took office in his place. Mr. Webster again became Secretary of State, whilst Mr. Crittenden, of Kentucky, whose name has been prominent of late years, became Attorney-General.

Mr. Clay's "omnibus" scheme was still pending when General Taylor died, and consequently at the date of the ratification (4th July, 1850) of what is known as the "Clayton-Bulwer convention" (19th April), between England and America, providing for the event of a navigable canal being established between the Atlantic and the Pacific. By this it was agreed that neither party should obtain or maintain any exclusive control over such a canal, erect or maintain fortifications commanding the same, or in its vicinity, "or occupy, or fortify, or colonise, or assume or exercise any dominion over Nicaragua, Costa Rica, the Mosquito coast, or any part of Central America ;" nor "make use of any protection which either afforded, or might afford, or any alliance which either had, or might have, with any state or people," for the purposes before mentioned. In case of war, the vessels of either party traversing the canal were to be exempt from blockade, detention, or capture. The body who should make the canal was to be protected, and the neutrality of the canal guaranteed, but such guarantee might be withdrawn if the canal regulations should contravene the spirit of the convention. It should be observed that England had long had a settlement of mahogany cutters on the coast of Honduras, and exercised a protectorate over a tribe of Indians, called the Mosquitos. On exchanging the ratifications of the treaty (29th June), Sir Henry Bulwer declared that it was not meant to apply to "Her Majesty's settlement at Honduras, or to its dependencies." Mr. Clayton admitted a tacit understanding that the treaty should not include British Honduras nor the small islands in its neighbourhood, but that the title thereto should remain as before.

Let us now return to internal matters. The "omnibus bill" failed as a whole, disjointed portions of it only becoming law. California was admitted as a state, without reference to slavery, but under a protest from the South, signed by such men as Jefferson Davis, Pierre Soulé, and others, on the ground of the non-extension of slavery to it. The reception of the protest was, however, refused, and Messrs. Gwin and Fremont took their seats as the first senators from

California. A Texas boundary bill was passed, by which 700,000 or 800,000 square miles of territory from New Mexico were at once handed over to Texas and slavery. Territorial governments without the "ordinance" (of 1787),—*i. e.*, without restrictions as to slavery, were given to New Mexico and to Utah. Lastly, the famous Fugitive Slave Act was passed (18th September, 1850), for rendering more effectual the provision of the Constitution as to the recovery of fugitive slaves.

It should be observed distinctly, that this Act introduced no new principle of legislation; it simply rendered that law efficient for its purpose, which was inefficient before. It was justified by its supporters by the temper of the South at this period. There was a convention of the slave-states at Nashville, Tennessee. It was proposed to assemble a Southern Congress; South Carolina passed an Act fixing the quota of her representatives at such a Congress. Mississippi passed also an Act for promoting it, subject, however, to the approval of the people. The grounds upon which this latter Act was passed were, "1st, That the legislation of Congress at the last session was controlled by a dominant majority, regardless of the rights of the slave-states; and, 2ndly, That the legislation of Congress, such as it was, affords alarming evidence of a settled purpose on the part of said majority to destroy the institution of slavery, not only in the state of Mississippi, but in her sister states, and to subvert the sovereign power of this and other slave-holding states." Secession was openly advocated by several speakers in the South Carolina legislature. The Secessionist (4th July) toasts at the South ranged from "The Union,—a splendid failure of the first modern attempt by people of different institutions to live under the same government;" to "The Union,—once a holy alliance, now an accursed bond." The scheme of a Southern Congress indeed failed, Georgia prominently opposing it. And when the Fugitive Slave Law passed, the South, no doubt, thought that it could rest content with its victory.

In connexion with the Fugitive Slave Law, let me mention an event almost simultaneous with it, which serves well to illustrate the temper of the American people at this period.

You will remember that I have long since left the Indians on one side in this history. The process of "shoving" them out of the way—for I can scarcely use any other term—has been always going on. An infinite number of treaties for removal and cession of territory has been concluded. One amongst others, a mere sample of the lot, with the Wyandots (17th March, 1842, under Tyler). In exchange for 109,000 acres of "reserves" in Ohio, and 6000 in Michigan, they were to receive 148,000 acres west of the Mississippi.

The Wyandots never received the lands promised to them. They were obliged to purchase lands from the Delawares. They became, however, a settled people, and came at last to the conclusion, that rather than preserve their precarious existence as a tribe, unrecognised by the civil law, it was better for them to merge in the great American community. So a treaty was entered into (bearing the ominous date of April 1), stating the above facts, and that the United States' Commissioner was induced to believe "that the Wyandot people had so far advanced in civilisation as to be capable generally of managing their own affairs, and were qualified and calculated to become useful citizens, a large portion whereof" (the grammar is not mine) "being already engaged in agricultural pursuits." And it was agreed that their existence as a nation or tribe should terminate, and that they should become citizens of the United States.

American officials had long been in the habit of pouring forth lamentations on the unimproveableness of these "unhappy people," the Indians, on the failure of all philanthropic efforts to civilise them. Here was a tribe at last improved, civilised, fit for, and desirous of, the duties of citizenship. What an opportunity to be seized! The senate did seize it, by striking out every word relating to the admission of the Wyandots as citizens, and reducing the treaty to a simple money bargain, whereby, in exchange for the Wyandots giving up all claim to the promised 148,000 acres, they were to receive 185,000 dollars, of which 100,000 was to be in United States' stock, and 85,000 in cash. The Wyandots, however otherwise qualified, were evidently too red to be citizens.

The infamy of such legislation, it will be observed, does not rest with the President or his cabinet, but with the senate, and probably with both parties in it equally.

Let us not, however, overlook one event which stands in pleasant contrast to the present staple of this history,—the expedition fitted out at his own expense by Henry Grinnell, of New York, which started in May, 1850, under Lieut. de Haven, in search of Sir John Franklin.

LECTURE VII.

FROM THE FUGITIVE SLAVE LAW TO THE JUDGMENT IN THE DRED SCOTT CASE (1850-6)—RESISTANCE TO THE FUGITIVE SLAVE LAW — FILIBUSTERING — REPEAL OF THE MISSOURI COMPROMISE — KANSAS — THE REPUBLICAN PARTY — FREMONT'S CANDIDATESHIP.

(Fillmore, to 1853; Pierce, from 1853.)

I HAVE said that the Fugitive Slave Law simply carried out a provision of the Constitution. Yet I believe that no single event contributed so much to produce that reaction of moral feeling in the North, which terminated in the triumph of the Republican party ten years later. How did this take place?

In the first place, then, it was the first Southern victory, which was at once palpable to the whole North. So long as the battle was waged in Missouri, or Texas, or Oregon, it was only known by hearsay to the most settled, orderly, stay-at-home portion of the North. To these men it now came home. The provisions of the Constitution on the subject might have seemed almost obsolete, so seldom did they see them attempted to be put in force. But there was no mistake about the vitality of the new law. Whether the principle of the recapture of fugitives were in the Constitution or not, clearly the South had won the use of some machinery for the purpose which the Fathers of the Republic had not deemed necessary, which was only now set to work. Every Southern slave-owner or slave-owner's agent who came North to hunt for a fugitive, every warrant of court for the apprehension of such, was a witness to Southern triumph.

Observe, moreover, that the law was not only a victory of the slave-power, but an insult to the lukewarmness of the North in the cause of freedom. For there can be no greater delusion than to suppose that evasions of slaves were frequent. As a French writer, M. Reclus, observes, in summer, when the Ohio is nothing more than a thread of water meandering through the gravel, the whole neighbouring slave-population of Kentucky and Virginia might easily escape to the land of promise—if the soil of the free states were such a land. It was not the river, not the law, not the federal authority which barred them out from freedom,—it was the selfishness, the hostility of the occupants of the opposite shore. The grievance of the South was one of nearly three-quarters of a century's standing (since it dated from the Confederation); yet it was in effect so trifling, that slavery had subsisted, grown, thriven, multiplied fourfold. And yet it was for this petty grievance,—this tiny leakage from the vessel of slavery,—most complained of by those who suffered least from it, the representatives of South Carolina and the Southern slave-states, not bordering by any part of their frontier on free territory,—that the South chose to do violence to the known traditional feelings of the North, by setting the whole machinery of the Central Government at work to catch a few runaways.

Again,—the nature of the institution on behalf of which this Southern victory was won, came home for the first time now to many of the optimists of the North. They believed in the talk about slavery as a patriarchal system, in which generation after generation of black men grew up on the same estate, never parted with by their benevolent masters. They now had to realise the unwelcome fact that slavery really meant kidnapping,—that it took hold of the man against his will, tore him from his home, from his wife and family, for the sole profit of his master; they had to realise the fact that this kidnapping was so profitable, that it paid a slave-owner to come or send to a distance of hundreds of miles, in order to catch a slave.

Again,—unluckily for the South, it was in the very nature of things that this ugly fact of kidnapping should be realised almost invariably in the most distressing cases. If there had slunk away to the North some idle black vagabond, only hating slavery on account of the toil which it imposes, only seeking freedom for the sake of doing nothing,—if there had come thither some reckless black savage, a fugitive not so much from slavery as from well-deserved punishment, and for whom freedom would mean but the gratification of every lust and passion not directly checked by the law —these were not the persons whom it would be worth while to bring back to slavery; or if they had been, from their homeless, vagrant habits, they would be the most costly to track and identify. No,—the slave-catcher's most precious and easiest prizes would be invariably the steady, the industrious, the gentle, the intelligent, the truly manly among the fugitives. If there were anywhere, in town or country, a coloured man or woman, or, still better, a household, noted among their white neighbours for thrift and sobriety and decency of demeanour, these would be the very ones whom common respect itself, more even than common rumour, would point out to his myrmidons. If there were anywhere a coloured artizan skilful enough to compete successfully with his white fellows, this would be the very man whom jealousy would too often denounce. Thus, wherever the blows of the Fugitive Slave Law might fall, they would make a void, they would leave a sore.

And for whom, after all, was the victory won, and all its miseries inflicted on the coloured race, all its shame on the whites of the North? For the sake of a minority of the nation, ever diminishing in ratio proportionately to the majority. At the census of 1820, as we have seen, the population of the free states was already half a million in excess of the slave. At the census of 1850 it was nearly four millions ahead—(13,434,922 against 9,612,769)—although spread upon a comparatively far smaller area, the population per square mile in the free states being twice as dense as in the slave. Three free states,—New York, Pennsylvania, Ohio,—now headed the census,—the first cotton-growing state, Tennessee, ranking only ninth, and restless

South Carolina only fifteenth. And out of the aggregate minority of under ten millions at the South, only 6,184,677 were free. So that, by the defects of the Constitution, aided by the besottedness or demoralisation of a portion of the North itself, six millions of Southern whites in fact dictated the law to more than double their number at the North; whilst a quarter of a million of slave-owners used even these six millions as their puppets.

Shall we wonder if, under such circumstances, when the new law comes to be put in motion, its action is resisted, sometimes by the coloured population, sometimes by the white? Shall we wonder if those free states, whose constitutions absolutely forbade slavery, whose soil was emphatically free soil,—above all, if those New England states, founded by the Puritan Fathers, and whose laws (*e. g.*, those of Connecticut) originally embodied literally many precepts of the Pentateuch, should have offered a collective resistance to a law which they deemed impious, and attempted by their state legislation to neutralise its action? No doubt, in so doing, they violated the Federal pact. No doubt they placed themselves in respect of it technically on the same footing as the Nullifiers of South Carolina. But (besides that the recollection of these days of Nullification, and indeed the whole doctrine of state-rights as expounded by Mr. Calhoun, should have effectually stopped the mouths of the South on the subject) let us not morally confound the two cases. South Carolina set the Constitution at nought out of sheer wilfulness, for the sake of its own selfish interests,—holding the Union cheap in comparison of a mere rate of import duties, which it complained of as excessive. If the North, in its turn, attempts to set at nought the Fugitive Slave Law, and thereby by implication the Constitution itself, it will be on no ground of self-interest, but because it deems that it ought to obey God rather than man. The children of the Pilgrim Fathers have read in their Bibles such texts as these:—" He that stealeth a man and selleth him, or if he be found in his hand, he shall surely be put to death " (Exod. xx. 16); " Thou shalt not deliver unto his master the servant which is escaped from his master unto thee; he shall dwell with thee, even among you, in that place which he shall choose in one of thy gates, where it liketh him best; thou shalt not oppress him." (Deut. xxiii. 15, 16.) They have read how St. Paul, in sending back the runaway Onesimus to his master Philemon, distinctly warns the latter that he should treat his late " unprofitable " slave as practically emancipated (" not now as a servant"), inflicting no punishment (" receive him as myself"), and that without any compensation for the loss of service, but only for actual wrong-doing (" if he have wronged thee, or oweth thee ought"). And they cannot reconcile such texts with the permission and facilities for kidnapping which the new law allows, with the delivering back into slavery, and for indefinite chastisement, the fugitives who dwell among them.

The first revelation to the North, however, of the dread reality of the Fugitive Slave Act was the dismay it spread among the coloured population of the free states. Mr. Palfrey tells us that 130 communicants of a single church in Buffalo left for Canada; that the coloured Baptist church in Rochester lost all but two of its 114 communicants; that the coloured Baptist church in Detroit lost eighty-four. Then came the actual enforcement of the new law. Attempts to execute it produced riots at Philadelphia, at Boston, where the coloured men, aided by an abolitionist journalist and a barrister, carried off Shadrach, a fugitive slave. An abolitionist convention was held at Syracuse, and even a black convention, at which Frederick Douglas, a fugitive slave, was spoken of as candidate for the Presidency of the United States. The South, on its side, unprepared, it would seem, for such results, grew more and more incensed. South Carolina refused to supply the vacancies among her representatives and senators, recommending her sole senator, Mr. Butler, and her representatives to abstain from taking part in the work of the Congress. She appointed, moreover, a committee to frame a bill forbidding all relations with states not executing the Fugitive Slave Law. Her Governor, Mr. Seabrook, in his message openly recommended separation. Governor Floyd, of Virginia, denied the right of Congress to legislate except to ensure the rights of slaveholders. A convention in Georgia declared the maintenance of the Union to be henceforth a secondary interest. A committee of the North Carolina Legislature denied the right of Congress to make laws on slavery, and declared the abolition of slavery in

California to be a violation of the Federal pact, and denied the right of Congress to obstruct the slave-trade between the states.

Ugly results these of compromise! Mr. Clay applied for increased powers of action for Government to enforce the Fugitive Slave Law; but they were not granted. He was more successful in his efforts to form a Union party. A greatly respected statesman of South Carolina, Mr. Poinsett, took manfully ground against disunion; and when General Hamilton, of South Carolina, urged the assembling of a Southern Convention, and an application to Virginia for the purpose, Mr. Poinsett, as well as General Houston, of Texas, opposed him with success. Notwithstanding this Convention, —which was now paralleled by the Black Convention, above referred to,—there was for a time a strong Unionist reaction. Mr. Howell Cobb, now a leader of Secession, distinguished himself then as the head of the Unionists of Georgia. The President, Mr. Fillmore (who seems to have been a well-meaning, though weak man), and his Secretary of State, Mr. Webster, both made tours throughout the country, endeavouring to allay the agitation.

With the slavery question so threatening within, one cannot feel surprised if American statesmen felt often tempted to turn the thoughts of their countrymen into other channels, especially that of foreign policy. A question which excited considerable hubbub at this time arose with Austria, out of the sending of an agent to report on the state of things in Hungary. Austria protested; Mr. Webster replied by quoting, somewhat ungraciously, the example of Austria herself at the time of the American revolution. Kossuth having, after escaping from Hungary, announced his intention of coming to the United States, a public reception to him was voted. He was accordingly most splendidly received; but when it was found that he was urging intervention by the United States, American enthusiasm for Hungary seems to have cooled down. No excuses were however made to Austria for these proceedings, certainly not complimentary to a still friendly power.

The question of Cuba came much more home to American feelings. An insurrection broke out in this island, Spain's brightest colonial jewel, and the queen of the West Indies. It might have been formidable, had a notorious adventurer, named Lopez, arrived in time. But an expedition, fitted out by him from the United States, only reached the island after the failure of the insurrection. He was defeated, but escaped; fifty of his men were shot, of whom forty were Americans. The event only caused an agitation for the annexation of Cuba to break out. At New Orleans, the mob destroyed the Spanish cigar shops, and threatened the Spanish Consul. The President (who, perhaps, had not been sorry to see Lopez rid the country of a certain number of desperadoes) now issued a proclamation against any undertakings against foreign powers, and in his message of 1851, blamed sharply the Cuba expedition. Salutes were given to the Spanish

Consuls who had been outraged, and an indemnity to the one at New Orleans; but all federal responsibility was declined for the damage done to private subjects of Spain, as being the result of purely local riots. Queen Isabella of Spain, on the other hand, pardoned and released all the prisoners taken in Cuba at the end of the year. But the agitation in reference to Cuba was not to be so easily put a stop to. By the end of the next year, there was much talk of an affiliation, or, in plain English, conspiracy, termed the "Order of the Lone Star," for the nominal enfranchisement, or rather conquest of Cuba, but which was intended, it appears, to serve as the starting-point of a great scheme of Southern or slavery extension. Even members of the senate, such as Mr. Douglas, of Illinois, and Mr. Yulee, of Florida, formed part of it. This, of course, gave rise to greater vigilance on the part of Spain, and to visits and stoppages of American ships at Cuba, all affording fuel for fresh agitation. To put a stop to this state of things, England and France proposed to the United States to sign a convention, by which all three parties should engage to abstain from attempting to annex Cuba, and to repel all aggressive attempts upon it; but this Mr. Fillmore refused to sign.

In addition to this Cuban affair, there were a number of other petty heats and broils with foreign powers. Differences with England, on account of the firing into a ship at Greytown, on the coast of the Mosquito territory, then under English protection; on account of the fisheries, and of the disputes of American and

English fishermen. Differences with Peru, on account of certain guano islands, called the Lobos Islands. Mr. Webster made warlike speeches, but eventually the American Government drew back in both cases. Add to these matters an expedition to Japan, and long discussions in Congress on the subject of intervention or non-intervention generally, with some violent speeches by Mr. Pierre Soulé, of Louisiana, and it will be seen that foreign questions occupied no small portion of the period of Mr. Fillmore's administration.

Two remarkable men passed away during this period, —Henry Clay, of Kentucky, born in 1777, who died 28th June, 1852 : and Daniel Webster, of Massachusetts, born in 1782, who followed him on the 24th of October in the same year. Both belong, with Mr. Calhoun, to that class of men to which I have before referred, created, it may be said, by the imperfection of the American Constitution, in reference to the establishment of the executive power,—of leading statesmen who never attained the Presidential chair, but were kept out of it, either by their own self-respect, which refused to bow before an irresponsible " convention," or more commonly by the mean jealousy of their own greatness entertained by the many.

To the latter end of Mr. Fillmore's administration belongs the publication of a book, which cannot be overlooked in treating of the history of the period,— " Uncle Tom's Cabin." Very few people, probably, now read the work; but most of us, probably, can call to mind the extraordinary sensation which we received from first perusing it. I believe myself that critics are now disposed most unduly to underrate it; that even in point of literary effect, it evinces a power of throwing off characters all alive, so to speak, perfectly individual, and, in themselves, solid and complete, so that you may view them, as it were, all round, like beautiful pieces of sculpture, which has never been equalled since Shakspere. But it was not by its literary power that the book achieved its effect, and sold by the 100,000. Its power lay in its reality. The writer's whole soul had gone into it. Believe or not in the reality of such characters as "Uncle Tom" on the one side, or "Legree" on the other,—I, for one, accept that reality implicitly in both cases,—yet you could not doubt for an instant that she believed in it. And there can be no doubt that to thousands and thousands this great and good book was the means of tearing asunder a veil, which, till then, had fatally obscured the truth from their eyes,—that to thousands of others who had seen that truth, the book gave, or mightily helped to give, the courage to proclaim it, to uphold it, to die for it.

Mr. Fillmore saw himself put aside as a candidate for the next election by the Whig party, to which he belonged, but this time in favour of no unworthy rival, General Scott, the Commander-in-chief of the Mexican war. It is refreshing, amidst all the low popularity-hunting of Presidential elections, to read of the worthy old General's letter, declaring that he would, if elected, allow no sedition or resistance to law, wheresoever it might be, and on whatsoever pretext. Of course he was not elected; and his opponent, a barrister, who had left his practice for the Mexican war, and had commanded in it the militia of his state, Mr. Franklin Pierce, of New Hampshire, was carried into office by the Democratic party, which, from henceforth until the actual Secession, is more and more identified with the slave-holding interest. Mr. F. Pierce, although he obtained the honour of a biographical puff from Mr. Hawthorne, afforded certainly no exception to the run of Presidential mediocrities, whilst, morally, he showed himself far inferior to his predecessor.

His " inaugural" (March, 1853) was enthusiastically received,—wherefore, it is difficult to perceive. He promised friendly relations with the states of the new world, non-intervention in the concerns of the old, but declared that American citizens must be respected. As respects internal politics, he pronounced himself in favour of the late slavery compromises. His choice of a cabinet, however, did not answer to these promises. Mr. Marcy, of New York, was his Secretary of State; the now notorious Mr. Jefferson Davis, his Secretary of War; Mr. Caleb Cushing (a Northern renegade, whom President Tyler had sent as envoy to China, and of whose proceedings while there Benton pungently says that, narrated by himself, they " bespoke an organisation void of the moral sense, and without the knowledge that any one else possessed it"), his Attorney-General. The struggle for office around him was unexampled. Among the nominations made was one which was to cast infinite discredit upon his administration, that of Mr. Pierre Soulé, one of the "fire-eating" democrats of Louisiana, the avowed partisan of the conquest of Cuba, as envoy to Spain. Differences soon broke out afresh with Spain, with Mexico, and the Attorney-General of the new cabinet openly declared himself in favour of the annexation, violent or pacific, of Sonora and Chihuahua, provinces of Mexico, and of Cuba. Never did enthusiasm fall so rapidly as that which had been worked up in favour of Mr. Pierce. Before the year was out, everything was at sixes and sevens. The cabinet itself was divided; there were "hard-shell democrats" in it, and "soft-shell democrats," Mr. Marcy leading the one faction, Mr. Jeff. Davis the other. Between the President and his Congress there was discord, such as had not been seen since the wretched days of Mr. Tyler.

We may now notice the entrance upon the scene of a new adventurer, Walker, the American "Filibuster," who far outstripped his Cuban predecessor, Lopez. His first expedition for the revolutionising of Lower California was, however, quite a failure, so that Mr. Pierce could afterwards safely launch a new proclamation against such expeditions. Perhaps, however, it was not without influence on the conclusion of a new boundary-treaty with Mexico, by which, for a sum of fifteen million dollars, Mexico agreed to give up a block of land 600 miles wide by 120, part of Chihuahua and Sonora; a desert about the size of Virginia, which, however, opened a new road to the Pacific (1854). The

Senate ratified the treaty, but "snubbed" the President, cutting down the payment to Mexico to ten millions of dollars.

The Cuban difficulty remained. The seizure by the Spanish authorities of a ship called the "Black Warrior," afforded the President a subject for a special message, and Congress the matter for a hot debate. The American cabinet set on foot negotiations for the purchase of Cuba (having at the same time legal proceedings taken to suppress some fresh filibustering preparations), and the President asked ten millions of dollars of Congress to provide for eventualities, *i. e.*, for purchase or war. Congress snubbed him again, and refused the money. The question became complicated by an act unheard-of in diplomacy. Three of the foreign ministers of the United States—Mr. Soulé, of Madrid, Mr. Buchanan, of London, Mr. Mason, of Paris—met at Ostend (18th October, 1854), to confer as to whether it were time to take possession of Cuba. They resolved that Cuba was for the United States a necessary acquisition, determined by Providence, and that if Spain refused to sell it, all laws, divine and human, authorised the United States to take it. Soulé, a Frenchman by origin, considered that France and the United States should share the world between them. A cabinet of ordinary dignity would have sent all three diplomats about their business. But Soulé was so perfectly indifferent to the orders of his superiors, that for eight months he had kept back conciliatory despatches from his own minister, sent in order to be communicated to the Spanish

Government, whom he kept irritating all the while by his insolence, and only communicated it on leaving Madrid. However, having given offence to Louis Napoleon by intrigues with the Republican party, he saw himself refused a passage through France, and before long America was rid of the discredit of being represented by such a personage. The cabinet was itself divided on the subject of the acquisition of Cuba. Mr. Jeff. Davis and Mr. Cushing were for obtaining it at any price; Mr. Marcy stood out for the *status quo*. The official Filibustering for Cuba may be said, however, to have been given up in the course of 1855.

But acts of lawlessness were multiplying on all sides within the sphere of American influence. The most shameful, perhaps, of these was the bombardment of Greytown, on the Mosquito coast. It arose out of a piece of murderous brutality by the captain of an American steamer, by which a fisherman, who had been told to keep off, and still hung about the ship, lost his life. This was turned into an outrage *upon* the United States by Captain Hollins, of the American navy,—the same, I presume, who, with a steam ram, has lately been trying to run down a Federal squadron near New Orleans,—and his act, instead of being reprobated, was adopted by the American Government, who held him free from all claims for damages through the bombardment. The Filibuster, Walker, again turns up in an expedition against Nicaragua, afterwards directed against New Granada, where he upsets the Government, has a President of his own choice elected, and sends a disreputable agent to Washington, to obtain recognition. This time the scandal was too great; the swindler-envoy was not received; an American consul, who had negotiated for Walker, was blamed; a new proclamation against Filibustering launched by the President, and two ships for the Filibusters actually seized. Another annexation, much talked of about this period, was that of the Sandwich Islands,—a convenient stepping-stone for the United States towards China and Japan. It happened, however, that the King of the Sandwich Islands, Kamehameha IV., although trained up, I believe, by American missionaries, had had his feelings galled to the quick through a voyage he had made to America, in which he had several times found himself treated with indignity on account of his colour. He was strongly opposed to annexation; nor was there any strong popular feeling in the United States in favour of it. The plan was given up, and although the President refused to sign a treaty proposed by the Hawaian envoy for a joint guarantee of Hawaian independence by England, France, and the United States, a treaty establishing free trade between the Sandwich Islands and the United States was accepted. Another treaty, negotiated with the Dominican Republic—*i. e.*, that part of the Island of St. Domingo formerly belonging to Spain, which had then lately established its independence of the Negro empire of Haiti, and which has now given itself back to Spain— failed, being rejected by the Dominicans through the want of protection which it afforded to their coloured citizens. Treaties with Denmark, ensuring the payment to that power of those sea-tolls called the "Sound dues," were refused to be renewed; and it is characteristic of the temper of the American people at this time, that they instantly began to speak about seizing St. Thomas, a Danish island in the West Indies, and a great centre of trade, as a compensation for the exaction of the Sound dues by Denmark, whilst at the same time indemnity was refused for the Greytown outrage. Add to this differences with Brazil and Paraguay, and an attempt to secure the protectorate of the Galapagos, and you will have some idea of the state of hot water in which Mr. Pierce's administration constantly kept the country. Nor was this all.

England had no greater wish than to remain at peace with the United States. The "Canadian reciprocity" treaty (5th June, 1854), for securing free trade and equal rights of fishery between the American Union and our bordering colonies, seemed to afford a great guarantee to this end. But the Crimean war was going on; and whilst the American government was sending its Commissioners to the allied camp to watch operations, one of whom was destined to be the leading Commander on the Federal side in the day of secession (the present General McClellan), some English Consuls had the unfortunate idea of trying to recruit men for our army in the United States. Considering the open way in which enlistments had taken place, at the beck of a Lopez or a Walker, for the invasion of almost every neighbour of the United States, the attempt seemed a harmless one. But America has always coquetted with Russia, and a storm of indignation at this unheard-of outrage on American neutrality burst forth. Lord Clarendon made excuses for the blunder committed, but refused to recall the Consuls. There were other points of friction between the two countries, just ready to fester into sores; a difference as to the construction of the "Clayton-Bulwer" treaty, which we alleged to have been intended to reserve, and the Americans to put an end to a protectorate which we claimed of the Mosquito coast, and our rights over certain islands off the coast, which we subsequently (17th June, 1852) erected into a colony by the name of the "Bay Islands." President Pierce's message of 31st December, 1855, was strong against England, both as respects the enlistment question and that of the Clayton-Bulwer treaty, and many speakers in Congress, of course, took the most violent tone against England; although, indeed, one plain-dealing man, Mr. Hale, of New Hampshire, declared that the agitation was all humbug. Mr. Dallas, an avowed partisan of Russia, was sent as envoy to England; and the British minister at Washington, Mr. Crampton, with three obnoxious consuls, received his passports. This took place about the same time as the reception at Washington, of one Father Vigil, a second envoy from Walker, who had committed all sorts of violences in Nicaragua, raised against him a confederation of the smaller states, and shot his lieutenant Schlesinger when the Costa Ricans had defeated him. However, we took the thing quietly enough; Mr. Crampton came back, and the Bay Islands were given up to the republic of Honduras. Two acts should, indeed, be noticed, as some set-off to so much that is discreditable,—one, the sending, at the joint expense of Mr. Grinnell and of the United States' Government, of a second expedition (under Dr. Kane) in search of Franklin; the other, the spirited rescue by Capt. Ingraham, off Smyrna, of the Hungarian refugee, Martin Koszta, who had been seized by the Austrians while under the protection of the United States' consul.

I have dwelt upon foreign politics first, as it is, perhaps, only through the mixture of insolence and vacillation, the lawless ambition, restrained by scarcely a shadow of moral control, the anarchical spirit, which are visible throughout the foreign relations of the United States during the period that the government of the country was thus given up to Southern influences, that we can credit the even greater demoralisation which the internal affairs of the country exhibited during the same period.

Slavery was winning fresh victories. None were sweeter, probably, than those won by Northern hands. Mr. Douglas, the slave-holding senator from free Illinois, was a most efficient ally for this purpose. A man of strong will, singular ability, deep craft, immense ambition, one of the recognised leaders in the senate, his weight was at this time, and for several years, thrown entirely into the scales of the pro-slavery party. One of his most note-worthy performances was the bringing forward of the Kansas-

Nebraska bill, to constitute governments for vast territories to the W. and N. W., the latter chiefly as yet inhabited by Indian tribes. The bill not only made the Fugitive Slave Law expressly applicable to these territories, but although they lie entirely north of the Missouri compromise line, instead of prohibiting slavery, it left the people of the territories free to decide whether they would have it or not, and as eventually modified, actually declared the Missouri Compromise Act inoperative and void. Thus the Southern party, which had originally devised the Missouri Compromise in order to drive slavery beyond the line of the ordinance of 1787, which had subsequently proposed to extend the line of that compromise to the Pacific, in order to have a chance of introducing slavery into regions yet free, now found itself strong enough to throw it completely overboard. In spite of a junction between the Whigs of the North, the Free-soilers and Abolitionists, the bill was carried in the senate by 37 votes to 14 (1854).

The opposition to the Fugitive Slave Law continuing, so that Federal officers attempting to execute it found themselves sued in the courts of the Northern states for violation of the state laws, a measure was brought forward for exempting Federal officers from all state jurisdiction. But it was soon felt that this was a two-edged weapon, and the bill was rejected by the House of Representatives. So defiant on the other side was the Free-soil spirit in the North, that Massachusetts passed an Act openly repealing the Fugitive Slave Law, enacted by Congress. I need hardly say how absolutely illegal such a proceeding must be. One regrets it the more, as in some sort retrospectively justifying South Carolina nullification. The great battle-field of the slavery question, however, began now to be the territory of Kansas.

The "struggle for Kansas" will be told you by my friend Mr. Hughes. It is sufficient to say here, that Kansas, lying, as I have said, wholly to the north of the Missouri Compromise line, had that settlement been adhered to by the South, would have been necessarily and unquestionably free soil. But the Missouri Compromise being now repudiated, and slavery treated as an open question, it became a point of vital importance for the future of the United States, whether Kansas should be slave or free, it being, to a great extent, the key to the yet unsettled lands further west. Both parties, therefore, free-soilers and slave-owners, endeavoured to secure it. Civil war ensued; rival constitutions were framed; the whole influence of Government was thrown into the scale of slavery. But before Mr. Pierce's administration was over, these local troubles of Kansas, as he termed them, were on the point of threatening to bring the very machinery of Government to a stand-still. How this came to pass is a singular story in itself.

There had grown up towards the beginning of Mr. Pierce's term of office a party called that of the "Know-nothings," whose watchword was "America for the Americans." A selfish, unpromising starting-point, which was followed by ungenerous and selfish acts. Emigrants from Europe were maltreated; a riot took place at New Orleans between Irishmen and Know-nothings, in which several deaths occurred; five persons were killed in a similar riot at St. Louis; other disturbances took place in Ohio. The quarrel between native Americans and foreigners easily ran into one between Protestants and Roman Catholics. Already, in 1853, the passage through the United States of the papal legate, Mons. Bedini, had given rise to rioting. Now (1855), at Newark, in New Jersey, the Irish attacked their Protestant fellow-citizens; these retaliated by sacking a Roman Catholic church; anti-popery feeling ran high in New York itself. Finally the Know-nothings held a convention in June, 1855, to organize themselves; but the convention split on the subject of slavery. They carried the elections of that year in various states, particularly in California; but they were too weak to subsist as a distinct party, and were composed, moreover, of too discordant elements. So the best of them combined with the remnants of the old Whig party in the North, and with the Free-soilers and Abolitionists. Hence the new Republican party—not to be confounded as respects principles with the party of that name which figures in the early history of the United States—which found itself at once in a slight majority in the House of Representatives, and succeeded after a struggle in giving it for Speaker Mr. Banks, of Massachusetts, a strong opponent of slavery.

An extraordinary piece of Southern brutality gave consistency to the Republican party. A senator from Massachusetts, Charles Sumner, one of the great speakers of the day, highly respected in private life, but somewhat extreme and violent in the expression of anti-slavery views, in a speech of his called tall senator Butler, of South Carolina, and short senator Douglas, of Illinois (the "Little Giant," so his friends named him) the "Don Quixote and Sancho Panza of slavery." A day or two after, as he was bending (he is very near-sighted) over his heavy senator's desk, a relative of Mr. Butler, member of the House of Representatives, Mr. Brooks, who had deemed his kinsman insulted by Mr. Sumner's speech, came behind, and struck him repeatedly over the head and nape of the neck with, I believe, a heavy cane. Mr. Sumner, a man of large frame and great muscular power, in starting up to meet his somewhat puny antagonist, wrenched from the floor his desk, which was fixed to it, but was so stunned and severely wounded, that he could not inflict on his opponent the chastisement which he deserved. He remained laid up for months from the effects of this outrage, which seemed at one time as if it would deprive him of his reason. The Senate, of which he was a member, instituted an inquiry, imposed a trumpery fine on Mr. Brooks, which was triumphantly paid; and, incredible to say, this brutal assailant of a stooping man, whose best deserts would have been the treadmill, leaped at one bound into the position of a Southern hero. Although expelled by the House of Representatives, he was immediately sent back to it. Addresses and eulogies were showered upon him; the so-called ladies of South Carolina presented him with a cane, as an emblem of his prowess, and when, about a year later (January 7th, 1857), a pitying Providence took him out of the world, he was openly compared in Congress, by a colleague (Mr. Savage), to Brutus.

I find some counterpoise,—though many would deem it a strange one,—to the moral enormity of the Sumner outrage, going, as it did, practically unpunished, in the singular events which took place in the course of 1856 on the seaboard of the Pacific. The gold-discoveries of California had, of course, for effect to draw to that country all that was most greedy and reckless, most impatient of all restraint,—in short, until similar discoveries in Australia served as a diversion to the process, to make it a *rendezvous* for the scum and refuse of the whole earth. So far from the central authority endeavouring to check the evil influence by a judicious choice of officers, the most worthless and violent men obtained office. Justice was sold, or rather absolutely ceased to be; its ministers were the first to break the laws; life was no longer secure; society seemed breaking up. And I believe it *would* have broken up in any other community than one in which the strong Anglo-Saxon element ruled paramount. But a "Vigilance Committee" (such a one had indeed sat already in 1851) was formed, and for three months took justice into its own hands (June—September, 1856). When present crime seemed stopped, it proceeded to get rid of old offenders,

—hanging one Philander Brace for a murder committed in 1854. And when order and security were restored, the committee threw up their, as I deem it, most righteous authority.

When the time came for nominating the Presidential candidates, Mr. Pierce, in his turn, found himself put aside by the Democratic convention at Cincinnati. His opponents were Mr. Douglas and Mr. Buchanan (he of Ostend), a Pennsylvanian; the South now endeavouring always to rule through Northern instruments; the latter was chosen, with Mr. Breckenridge as candidate for the Vice-Presidency. The Republican party, on the other hand, chose Fremont, of exploring fame, Mr. Benton's son-in-law, but an avowed Free-soiler. The contest was at its height, both within and without the walls of Congress. The war in Kansas continued, wearing out governor after governor. The Republican party stopped the appropriations for war purposes, on account of the illegalities committed in Kansas. Congress was called together in an extraordinary session (21st August, 1856), and for some time the Senate and the House remained in conflict, the House always refusing to appropriate. At last it yielded, the President signed the appropriation bill, and Congress adjourned. Out of doors, no accusation or slander was spared to Colonel Fremont by the Democratic party. So hot already was the South, that Governor Wise, of Virginia, threatened, if Fremont were elected, to march on Washington, and seize the Capitol and the national archives. When the election came, the Democrats carried the free states of Ohio, Pennsylvania, and Indiana and returned their candidate by 174 votes to 126 given for Fremont; the state of Maryland alone voting for Mr. Fillmore, who stood as the candidate of the Native American party, *i. e.*, of that portion of the Knownothings which had refused to enter into the Republican party.

The last months of Mr. Pierce's administration saw the return of Walker the filibuster from Nicaragua. He had now a grand project of a federation, to be composed of Mexico, Central America, Cuba, and Hayti, which was, however, prematurely divulged by an associate. As an earnest of his intentions, Walker re-established slavery in Nicaragua. But he had rendered himself thoroughly unpopular, and had to withdraw. The annexation propensity amongst his countrymen was not, however, yet subdued. There was at this time considerable excitement in reference to a riot at Panama (through which place a constant stream of American emigration to and from California was passing), where the native population, —a mixed and mongrel race,—often treated with great brutality by American travellers, had at last risen upon them. The Committee of Congress appointed to consider this "Panama outrage," concluded in their report to annex the isthmus itself. The little republic of New Grenada, however, stood firm, and the project was given up or put by. Let us notice, however, as one act of truly graceful, as well as manly, international courtesy, the sending back to England of

Franklin's ship, the "Resolute," which had been found derelict in the Northern seas by an American vessel, and which was restored to us in a state of full repair and re-equipment. Such acts as these make us feel that the old kindred blood was strong in American bosoms yet, even during the baleful period of the ascendency of the slave power.

Mr. Pierce, in his last message to Congress (2nd Dec., 1856), endeavoured to sink out of office as handsomely as he could, declaring that Mr. Buchanan's election was a triumph of his own views. He further took this occasion to pronounce his opinion, in addition to the vote of Congress, that the Missouri Compromise was unconstitutional,—in other words, that no limit must be placed to the development of slavery. From that question of slavery there was now no escape. Again the Kansas civil war roused loud discussions in Congress. So united was the North rapidly becoming, that even leading Democratic senators, like General Cass, admitted that they should prefer to see Kansas free. Even more serious was the discovery of a negro plot at Nashville, Tennessee, with branches in Kentucky and Louisiana. What had it sprung from? Strange to say, the pro-slavery fanaticism of the whites. The tumult of electioneering, the furious speeches of their own masters, had been the enlighteners of the slaves. Not that the conspiracy was a very formidable one. It only contemplated a collective rush to Canada, that land of promise to the slave. But the repression of it was not the less severe. Yet the masters could not help talking on the dangerous subject. The South held a Commercial Convention at Savannah, in the early days of December. Here the re-opening of the slave-trade was publicly discussed. Delegates from Virginia, Texas, and Alabama, supported the proposal; but it was repelled by other members, chiefly Virginians; and even in the House of Representatives of South Carolina, Mr. Orr protested against the idea. It was about a month later that hero Brooks died (Jan. 7, 1857).

But the great event in the history of the slavery question which marks the close of Mr. Pierce's administration, was the decision of the Supreme Court of the United States, in what is known as the "Dred Scott case" (*Dred Scott* v. *John F. A. Sandford*, December Term, 1856; 19 Howard's Reports, pp. 393-633). The circumstances of the case appear to have been simply these: A negro slave from Missouri was taken by his master to the state of Illinois, where slavery was prohibited by law; thence to a territory north of lat. 36° 30′, part of the Louisiana cession, where, consequently, slavery was equally prohibited by the Missouri Compromise Act; thence back again to Missouri. Here he sued for and obtained a verdict and judgment in the Circuit Court, declaring his freedom; but, on appeal, the Supreme Court of the state reversed the judgment, and remitted the case to the inferior Court. Meanwhile, his old master's administrator laid hands on him, his wife, and two children (whose cases were much the same as his own). He brought an action of trespass, as a citizen of Missouri; the defendant pleaded that he, his wife, and children, were slaves. It was upon this plea that appeal was made to the Supreme Court. It has been ingeniously urged* that the decision amounted strictly to this, that the condition of citizenship within a state must be decided by the law of that state itself; a decision which itself would seem to offer the gravest obstacles to the due ascertainment of freedom. But the ground taken up by C. J. Taney and the majority of the Court was far more extensive, and the decision was, it may be said, accepted by public opinion as establishing, or endeavouring to establish, 1st, That free negroes could not be citizens of the United States, but only within the jurisdiction of particular states; 2nd, That so much of the Missouri Compromise Act as prohibited slavery in territories N. of lat. 36° 30', was unconstitutional, and that, consequently, Congress had no power to forbid slavery in any territory; 3rd, That the slave-owners of the South could go with their slaves wherever they pleased, into or out of states where slavery was most expressly prohibited, without the slaves acquiring any right to claim their freedom. It is difficult for an English lawyer to conceive the extent to which pro-slavery partizanship warped in this instance the judgment of one who is reputed a really great judge in his own country. Nothing, for instance, could seem clearer than the provision of the United States Constitution, that the

---

* See "A Legal Review of the case of Dred Scott, as decided by the Supreme Court of the United States, from the Law Reporter for June, 1857." Boston: Crosby, Nichols & Co., 1857.

citizens of each state should be entitled to all the privileges and immunities of citizens in all. But in order to exclude negroes from citizenship, the Chief Judge held, 1st, That this provision was confined to those who were citizens of any state when the Constitution was adopted; 2nd, That negroes were not such citizens. He was not ashamed to argue this from the terms of an Act for the enrolment of "every free able-bodied white male citizen;" to which a colleague (Justice Curtis) answered very simply, that he might just as well have argued that all citizens were able-bodied or males, as that all were white. I cannot dwell here at length upon this monstrous judgment. But you will now feel for what purpose, in an earlier portion of this history, I called your attention to the fact, that out of the four men claimed by Jefferson from England as "American citizens" after the searching of the "Chesapeake," were men of colour; and to the style in which Jackson addressed the free coloured men of Louisiana during the war with England, treating them as "fellow-citizens" of the whites. Observe that, even prior to the date of this judgment, the Executive had issued orders to its foreign ministers to refuse passports to American-born persons of colour.

Note also the refusal by the United States to accede to the terms of the Paris conferences of April, 1856, by which the chief European nations agreed to abolish privateering,—to allow a neutral flag to cover enemy's goods, not being contraband of war,—to exempt from seizure under the enemy's flag neutral goods, not being contraband of war,—and that blockades, to be respected, should be effectual. Every leading principle that America had ever contended for in such matters was thus granted; still she would not be satisfied, unless all private property at sea should be declared exempt from seizure. "Sumters" and "Nashvilles" have, ere this, made her bitterly feel the folly of her refusal.

LECTURE VIII.

FROM THE JUDGMENT IN THE DRED SCOTT CASE TO SECESSION (1856-1861)—THE SLAVE POWER AND THE SUPREME COURT—FREESOIL VICTORY IN KANSAS—OFFICIAL SCANDALS—HARPER'S FERRY—BREAK UP OF THE DEMOCRATIC PARTY—ELECTION OF LINCOLN—NATURE OF THE PRESENT CONFLICT.

(Pierce, 1853 to 1857 ; Buchanan, 1857 to 1861.)

It is impossible to exaggerate the historical importance of the Dred Scott case. The Supreme Court of the United States is invested with a quite peculiar importance among earthly tribunals, as the sovereign interpreter of the Constitution of a great nation. It represents the attempt to create a moral power, which, within certain limits, shall be superior to that of the nation itself, acting at once through its representative and its executive bodies. For, whilst with us, Parliament, as composed of King, Lords and Commons, is for all earthly purposes literally omnipotent, and any interpretation of the law by the very highest Court of Appeal can be nullified at once (and, indeed, in practice is nullified not unfrequently) by Act of Parliament; in the United States, on the contrary, there is no direct practical appeal from a decision of the Supreme Court, interpreting the Constitution, but either to itself on another occasion, or, by means of amendment to the Constitution, to the nation at large, according to a certain specified and jealously devised procedure, requiring 'the assent of three-fourths of all the states; or, lastly, to the necessities of military law, in case of foreign or civil war.

This enormous moral power with which the Supreme Court has been invested would evidently require for its exercise almost superhuman wisdom, moderation, and prudence. And it is to the credit of the American judiciary, that, in despite of the vagaries of many of the inferior and local courts, the decisions of the Supreme Court had, up to the time which we have reached, commanded universal respect. But now it was seen that this sovereign tribunal was itself enthralled to the slave-power; the national justice was corrupted in its very head-springs; right and wrong became henceforth no more judicial, but solely political questions, the arbitrament of which was to be sought only at the ballot-box, or, if the worst came to the worst, as it has now, at the cannon's mouth. For we must not forget that the "Dred Scott" decision came just in time to supplement, by legal authority, the numerical weakness of slavery; at a time when a Southern delegate was warning the Democratic connection that Kansas, Nebraska, and the other territories, could only be peopled with slaves at the expense of Maryland, Virginia, and Missouri, which would then become free; so that that decision could only be taken by the free states as judicially robbing them of the fruits which they felt themselves sure to reap from the exercise of their greater colonizing energies.

It is essential, I think, for us to bear this in mind in considering that practical lawlessness, that visible contempt for the most cherished prerogatives of civil liberty, which surprise and grieve us at the North in the present day. Accustomed as we are to respect the passionless impartiality of our Courts of Justice, wisely kept aloof as they are from all political action, we can neither realise the vertigo which the "Dred Scott" decision shows to have been induced among the judges of the Supreme Court, by their political privilege of constitutional interpretation, nor yet the coarse matter-of-fact expediency which the Executive is now content to allege in thwarting or forbidding a *habeas corpus*. We do not see that the one is the consequence of the other. We do not see that the contest, unseemly in itself, between the Supreme Court and the Administration is one between political opponents. We are apt to forget that, by one of the most striking ironies of history, the same Chief Justice Taney who was just now doing battle for the rights of citizenship of white Southern traitors or their adherents, is the one who, to exclude the free coloured man from citizenship, has done violence to the Constitution, and set at nought the tradition of almost all the great founders of the republic, and of at least one-half of its history.

From the time of such a decision, then,—the battle having become exclusively a political one,—if the free North was not to see the whole territory of the United

States poisoned with slavery, under colour of law, it must win the upper hand in Congress and in the Executive, and keep it, so as to be able practically and in detail to forbid any further extension of the slave-power, which in principle could no longer be resisted, until such time as the requisite amendment to the Constitution could, under the three-fourths rule, be enacted.

To the latter part of Mr. Pierce's term of administration, and to that of Mr. Buchanan, belongs the publication of a series of works which must have greatly contributed to form or fix the judgment of the North on the question of slavery,—Mr. Olmsted's "Our Seaboard Slave-States," his "Texas," and his "Journey to the Back Country." A Northern farmer, as he tells us, who had visited the South, fully persuaded that the evils of slavery were grossly exaggerated, and intending to settle there himself, he returned, after a leisurely examination, with a conviction of the false economy and radical immorality of slavery, of which the picture, as given in the three works above referred to, must amount, for any unprejudiced mind, to an absolute demonstration of the conclusions to which he has himself been led. The "Biglow Papers" had held up the humbug of the slave-power to the scorn of the world; "Uncle Tom's Cabin" had shown the outrages upon human nature to which it may lead; Mr. Olmsted's works now brought home to every thinking mind the proof that it is in itself a moral and economic nuisance, of which, as a mere matter of business, the further progress must be stopped.

The task was not an easy one. Both Congress itself and the Administration had, before all, to be purified. Throughout the whole of Mr. Pierce's administration, complaints were rife as to the abuse by members of the privilege of franking, to which the Postmaster-General attributed the deficiency in the receipts of his department;—of the privilege of "mileage," for coming to and returning from Congress ;—lastly, of actual sales of votes. To such a height had this come, that in the last session under Pierce four members were expelled by the House of Representatives, three of them for actually selling their votes, the fourth for speaking of all as doing the same. Note that of the four, two were from New York, and one from Connecticut. A Southern gentleman like Mr. Jefferson Davis advocates openly repudiation of its debts by a whole state ; the Northern riff-raff, whom a period of Southern ascendency floats uppermost, indulge in petty personal peculations.

And now came (1857) that last Presidential term of office which was to see closed, at least for a time, the history of the "United States." It seemed difficult to outdo the disgrace of such an administration as that of Mr. Pierce. Mr. Buchanan was to achieve that marvel. A Pennsylvanian full of years, who had filled the highest subordinate offices of the State, with full experience both of foreign and of home politics; consummate, it was held by his admirers, in state-craft, in craft simply by his opponents, he might at least, one might think, have wiped out the recollections of past inexperience in the Presidential chair. Never were expectations more disappointed than they were in him.

Not unwisely, indeed, judging from past experience, did the new President in his "Inaugural" (4th March, 1857) declare that he would only hold office for a single term. He praised the Union, of the maintenance of which he represented himself as the living symbol. He deplored past scandals.; recommended economy and reduced taxation, and the formation of a great highway to the Pacific, daily more and more needed by the growth of California and its sister-states on the Pacific; contrived skilfully to throw an indirect blame upon illegal undertakings. For a time this promise of prudence was kept up. Although General Cass, the fanatical opponent of England, was named Secretary of State, and the cabinet was filled with Southerners and future Secessionists, still Mr. Howell Cobb, of Georgia, might seem to offer a grateful relief from Mr. Jefferson Davis; nor was it foreseen, in the North at least, to what purpose Governor Floyd might turn his secretaryship-at-war. One or two irritating questions of foreign policy were set at rest, or put in train for being so. A convention was concluded with Denmark for the redemption of the Sound dues; a commission named under a treaty with New Grenada for settling the Panama indemnities. Not less wisely, perhaps, did the Cabinet refuse to co-operate with England and France in the China war.

But the slavery question was the rock on which all this seeming wisdom was to split. The Dred Scott decision was convulsing the North. The illegality, at least of the positions laid down by the Chief Justice, and of the conclusions drawn from them by the partizans of slavery, was felt instinctively on all sides. The idea, above all, of seeing slave-owners come and parade their slaves on free soil, in spite of the most positive state laws for the exclusion of slavery, galled men to the quick. The Senate of New York resolved that that state would not tolerate slavery within its limits under any shape or pretéxt, or for any period, however short. The Senate of Pennsylvania declared the judgment of the Supreme Court to be a violation of the spirit of the Constitution. The illegal judgment was too often met by illegal acts. Fugitive slaves arrested in Ohio were rescued, the Federal officers arresting them were imprisoned, and only released on *habeas corpus*. The Kansas struggle, on the other side, ran to its height. Although each pro-slavery governor in his turn became converted by the force of things to the conviction that the true rebels in Kansas were not the free-soilers, but the Missourians, the President continued to show himself even more shamelessly partial to the pro-slavery party than his predecessor, and attempted to maintain its fraudulent constitution (the "Lecompton" one) even after such men as senator Douglas, of Illinois, leader of the Northern Democrats, and the author of the Nebraska bill, had pronounced himself against it, and Governor Wise, of Virginia, had acknowledged the triumph of the free-soil party in Kansas, and Southern veterans like Mr. Crittenden, of

Kentucky, and Mr. Bell, of Tennessee, felt themselves constrained to condemn Mr. Buchanan's conduct. The House of Representatives had long been opposed to the Lecompton Constitution; the Senate yet clung to it, in spite of the adoption by Congress of a Machiavellian suggestion by a Northern Democrat, Mr. English, of Indiana, for bribing Kansas into the acceptance of slavery, by the two-fold bait of immediate admission as a state and the free gift of three millions of acres of public lands for schools and railways. Kansas firmly stood by her free-soil principles, rejecting the "English Ordinance" (2nd August, 1858) by a majority of about six to one. Hence it has happened that Kansas has had to wait till 1861 for its admission as a state.

The same period, however, that saw the Kansas contest practically settled, saw also the admission as states of Minnesota and virtually of Oregon, both free, —thus giving in the Senate an addition of four votes to the free states, and breaking up the custom of the alternate admission of free and slave-states. But it should not be overlooked, that in the free states of the present day freedom is too often only a practice, not a moral principle. Slavery is excluded, because it is felt to be economically and politically mischievous; but there is no genuine feeling even of justice, let alone brotherhood, as towards the coloured man. Thus the constitution of Oregon forbad free coloured persons to live or acquire property in the state, or to sue in its Courts; and it was on this account that the pro-slavery party voted in favour of the admission, which, after passing the Senate in 1859, was carried in the House by 114 to 103 (12th Feb., 1859). Let it be observed, that Oregon was admitted with from 10,000 to 15,000 inhabitants only, whilst Kansas, with a considerably greater population, was kept out till it should have 93,000. It is painful, indeed, to have to add that Kansas herself yielded to the example of Oregon, following up the exclusion of slavery by an absolute exclusion of the coloured race from her limits.

To dispose of a subject which has close moral connection with that of slavery, and which will, perhaps, become the most prominent question for America when that of slavery is once settled, let me say a few words of a "Mormon difficulty," which formed one of the thorns of Mr. Buchanan's administration. The church of the "Latter-day Saints" had by this time grown in the valley of the Great Salt Lake into a community of many thousands, nominally subject to the United States, in the person of the Governor of Utah territory (organised in 1850), and to the jurisdiction of the Federal Courts of Justice. But the Prophet-governor, Brigham Young, supported by the Mormonite hierarchy, had contrived to reduce the Federal authority to a mere nullity. If the Federal Court gave sentence on a Mormonite criminal, the Governor pardoned him; and, at last, he went so far as to burn publicly the registers of the Court, the Federal laws, and other documents. The feeling of the American people was strongly roused by these outrages; the

Republican party, in particular, took up ground openly against the allowance of polygamy in Utah. A military expedition was sent to coerce the rebellious governor and his people; and although it failed in the main through the hardships of the march, Brigham Young thought fit to yield a nominal submission. Matters still remain in that direction till now nearly *in statu quo.*

Putting slavery and polygamy aside, the internal condition of the United States was far from prosperous, and far from creditable. There was a financial crisis in 1857, which the President in his message attributed to over-discounts and over-railway speculations; probably with justice, since it coincided with a good cereal and cotton harvest. Specie payments were resumed by the 14th December in New York, and the chief loss, it appears, fell on the foreign creditors,—much of the debt to Europe being, to use the cool expression of the "New York Herald," "spunged out." And long after the resumption of specie payments, it was very difficult for the foreign railway bondholder to obtain justice in the western states. Meanwhile, the scandals as to the sale of votes in Congress continued, and grave charges of corruption began to be brought against members of the Cabinet itself. The future Secessionist, Mr. Floyd, Secretary at War, was accused of having procured large sales of public lands in Minnesota to be made *to* his friends cheap, and purchases of lands for the public near New York to be made *from* his friends exorbitantly dear. The state of things in the Union at large was aptly mirrored in its greatest city. The municipal scandals at New York outvied the Federal scandals at Washington. The municipal government had fallen into, and for several years remained in, the hands of a clique of the Democratic party, hotly sympathetic with the South, with whose proceedings no respectable man of any class cared to be associated. Inefficiency and peculation ran riot on all sides. School-trustees were as ignorant as they were dishonest; 500,000 dollars were paid for sweeping the streets, and they were never swept from June 1856 to April 1857, through a severe winter, when the snow lay several feet thick on the ground. When the public feeling of the community at last rebelled against such a rule, and the sweeping of the city was given to a new contractor, his men were beaten by the old sweepers, and for several nights the streets could only be swept under the protection of an armed force. Murders were frequent, and often unpunished. The Republican party having succeeded in carrying an Act for taking away the control of the police of New York from the municipal body, a perfect state of anarchy ensued; the mayor, Fernando Wood, refusing to give up his authority, so that there were two rival authorities under arms against each other. Mayor Wood was indeed at last turned out, but I am sorry to say he has since regained office. Another extraordinary local outrage was the destruction of the lazaretto at Staten Island, near New York, the site of which seems indeed to have been ill chosen, and had been fruitlessly complained of by the inhabitants. Martial law was indeed proclaimed in the county, but no legal proceedings were taken, and the lazaretto was transferred. One cannot be surprised to hear, under such circumstances, that William Walker attempted a new filibustering expedition to Nicaragua; that when it was stopped by the straightforwardness of the American Commodore Paulding (1857), and himself brought to trial at New Orleans, he was acquitted, and achieved a triumphal progress through the South. The very next year saw him prepare a fresh expedition, which started in spite of a new Presidential proclamation, but failed through the striking of the ship on the coast of Honduras. Let us dispose of this troublesome individual at once by saying, that he was at last shot by order of a British officer.

A somewhat unexpected event of this period was the capture, by an American vessel of war, of an American slaver. Long had we complained of the carrying on of the slave-trade under the American flag, which, as America had refused to concede a mutual right of search, effectually covered the offenders against the British cruisers. Although slave-ships had now and then been captured by American vessels, such events were apparently so rare, that a slaver, named the "Echo," being chased by the American ship "Dolphin," and unable to credit the portent as a reality, ran up the "Stars and Stripes" to stop the supposed "Britisher," and found herself a prize, with 314 negroes on board. Of all places in the world, she was taken into Charleston. Such an opportunity of securing to the black man the blessings of the "peculiar institution" was not to be thrown away, and the state authorities at once claimed the negroes. The claim was, however, resisted, and they were sent over to Liberia at a cost of 150 dollars a-head. It was said that the whole cost of the capture amounted to 400,000 dollars,—a sum large enough, and perhaps meant to be large enough, to disgust America with the attempt to fulfil her engagements against the slave-trade. Another slaver, called the "Haydee," fitted out from New York, was stranded, and taken possession of by the Federal authorities. But it is sufficient to say, that although trials were instituted in both the cases of the "Echo" and the "Haydee" for the slave-trading, no conviction was obtained in either.

I may as well mention an expedition against Paraguay, which went up the great river Parana, to avenge the so-called outrage of a shot being fired against, and a sailor killed on board of, an American ship-of-war, which had ascended that river, as the Paraguayans alleged, in breach of the law of Paraguay, but, according to the Americans, by permission of the proper authorities. Nothing came of the expedition, as in the course of the following year President Lopez, of Paraguay, under the mediation of General Urquiza, consented to give an indemnity for the alleged wrong; but the expedition is remarkable as an instance of the reckless audacity of American statesmen at this period. For Paraguay is an entirely inland state, and the expedition was really as foolhardy a one as if we, having some grudge against Switzerland, were to send one up the Rhine, running the gauntlet of all possible stoppages on the way by Dutchman or Prussian, Frenchman or German. It is equally curious to observe that when, at this period, a convention was concluded between England and Nicaragua, the "New York Times," the organ, not of the Democratic, but of the Republican party, doubted whether the United States could consent that any European power should be put on the same political footing with themselves in reference to the Isthmus.

We have now to notice the wane of the President's influence. The elections to Congress of the summer of 1857 had generally been favourable to him; although one portentous fact had occurred—the election of an abolitionist representative for the great city of St. Louis, in slave-holding Missouri, a circumstance mainly attributable to a sort of reflex action from the Kansas contest. For the tide of emigration from the free states to Kansas flowing partly through St. Louis, left behind it a sort of *alluvium* of free-soil principles; whilst the personal influence in St. Louis of the Benton family, and the personal popularity of Colonel Fremont (a member of it, as you will recollect, by marriage), did perhaps even more at this time to decide this very remarkable election.

But before the session was over, the prospects of the President were changed. His Kansas policy, as you will recollect, had been so insane as to disgust even senators from the northern and middle slave states, as Kentucky and Tennessee, and to give a most dangerous rival, Mr. Douglas, a ground for openly detaching himself from him. He saw himself refused an addition of five regiments to the army, which he had asked for. A long session was chiefly spent in a wrangle over appropriations. At the next elections (1858), the Republicans obtained signal success. In Pennsylvania, the President's own state, they carried twenty-one representatives out of twenty-five, besides all elective functionaries. In New York they carried twenty-nine representatives out of thirty-three; in Massachusetts, Iowa, New Jersey, not a single Buchananite was elected. Mr. Douglas—passing from opposition to the most violent hostility—stayed in Illinois to carry the elections for his friends. The whole resulted in a loss for the President's influence of thirty votes, twenty-five of which were gained by the Republicans and five for the Douglasites. Instead of bearing up manfully against the blow, the President lost heart, and indited a doleful letter in reply to an invitation from Pittsburg, deploring public dishonesty (of which his cabinet gave the example), and expressing fears of disruption (which he was to verify by his incapacity).

His message of this year (2nd December, 1858) was fitly communicated beforehand, contrary to custom, to the disgraceful "Herald," thereby of itself exciting no small amount of animadversion. In it he praised the "Dred Scott" decision; dilated upon Kansas troubles, which, he was "happy to say," were nearly at an end;

showed that there had been a great fall in the customs' receipts since the passing under Mr. Pierce of a low-tariff Act, and recommended a raising of duties, and making them specific; declared that a free transit over the Isthmus of Panama must be maintained, and asked for permission to use force by sea and land to secure it; complained of Mexico, and recommended the establishment of an American protectorate over the provinces of Sonora and Chihuahua, with a chain of military posts; lastly, complained of Spain, and asked money to buy Cuba. He put the need of the annexation of Cuba, amongst other things, on the ground of the extinction thereby of the slave-trade. "It is the only spot in the civilised world," he said, "where the African slave-trade is tolerated. . . . As long as this market shall remain open, there can be no hope for the civilisation of benighted Africa."

Cubans, however, like other men, have a dislike to be bought and sold. When the news reached Havana, the President's proposal was protested against as "the grossest of insults." When it reached Spain, the tone of its reception was no less decided. On the 31st December, the Minister of State declared that any proposition to the country to "dispossess itself of the least part of its territory" would be "considered by the Government as an insult offered to the nation,"—the leader of the Opposition moved a resolution in the lower House of the Cortes, approving of the explanations of the Ministry, and declaring the readiness of the Cortes to support them in preserving the "integrity of the Spanish dominions;" and such resolution was unanimously adopted by the House, whilst an equally positive and unanimous one was adopted four days later (4th January, 1859) by the upper House. So that when, on the 10th January, Mr. Slidell, of Louisiana (now one of the commissioners to Europe from the Confederate states), introduced a bill for placing 30,000,000 dollars in the President's hands, "to facilitate the acquisition of Cuba by negotiation," this attempt to brazen out a hopeless proposal was felt to be abortive. Mr. Thompson, of Kentucky, in fact, killed the measure by simply asking what could be the use of giving money for a purchase which had been already refused by Spain? Whilst a message from the President (18th February, 1859) to allow the use of force in respect to Cuba, came also to nothing. Not, indeed, that the pro-slavery party in the least gave up the scheme of Cuban annexation. Senator Brown, of (now seceded) Mississippi, speaking at New York on the 14th March, declared that three modes had been proposed for acquiring Cuba—purchase, "the most honourable;" conquest, "the most certain;" and "the mysterious operation known as filibusterism," . . . "the most probable; but by one or the other, or all combined, Cuba must and shall be ours."

The tide of scandal continued flowing. This time it was against Federal judges that complaints came in of partiality or corruption. The President and Congress fell to loggerheads, the bills brought in by Government being thrown out, those of Congress being vetoed. Treasury bonds, issued by Mr. Howell Cobb, for a time found no customers. An inquiry was instituted by Congress into the abuses of the Navy. The President's affectation of energy against the slave-trade was met by declarations by twenty-five representatives of opposition to all laws against it, and by the actual landing of 400 slaves in Georgia by the yacht "Wanderer," whose starting for the trade had been openly announced beforehand. When it had been seized and condemned, its owner or part-owner, Lamar, came openly to the sale, thrashed the sole adverse bidder against him, and was declared the purchaser amidst the applause of the crowd at the sum of 4000 dollars, or one-tenth of its value. Two more ships, meant for the slave-trade, were seized by the Federal authorities. But when they laid hands on the smuggled negroes themselves, these were rescued from them, and the Federal officers themselves, and the citizens who helped them, arrested on a charge of negro-stealing. The senate of South Carolina voted a resolution in favour of the slave-trade; Mr. Stephens, of Georgia (now Vice-President of the Confederate states), in resigning his senatorship, indicated the reopening of the trade as a necessity. Mr. Douglas, on the other hand, expressed himself in the strongest terms against it. Forced, perhaps, to outdo a formidable and hated rival, and, perhaps, stung somewhat by the open defiance of the South to Federal authority, Mr. Buchanan took the only step of real efficacy in the matter, by increasing the American squadron off the coast of Loanda.

If the slave-trade question gave trouble to the President with the South, the Fugitive slave law gave him no less with the North. Vermont passed an Act, the Supreme Court of Wisconsin gave judgments, and both houses of the legislature of Wisconsin passed resolutions, practically setting that law at nought. Rescues multiplied in the free states. Kansas, meanwhile, was growing more peopled through some gold discoveries, not, indeed, of great importance. Though the civil war, properly so called, was at an end, a guerrilla warfare was still going on upon its borders. Partizan chiefs whom persecution had raised up among the free-soilers, the John Browns and the Montgomerys, replied to the incursions of the Missourian border ruffians to force slavery upon Kansas by raids within the Missouri border to carry away slaves into freedom. Terror spread in the neighbouring slave-district, so that throughout Western Missouri the slave-holders either sold off their slaves or moved away with them further South (1858), in either case clearing the ground for the occupation by free labour. The Abolitionists had a majority of 3000 in St Louis, and were the stronger party also in two neighbouring towns. Thus, there grew up in Missouri a genuine free-soil party, which is now the mainstay of the Union in that state. The South on its part subscribed to introduce slaves into the territories of Arizona and New Mexico, and Mr. Jefferson Davis asked in Congress for a slavery protection code, to be in force throughout the territories. Supported by the Southern members, he found himself opposed by the Northern Democrats, so long their allies; and though the "fire-eaters" of the party carried the elections in Virginia, it was not without loss.

And now occurred (October 17, 1859), an event, of which, perhaps, the main importance was, that it gave a pretext for secession,—the strange, mad Harper's Ferry expedition of John Brown. I have no leisure to dwell on the detail of this attempt, the necessary sequel to the "Struggle for Kansas," of which Mr. Hughes will no doubt tell you, in which an old partizan chief, with twenty-one followers, took possession of a United States arsenal, seeking, apparently, nothing more than to facilitate the escape on a large scale of Southern slaves; and after sending six of his followers to the hills to raise the slaves, with the remaining fifteen, and a few liberated slaves, held the engine house of the armoury until it was stormed by ninety marines. A noble madman, he was sentenced on the 31st October, hung on the 3rd of December, and met his death like a hero and martyr, perfectly satisfied, as he said himself, that he was "worth inconceivably more to hang than for any other purpose." Yet, though the attempt was a complete failure as respected its immediate object, so great was the terror which it spread through the South, that not only was the militia of Virginia kept under arms till the middle of November, but, far to the South, Carolina was placed under martial law. The frenzy of the South, indeed, knew no bounds. Even a woman was among the many applicants for the honour of hanging John Brown, and various Southern states disputed amongst themselves that of supplying the hemp for his execution. The North looked on, bewildered and amazed; for the most part disavowing the act, often basely and shamefully. Only a few fanatics held grimly their peace, leaving time to do justice to "old John Brown."

And time has done justice to him. He struck too soon, no doubt. He violated the law; he died justly, the law being too strong for him. But what was that law, when such a man as he, righteous, God-fearing, utterly self-devoted, the choicest model, I take it, of Christian chivalry that has been seen in these days, could spend the last days of his life in breaking it? John Brown died justly, but the law which sentenced him doomed itself thereby to death; Virginian slavery hangs for ever gibbeted with the noble madman's corpse.

From this time forth the history of the United States is little more than that of the preparations of the South for secession. It is made a crime to a Northern Republican in Congress, that he had subscribed for a cheap edition of a book,—extreme and violent indeed,—by Mr. Helper, of North Carolina, formerly a slave-owner, who professed to have been converted to anti-slavery principles by a journey through California and the North, whilst his opponents accused him of having quitted the South under not very creditable circumstances. The Governor of Mississippi asks for a duty of twenty-five per cent. on

Northern manufactures, and power to call a convention if a Republican President were elected in 1860. The Governor of Virginia declares that the time of compromise is past. South Carolina votes 100,000 dollars for providing arms and otherwise guarding against emergencies.

The President's message (27th December, 1859), as usual, pleased nobody. Although the trial of John Brown had failed to connect the Harper's Ferry outbreak with any party or politician in the North, Mr. Buchanan treated the Abolitionists as implicated in it. He praised anew the pro-slavery decisions in the Supreme Court. There was just then pending a "difficulty" with England on the Pacific, through the unwarrantable occupation by the American general, Harney (a Southerner) of the Island of St. Juan, in a channel nigh to our colony of Vancouver's Island, and which difficulty General Scott had been sent to settle; Mr. Buchanan palliated General Harney's conduct. In spite of the rebuffs of the previous session, he again asked for authority to occupy Mexican territory, and to use force in Central America. Again he reiterated old grievances against Spain, and dwelt on the advantages of securing Cuba. After treading thus at every step on the feelings of the North, he proceeded to irritate the South by advocating a high tariff.

Whilst the Senate instituted an inquiry into the Harper's Ferry affair, the House of Representatives wasted time in vainly attempting to constitute itself. South Carolina meanwhile was deputing Mr. Memminger (now finance minister of the Confederate states) to the legislature of Virginia, urging the latter to invite a conference of the slave-states, and maintaining that a dissolution of the Union had become necessary, unless the Constitution should be amended. The amendment suggested was much the same as that which Calhoun had hinted at in his last speech—consisting of a double President and a double Senate. Mr. Memminger spoke for four hours, but the Virginian legislature declined the proposed conference. The committee of the Senate on the Harper's Ferry affair, although presided over by Mr. Mason, of Virginia, failed to inculpate any Northern politician. Stevens and Hazlett, two of John Brown's associates, were executed on the 16th March, 1860, maintaining to the last that they had not known their destination till at the very gates of Harper's Ferry.

In Congress, the President's majority had been completely broken up by Douglas's opposition. Mr. Buchanan seemed to have lost all common sense and all memory of the past. He sent in a bill for authorising the Federal authorities to repress attempts against the States, and to prosecute offenders. The Republican party would vest no such power in a Federal government grossly biassed in favour of slavery. The Southern party would permit no such attack on their favourite democratic doctrine of states'-rights, on which Secession had to be grounded. The bill was not even taken into consideration. The two parties now proposed each extreme measures. Mr. Jefferson Davis, of Mississippi, offered resolutions, making it the duty of Congress to protect slavery in the territories, and embodying a scarcely-disguised threat of separation. Mr. Seward, of New York, presented a bill for the immediate admission of Kansas (28th February, 1860). All this while the House of Representatives had been still trying to constitute itself. The contest ended by a Republican triumph, in the election of Mr. Pennington, of New Jersey, as Speaker. Meanwhile the administration was almost disorganised. The postal service had been carried on on credit since the 1st July, 1859. Congress refused to renew twenty millions of dollars of treasury bills, proposed to be converted into a loan. The President retorted by new vetoes. Mr. Covode, of Pennsylvania, his personal enemy, proposed and obtained in the House a commission of five members to inquire into Government patronage and its abuses, and the expenses of elections. Scandalous disclosures took place. Mr. Buchanan sent in a protest, taking the high ground of being the sole direct representative of the people. It was simply sent on to the "judicial committee." The most remarkable exposure which took place was that of the Government printing system. The yearly cost of this to Congress was 700,000 dollars, giving a profit of from forty to fifty per cent. Such a rate of profit was only fit for very fine gentlemen, and accordingly, the official printer treated with a working one to do what was required. The ministerial printing cost 100,000 dollars a year, and was hampered with various conditions, such as that of printing the "Union," the Government organ. During the latter years of Mr. Pierce's administration and the three first of Mr. Buchanan's, Mr. Wendell, the official printer, was shown to have subsidized for ministerial purposes three newspapers (including two Philadelphia ones); one of the purposes having been, in 1856, to push the candidateship of Mr. Fillmore, to the sole end of dividing the non-slavery votes, and thereby giving Mr. Buchanan the majority; whilst in 1858 Mr. Wendell had paid money directly as "political expenses" in districts where democratic candidates were in danger. Another case of political corruption, scarcely less glaring, was that of Schell, collector of customs at New York, who had required his *employés* to give up part of their salary for an election expenses' fund. On being examined, however, he refused to give up the names of the contributors to the fund, and was not compelled to do so. Mr. Hickman, a bitter enemy of the President, drew up the report on these scandals for the judicial committee, controverting in it the allegations in the President's message (8th April). The report was adopted by eighty-seven to forty; but, for his pains, Mr. Hickman got beaten by some representatives from Virginia, whilst one or two more "rows" or duels between members of Congress, added to the unseemliness of the affair. Strong in its majority, the Republican party passed a bill for abolishing polygamy in Utah, and (by 134 to 73) another for admitting Kansas as a state, with its new Wyandotte or free constitution; whilst a Presidential treaty with Mexico was rejected.

Mr. Douglas, who, with his Northern Democrats, turned the scales of party, felt assured of success in his candidateship for the Presidency, now the third already. The President, on his side, was stung to the blindest hatred against him, and Federal officers were ordered, under pain of dismissal, to support any party which should be hostile to Mr. Douglas.

The struggle for the Presidency was now the life and death question for the Union. The turning-point of the election was probably the Democratic Convention at Charleston (April 23, 1860). A programme had to be drawn up. That of the South claimed the territories absolutely for slavery; declaring, that whilst the stage of territorial government lasted, every citizen had a right to establish himself with all his property in a territory, without either the Congress or the territory itself having the authority to diminish any of his rights of property. The Northern Democrats claimed to abide by a former manifesto of their party, issued at Cincinnati in 1856; it adhered to the decisions of the Supreme Court as to slavery within the territories, but claimed for the people of the territories the right to decide on the admission or exclusion of slavery. This doctrine of "squatter sovereignty," as it was now termed, though long held by Mr. Calhoun, the South openly repudiated. It was even worse, they said, than the Wilmot proviso, fixing geographical limits to slavery. The Convention came to a vote, and the programme of the slave-states was rejected by 165 to 138, while that of the free states was adopted article by article. Before a vote was taken on it, as a whole, Mr. Walker, of Alabama, rose, and withdrew from the Convention the delegacy of Alabama. The delegates from Mississippi, Louisiana, South Carolina, Florida, Texas, Arkansas, followed his example, leaving Mr. Douglas with a bare majority of the whole Convention. The session came to nothing, and the Convention adjourned till the 18th of June at Baltimore. The sensation was enormous. It was felt that the Democratic party was broken up. Violent attacks were made on Mr. Douglas in the Senate. It came out, through a speech of Mr. Benjamin, of Louisiana, that, in 1856, when the Democrats had supported the abolition of the Missouri Compromise, an ambiguous wording of the declaration of principles had been adopted, which was differently understood by the Northern and Southern factions, under an agreement to obtain a judgment of the Supreme Court, which was given in the "Dred Scott" case. Mr. Douglas retorted by an elaborate exposure of the many variations of principle to which the South had successively committed itself.

The next Convention was the "Union" Convention at Baltimore; small in number, but very respectably composed,—representing a tradition of compromise and mutual forbearance for which the time had long gone by,—its members were termed the "old gentlemen," the "silver heads." They durst not venture upon a manifesto, but took as their motto "the Union, the Constitution, and obedience to the laws," selecting for candidates to the Presidency and Vice-President, Mr.

Bell of Tennessee, a slaveholder opposed "in principle" to slavery, and Mr. Edward Everett, of Massachusetts, one of the most elegant writers of America, who had been minister to England, and for a short time Secretary of State under Mr. Fillmore, both men highly respected. The "Union" party had no thought of obtaining a majority, but built its hopes on the chance of dividing parties, so that, no other candidate carrying an absolute majority, the election might fall into the hands of Congress, with whom its candidates were supposed to be in favour.

The Republican Convention met, on the 16th May, at Chicago. Its foremost man, beyond all shadow of question,—the first political orator of the day,—was William Seward, of New York, who was accordingly put forward in the first instance. But, as usual, he was too eminent to please all, and some one suggested an Illinois advocate, popular in his own state, and thereby a dangerous rival to Mr. Douglas on his own ground, who had been heard at New York, at the Cooper Institute, on the 27th Feb.,—the day before a great speech of Mr. Seward's, for the immediate admission of Kansas. Abraham Lincoln was grandson to one of the companions of Daniel Boone, a celebrated chief among the first emigrants from Virginia to Kentucky. His father had died young, in 1815, leaving a wife and several children, little Abraham the eldest, and only six years old. He had had but six months' schooling, but soon learnt to handle the rifle and axe, and to drive the cart; earned his bread first by keeping flocks, then as apprentice in a saw-mill, then as "deck hand," or otherwise, on river-steamers, on the Wabash and the Mississippi, then as rail-splitter. At twenty-one he emigrated to Illinois, worked a year as a journeyman in a firm near Springfield, became a clerk in a store, educating himself the while; then served as a volunteer in Black Hawk's War, and was elected captain of his company. Two years later he was elected a member of the House of Representatives in his state, where he served during four sessions. He now made a successful *début* at the bar, became a leading Whig politician in Illinois, was elected representative to Congress in 1846, but gave up politics for some years to devote himself to his profession and to the education of his children; returned to them finally in 1859, and boldly competed with Mr. Douglas for the senatorship of Illinois in Congress, obtaining an actual majority in votes, though not that of districts which was requisite to return him. Fortunately, I think still, on this occasion, the great orator was put aside; and the provincial advocate, Abraham Lincoln, adopted as the Republican candidate. The choice at once gave immense strength to the party, by engaging heartily in its cause the great West, whose admission to political power may be said to date from Mr. Lincoln's election. The Republican programme, whilst expressing a determination to maintain the rights of the states, declared the new doctrine, that the Constitution of itself carried slavery into the territories, to be a dangerous heresy.

It asserted freedom to be the normal state of all the territories, and denied the power either of Congress, of the territorial legislatures, or of individuals, to legalise slavery within them.

The adjourned Democratic Convention at Baltimore now came off (14th June). The Southern delegates who had withdrawn from the former session were excluded from it, whilst delegacies of Douglasites were admitted for Alabama and Louisiana. Seeing this, the delegacy from Virginia withdrew, followed by nearly all the Southern and some Northern members. The Seceders chose for their candidates Mr. Breckenridge, of Kentucky, and General Lane, of Oregon. The whole strength of the "White House" (*i. e.* of the President and his Ministers) was exerted in their favour, and *employés* at Washington were invited to give up fifteen days' pay towards the expenses of the contest.

Meanwhile, a new conflict had arisen between the President and the House of Representatives. The Navy Committee of the latter asked of the Secretary of the Navy a list of witnesses and subjects for examination. These were refused, and the proceeding declared a usurpation. Hereupon, a vote of censure was come to by the House (by 120 to 65) upon the President and the Secretary of the Navy (13th June). On the last day of the session (25th June), when he was sure that he could no more be answered, the President sent a message to Congress, protesting against several of its acts, such as the reduction of the printer's bill by 40 per cent.

The question at issue was, however, to be decided out of doors, not within. Derogating from all usage, Mr. Douglas "went the stump" throughout the South, urging his pet doctrine of "squatter-sovereignty," denouncing Republicans and "Fire-eaters," as equally conspiring for the ruin of the Union. But the Republican party grew stronger every day. Not only was the Republican candidate Blair re-elected at St. Louis, Missouri, but Republican committees for the Presidential election were founded in various slave-states; in Kentucky (where stout-hearted Cassius Clay had for years maintained abolition principles in the teeth of all opposition and persecution), in Tennessee, in Maryland, in Delaware. Even the irritation of the manufacturers of New Jersey, the ironmasters of Pennsylvania, at a late rejection of the Senate of a Northern high tariff promoted by the President, did not avail to stop the progress of the Republican cause. The results of the census of 1860 just being published, gave it sure hope moreover for the future. It showed the South declining in population, so that Virginia would lose at the next elections for Congress two or three representatives, South Carolina one, the South generally six or seven.

The South was still more energetic. Whilst its wildest enthusiasts enrolled themselves as "Knights of the Golden Circle," in an order destined to form a new confederation, including with the South Mexico, Cuba, &c., all of course on the basis of slavery, its "Vigilance Committees" stopped the distribution of Northern newspapers, opened letters to or from the North. "Minute-men" were enrolled, and "Southern rights volunteers," to defend by arms the rights of the South. By the end of the autumn, seven or eight cotton states had each a regiment or two of volunteers on foot, while the Republicans had only "Wide awake Committees" to watch the mischief. But the most efficient allies of the South were in the cabinet. Mr. Toucey at the Navy, Mr. Floyd, of the War Department,—both "fire-eaters," both strongly implicated in the late disclosures as to political corruption,—were preparing beforehand the work of Secession. Mr. Toucey dispersed the navy on all the seas; Mr. Floyd emptied the Federal arsenals of the North, leaving, it is said, neither a musket nor a cartridge, but having all arms and ammunition conveyed into the Southern arsenals, whilst,—like Mr. Toucey with the navy,—he scattered the regular troops far and wide, placing moreover Southern partizans as far as possible in command of all important posts.

Already, since the month of February, the Alabama legislature had required its governor to convoke a committee, if a Republican President were elected, to consider the Secession question. The Governor of South Carolina, on opening in October the session of the state legislature, recommended taking the measures necessary for leaving the Union if Mr. Lincoln were elected. He was elected, and by 173 votes, or 21 more than the absolute majority,—a figure which the subsequently known votes of California and

Oregon eventually carried to 180. The North and North-west had voted for him as one man. On the other hand, four of the Northern slave-states (Delaware, Virginia, Tennessee, Kentucky) had voted for Bell; the bulk of the South (Texas, Louisiana, Arkansas, Alabama, Mississippi, Florida) for Breckenridge. Douglas was completely distanced. He had simply secured Lincoln's triumph by promoting division. In slave-holding Missouri itself, 17,000 votes had been given for Lincoln.

On the news of the election, a meeting at Charleston resolved in favour of separation from the Union. The Federal flag was pulled down, a "palmetto" flag (badge of the state) hoisted in its stead. The legislature accepted the resignation of the senators of the state in Congress. Most of the Federal *employés* threw up their offices. Votes were passed by the legislature of 10,000 volunteers, 100,000 dollars for arms, a loan of 400,000 dollars, a credit of one million and a half for fortifying Charleston and the coast. The banks were authorised to suspend specie payments. The payment of debts due to the North was forbidden.

As yet, this was but the act of a single state, and that notoriously the most hot-headed in the Union. Had the Presidential chair been occupied by a man of common sense, or common honesty, or common pluck, further defections might perhaps yet have been staved off. When Congress met in December, Mr. Buchanan addressed it in the most incredible message that had ever been heard within its walls. Forgetting that self-preservation is the first law of life,—amidst a flood of prolixity, and lamentations over the insecurity of Southern rights,—he declared at once that Secession was unlawful and revolutionary, and that there was no power in President or Congress, or both, to prevent it. Between the impotency of the administration and the audacity of the South, the Republican party quailed for awhile. Compromise was suggested by their journals. The free states had put themselves constitutionally in the wrong in some cases by their "Personal Liberty Acts," passed in defiance of the Fugitive Slave Law. They proceeded to repeal these. Mr. Crittenden proposed terms of compromise; Virginia offered mediation. Meanwhile the tone of the South rose higher and higher. Mr. Iverson, of Georgia, announced further Secessions to the Congress as impending, and violently denounced General Houston, of Texas, for his adherence to the Union. A South Carolina convention of the 19th December decreed separation, but sent commissioners to Washington. Mr. Howell Cobb, of Georgia, resigned his Secretaryship of the Treasury to go and work for separation. Public meetings, or vigilance committees, in South Carolina, Louisiana, Mississippi, offered rewards for the heads of those whom they deemed their enemies; even a governor of Georgia offered 5000 dollars for Garrison, the editor of the "Liberator." The cabinet was as impotent as ever. General Scott proposed plans of defence for the Federal capital; they were rejected, and old General Cass, the last man of any eminence who had stood by

Mr. Buchanan, withdrew in disgust. Almost immediately a new ministerial scandal burst forth. There was a deficiency of 870,000 dollars in what was called the "Indian Fund." The cashier of the fund was Mr. Floyd's nephew, and Mr. Floyd's name, as Secretary of War, was attached to a swarm of fraudulently-issued bonds. Presently came the news that, resuming violent possession of property duly sold and conveyed by her to the Federal Government, South Carolina had seized the Federal fort Moultrie, and that Major Anderson, the Federal officer in command, had been forced to withdraw to Fort Sumter, a better position. The example spread like wildfire. Without even taking the trouble of previously seceding, other states took possession of Federal forts at Savannah, Pensacola, Mobile, &c. Everywhere they found, either nobody to defend the positions, or willing traitors in command. Then came more actual secessions; of Mississippi, on the 8th January, 1861; of Alabama, Florida, on the 11th; then of Georgia; then of Louisiana, January 26th; followed in the latter state by the confiscation of the funds of the Federal post-office and mint at New Orleans. In Texas, the legislature voted Secession, in spite of all the efforts of Governor Houston. By the end of January seven states had seceded from the Union; throughout all which specie payments were authorized to be suspended, and debts to the North forbidden to be paid. The following passages from the Ordinance of Secession of Louisiana give clear proof of the spirit of the whole movement:—

"Whereas it is manifest that Abraham Lincoln, if inaugurated as President of the United States, will keep the promises he has made to the Abolitionists of the North; that these promises, if kept, will inevitably lead to the emancipation and misfortune of the slaves of the South, their equality with a superior race, and, before long, to the irreparable ruin of this mighty Republic, the degradation of the American name, and corruption of the American blood;—Fully convinced, as we are, that slavery is the most humane of all existing servitudes, that it is in obedience to the laws of God," &c. &c.

Delegates from the seceded states met at Montgomery, in Alabama; and here, on the 9th February, the Constitution of the "Confederate States" was adopted. It is almost identical with that of the United States, with the exception of the significant substitution of the word "slaves" for "persons bound to service." Mr. Jefferson Davis, the fire-eater and repudiator of Mississippi, was elected President; Mr. Alexander Stephens, of Georgia, who was soon to declare that slavery was the "corner-stone" of the new republic, Vice-President; 50,000 volunteers were voted; a loan of fifteen millions of dollars; Washington was openly threatened.

Here then the history of the United States closes necessarily for a time,—it may be for ever.

And now let me add a few words as to the nature of the present conflict between North and South.

What I have said to you will, I trust, have been

sufficient to show you the utter unlikeness of the present Secession movement to the revolt of the American colonies, with which it is so often paralleled. The thirteen colonies threw off the dominion of England because they were taxed and ruled without their consent and against their will, by a Parliament in which they were wholly unrepresented. The South seceded from a Union in which it has not only enjoyed all rights of representation, taxation, and government equally with the North, but has been allowed a special property franchise not recognised elsewhere; and has, although from the first composing a numerical minority, virtually ruled the majority from the first Articles of Confederation until 1860 : it secedes, simply because it has lost that rule. On such grounds, evidently, the North would have been justified in seceding at any time within the last forty years at least, or since the Missouri Compromise.*

But we hear it frequently said : There is nothing in the American civil war to enlist the sympathies of Englishmen on either side. Slavery is really not in question— Neither party desires to see it abolished. The tariff question is far more important. The North seeks to force a high tariff on the South. The South seeks free-trade with all the world. The interests of the South, therefore, fit in more with our own. They have

* The latest pro-secession fallacy, that sovereignty could be reserved by the states when all the main attributes of sovereignty were parted with, is sufficiently disposed of, I trust, by what I have said or quoted ere this—see pp. 41, 42, 139, 140, 141.

even more real freedom. It is not they who thwart the action of Courts of Justice, and violate the right of *habeas corpus*.

Well, it is quite true that neither party to the conflict goes to war in favour of the rights of the slave. It is very likely that the North does not yet really so much as desire to see slavery abolished, if the South could be otherwise overcome. Nay, it is quite true that the coloured population is still on the whole disgracefully treated at the North; that the repulsion of colour seems greater there than at the South. And, on the other hand, it is quite true that the haste with which the protective Morrill tariff was passed through Congress immediately after the retirement of the Southern members was most indecent. It is quite true that our exports to America have greatly diminished, and that our manufacturers and artisans have seriously suffered by it. It is quite true that the South, if only it can obtain national recognition, declares itself quite ready to throw its ports open. It is quite true that the South has not taken the trouble to suppress *habeas corpus*, or to interfere with the action of the law courts. Nevertheless, I believe, there are ample grounds why England should sympathise, not indeed with the North, but with the struggle which it is carrying on; I believe, above all, there is the strongest necessity for her to stand wholly aloof from and reprobate the South.

The tariff question may be easily disposed of. I trust to have shown ere this that no high tariff can account for Southern decay, that no low tariff can restore its prosperity; that it is the most egregious fallacy for our merchants and manufacturers to expect to drive a profitable trade with a country which seeks to perpetuate slavery. The smallest consideration will moreover show, that if duties on imports have been the financial mainstay of the Union hitherto, duties on imports, or, what would be equally mischievous to ourselves, an export duty on cotton, must form still more necessarily the mainstay of a Southern confederacy, where the thinner population, its ruder and more lawless habits, must render the permanent collection of direct taxation absolutely hopeless. And let us remember, that, so far as the high Morrill tariff having been the cause of Secession, it only became possible through Secession. Had Secession not taken place, and Southern members stood at their posts in Congress, it never would have been passed. The South is as guilty of it through omission, as the North through commission. So far from American tariffs having been hitherto imposed by the North on the South, I believe it to be strictly correct, that "no protective tariff has ever been enacted without a considerable vote of Southern representatives, a vote always large enough, if given in the negative, to have defeated such tariff;" that "for near fifteen years" prior to Secession, "the tariffs in force were such as had been passed by a majority of Southern votes against a majority of Northern votes;" as in the case of the tariff of 1846, for which there were fifty Northern votes given, and seventy-three against it, but of Southern sixty-four for, and only twenty-two against; and of the tariff of 1857, for which sixty Northern votes were given, but sixty-five against, and sixty-three Southern votes, with only seven against.* This last, emphatically a Southern tariff, imposed a protective duty on rice for South Carolina, and on sugar for Louisiana—one of 15, the other of 25 per cent.

As to the Southern vaunt about free courts of justice, and respect for *habeas corpus*, a more audacious mockery was never sought to be palmed off upon the credulity of Europe. *Habeas corpus*, indeed! Where is the free coloured person, the abolitionist, the mere friend to the Union, who would dream of suing one out of a Southern court of justice? Where is the master at the South, of late years, who has been punished for the murder of his slave, unless under circumstances of quite exceptional atrocity? What year has passed by of late at the South without some unpunished tarring and feathering, or worse, of a suspected abolitionist? some burning alive of a slave or free negro for a crime which justice would have unfailingly punished with the utmost severity; but over the chastisement of which the passions of the white mob claimed a jurisdiction paramount? "Why, sir, I wouldn't mind killing a nigger more than I would a dog," was said to Mr. Olmsted by an overseer, "superior to most" of his class, on one of the plantations, "much the best in respect to the happiness of

* Details supplied by an American gentleman, in a letter to Mr. E. Chadwick.

the negroes" that he saw at the South. Is this the habit of mind to respect a *habeas corpus?* to value forms of justice?

But grant that the North did not go to war to abolish slavery. Yet I venture to think that in going to war for nationality, it did go to war for a very high and holy thing. As has been well asked by the present President ere this, if the right of Secession be once admitted, where is it to stop? If a state may secede, why not a county? If a county, why not a parish or township? till at last you reach that state of utter lawlessness and anarchy, where every man "doeth that which is right in his own eyes." The rankest revolutionary individualism was thus at the root of Southern Secession. There can be no settled government, no national life, upon the principles which it contends for. No man who values true and manly freedom, that self-possessed freedom which alone can teach willing and intelligent obedience, which alone can evolve a living and lasting order, can wish otherwise than for the success of Northern efforts, as against the mere freedom of self-will, the freedom to do wrong, now in effect being fought for by those, who alas! are shedding their heart's blood simply to realise the Yankee Joe Miller, of a "land of liberty, where every man is free to wallop his own nigger." Quite apart from the slavery question, the struggle of the North for the principle of national unity appears to me a protest of momentous value, above all upon that American continent, where so many republics have split and resplit without other check than the occurrence of some temporary ruler of stronger will than his fellows. Even if it should not succeed in establishing that principle, it is better for it to yield to facts, than passively to compromise rights. It does not follow, because I have not strength enough to knock down a thief whom I see robbing a church, that I should have done better to help him off with the sacramental plate. And if the Federalists themselves show often so little comprehension of the principle they are defending, that Western Virginia, on the score of its loyalty, seeks to secede from Eastern, and Raleigh county from North Carolina, and General Fremont's followers talk of establishing a South-Western republic if they are not allowed to follow him in conquering a Southern one, what does it prove but the deep root which the anarchical tendency has cast in the North itself, and the urgency of striking a death-blow at it, if it may be, at the South?

The war at the North is not one for the abolition of slavery. But it cannot be one under the yet unamended Constitution. Abolition might no doubt be justifiable, according to circumstances, by the necessities of military law; under the somewhat unworthy name of " confiscation," it is practically proceeding with the progress of the war, and the resistance opposed to it. But it will only become practicable, as a deliberate act of the national will, through an amendment of the Constitution; and this again will only be possible when, either through an addition to the present nominal number of states,* or through a reduction of that number, by recognising the Southern Confederacy, the requisite assent of three-fourths of the states can be obtained. But, in the meanwhile, the war is all, or nearly all, that it can be under the present Constitution. It is a war to prevent the spread of slavery. The ground taken up by the South proves it. Does not the South go to war to maintain and perpetuate slavery? Is it not proclaimed to be the corner-stone of the new Republic? Since Christ came into the world to die for all men, was it ever heard in the history of Christendom that a nation sought to constitute itself upon the basis of slavery,—upon the right of one man to buy and sell his fellow-man unchecked? What colour is there for Secession but the declaration by the Republican party that slavery was to be kept out of the territories,†—that it was not to be allowed to pollute

---

* These are now 34 in number, of which 19 Free (Maine, New Hampshire, Vermont, Massachusetts, Rhode Island, Connecticut, New York, New Jersey, Pennsylvania, Ohio, Indiana, Michigan, Illinois, Wisconsin, Iowa, Kansas, Minnesota, Oregon, and California); and 15 Slave (Delaware, Maryland, Virginia, North Carolina, South Carolina, Georgia, Florida, Alabama, Mississippi, Tennessee, Kentucky, Missouri, Arkansas, Louisiana, and Texas).

† I may observe that the following, at the date of Secession, were "territories" of the United States :—Utah and New Mexico, organised 1850; Washington, organised 1853; and Nebraska, organised 1854. Utah is understood to be entitled to, and has applied for, admission as a State on the ground of population. Both Utah, and a large portion of the tribes of the Indian territory, it is said, have slaves, but it seems doubtful whether they side with the South. Three new territories, Da-

and waste any more of God's earth within the limits of the United States than what it stood on already,—anything in "Dred Scott" judgments to the contrary notwithstanding? To sympathise with abolition may not be to sympathise with the North. But to sympathise with the South is to sympathise with the extension and perpetuation of slavery.

And if you have followed me thus far, you will have seen that to check the extension of slavery is, unless upon one condition, to extinguish it sooner or later. There is, indeed, one condition upon which slavery can subsist within the same area, without immediate ruin. It is that upon which for several years a large portion of the South has been insisting,—an open slave-trade. If you can buy live human flesh cheap, no doubt—as in Cuba—slave cultivation may pay for yet awhile. The profits that would otherwise have gone to defray the enhanced price of slaves, may then be spent in the application of guano and other costly manures, and, within certain limits, in the improvement of agriculture. Are we going to deny and stultify our past,—to cast dishonour on the noble names of Clarkson and Wilberforce, of Buxton, and Lushington, and Sturge,—to oppose new obstacles to the progress of our West India colonies, now and for several years past slowly rising to a healthier and more solid prosperity than they have

cotah, Nevada, and Colorado, have been carved out by the North since secession. But the territories at large have sided with the North, so that the South has virtually lost what it went to war for,—the chance of extending slavery.

ever enjoyed,—to stop the rapid development of our Indian empire,—for the purpose of tolerating a hideous wrong, and wringing from it some fraction of temporary profit? Yet such, I am convinced, are the conditions upon which alone we can favour the Southern Confederacy. Hemmed in, as it will be on all sides, by the free-soil populations of the North and West, which, ere many years are over, I cannot help thinking, will have won a control over Mexico, from whence, in the meanwhile, the South will probably be stopped out by European intervention, the South can only subsist by re-opening the slave-trade. It may legislate against that traffic; but when we recollect that, in the teeth of all legislation, more slaves were said to have been imported in 1859-60 than in any one year before, even while the trade was legal—15,000 being the reputed number,—what credence can be given to any laws that the South may thus pass, having the full power to disobey them, and the sanction for its disobedience of the right to secede?

You may think, perhaps, that I have made but few allowances for the South. I am far from thinking that there is not a large proportion of sincerity and earnestness and self-devotion on the side of the Secessionists. So you may find, no doubt, in any madhouse in England. No one has ever conversed with any well-meaning Southern slave-owner without feeling that, on the subject of slavery, he is possessed with what cannot be termed otherwise than a moral monomania. The benevolent slave-owner of the last century looked upon the slave, black or white, as a man entitled to freedom when fit for it; if not fit, then to be trained into fitness. The benevolent Southern slave-owner of our days looks upon the slave, white or black—ay, though he could only be told from a white freeman by the quailing of his eyes when you look into them,[*] though he should be the slave-owner's own brother, or son, or grandchild— as less than a man, doomed to perpetual slavery, perpetual ignorance, perpetual exclusion from the rights of the husband and of the father. The slave-owner of old days looked upon slavery as doomed in principle from the day when Christ said, " Ye are all brethren." The slave-owner of the present day maintains that slavery is mentioned and commanded by the Bible, and is ready to declare, with ex-governor Hammond, of South Carolina, that slavery is an Eden, and that Satan enters it "in the shape of an Abolitionist!" This moral monomania is so complete, that the slaveowner is unable to see the incoherency of his own statements and reasonings, the discrepancy between his principles and his practice, the bearings of the most obvious facts; whilst his ignorance in many respects is generally as great as his dogmatism. Argument is, for the most part, wasted on him; nothing can bring him round but the gradual influence of a long residence in a different moral atmosphere, helped, perhaps, by some occasional short visits to his own, when the foul miasmata with which it reeks may, perhaps, become visible

[*] Olmsted, "Journeys and Explorations in the Cotton Kingdom," vol. ii. p. 211.

to his purged eyes. Now the fact is, "Dixie's Land" is simply one huge madhouse, in which such monomaniacs abound, and where, instead of being harmless, as they are when in the midst of ourselves, they are excessively dangerous, having (together, unfortunately, with a set of rogues and villains who use the good qualities of others as a cloak for their own rascality) the control of the house and of all the weapons of offence and defence which it contains, and which they are both able and willing to use against all sane persons who wish to hinder both madmen and rogues from doing mischief, and to turn the house to better account than they know how to do. The safety of the world, I believe, demands that these dangerous monomaniacs, however estimable they may be in private life, should be put down, and the sooner the better.

Why, you may ask me, for the interests of the world? How are we concerned, except on moral grounds, to prevent the extension of American slavery? I will tell you. Because the principles put forth by the South in defence of its slave-system are such as threaten the freedom of the working classes throughout the world. Listen to Mr. Cobb:—"There is, perhaps, no solution of the great problem of reconciling the interests of labour and capital, so as to protect each from the encroachments and oppressions of the other, so simple and effective as negro slavery. *By making the labourer himself capital, the conflict ceases, and the interests become identical*" (Historical Sketch, p. ccxiv.). Is there a working man here, or anywhere, whose freedom is not involved by such a doctrine? Are you prepared to be made "capital," that the problem of reconciling labour and capital be solved? Is it not *your* cause, then, that the North is fighting at this moment? No,—it is not a war between black and white which is being waged beyond the Atlantic; it is *the* war, the world-old war, between freedom and tyranny, between God and the devil. For the sake of all mankind, once more, these dangerous Southern lunatics must be put down.

But make, if you like it, all possible allowance for the moral hallucination of the South on the subject of its pet nuisance, slavery, provided that allowance does not extend to the enabling it to plant it on a foot of ground that it does not pollute already. Yet make also some allowance for the North, now at last emancipated from three-quarters of a century of Southern ascendency, from nearly a quarter of a century of the direct ascendency of the slave-power, in league with all that was most heartless and most vicious at the North itself. Nations cannot be regenerated in a day. A true and Christian morality, when once seemingly trampled out of a nation's policy, does not spring up again after a single shower. But unless the tree can no longer be judged by its fruits, it is from the North alone that that morality can be spread. "It would be difficult already," says a writer whose national sympathies would rather lead him to prefer a society more in harmony with that of his own country, as that of the French creoles of Louisiana, "to find in any part of the earth societies morally superior to those of Vermont, Massachusetts, Rhode Island, New Hampshire. The majority of those composing them are conscious of their freedom and of their worth; instruction is general; the spirit of invention is active to the last degree; a love of the fine arts is developing; every commendable undertaking is supported with unexampled generosity; progress in all things has become the general end. And what freedom has produced in this corner of the land, she will doubtless produce throughout the vast Anglo-Saxon republic, when the crime of slavery is expiated, and the black, delivered at last from his chains, shall be able to press in his hands that of his former master.* The present contest has been till now nothing more than a free-soil one. The transition Presidency and cabinet of the present day will be succeeded by one of clearer views and firmer purpose. Under the stern teaching of civil war and domestic distress, the North will gradually, I trust, discern more and more the principles which underlie the contest, the deep moral ground of equal rights and common brotherhood, upon which alone it can finally triumph. "Whom the Lord loveth

---

* M. Elisée Reclus, "Revue des Deux Mondes," for 1st Jan. 1861, p. 154. I need hardly repeat here what has been said so often, that the word "creole," which I have used above, is only by a vulgar error supposed to imply African descent. It is applied simply to persons and animals born within the tropics; there are creole whites, creole negroes, creole horses, &c.; and creole whites are, of all persons, the most anxious to be deemed of pure white blood.

He chasteneth;" and I cannot help trusting that, through these bitter lessons of defeat and humiliation, through the ungenerous, but not undeserved scorn and mockery of other nations, through many a sharp trial yet in store, the American nation will yet pass on to a more glorious future than any past which it has yet enjoyed, purified as silver in the fire, to be wrought under God's hands into one of His chosen vessels for the civilising and evangelising of the earth.

THE STRUGGLE FOR KANSAS.

BY

THOMAS HUGHES.

THE STRUGGLE FOR KANSAS.

THE SUBSTANCE OF TWO LECTURES

DELIVERED

AT THE WORKING MEN'S COLLEGE, GREAT ORMOND STREET.

I AM glad to be able to give my term lecture here on this subject of the struggle for Kansas between the two great parties of the United States, the Free-soil party and the Pro-slavery party.

I need not tell you here that my deepest sympathies are with those who are struggling for freedom all over the world, that I hate slavery of every kind,—of the body, of the intellect, of the spirit,—with a perfect hatred. I believe it to be the will of God that all men should be free, and that Christ came into the world to do God's will, and to break *every* yoke. That was His work, and that is the work of every true follower of Him. Therefore, I do not pretend that I am not a partisan in this struggle in Kansas. I think that the free-soilers were as much in the right, and the pro-slavery party as much in the wrong, as parties composed of human beings are ever likely to be. But I hope, notwithstanding my partisanship, that I may be trusted, and can trust myself, to put before you a temperate and fair statement of the facts of the case. Indeed, the most simple and naked statement of facts which can be made is likely to be much more effectual than any advocacy, however ingenious. The only difficulty,—and it is not a small one,—is to make oneself sure as to the facts where the evidence is so very conflicting. In order to be on the right side, I have accepted no statement on the authority of one witness only, and have in no case repeated any story which rests on the sole evidence of the free-soil party, however numerous the witnesses might be.

Our special subject to-night is interesting, not only as a story, but because it was, in fact, the first outbreak of that desperate struggle which is now raging in America; and because it illustrates remarkably the strength and the weakness of the great nation engaged in that struggle,—the strength and soundness of the great body of the Northern people,—the doers, not the talkers,—the sad weakness and unsoundness of the United States' government, the atrocious corruption of the press and of official life, and the demoralising effect which slavery has exercised on the mass of the Southern people.

In speaking to you to-night, I shall assume a considerable amount of knowledge on your parts of late American history, as I may safely do coming after Mr. Ludlow.

You are aware, then, that until the year 1820, slavery was prohibited for ever in all the United States' territory lying N.W. of the Ohio river. In that year, to avoid a dangerous collision between the free and slave states (which threatened even at that time, forty years ago), the arrangement, known as the Missouri Compromise, was come to, by which slavery was admitted into the territory which afterwards formed the state Missouri. Nearly the whole of this territory is north of the Ohio river. To this infringement of the old engagement the North was only induced to agree on the understanding that it was to be final.

You will find many instances of such attempted compromises in your readings of history. Men in all parts of the earth, and in all ages, have tried to *compromise* one part and another of its surface as though it were theirs; as though they could say, we, for our purposes, will allow this wrong to occupy here, that robbery to stand there. But the old earth laughs at them. They have forgotten to make one person a party to their contract, and He is the Lord of the whole earth. And one of the lessons which stand out in letters of sunlight on the face of History is, that He is against all such compromises,—that He will allow no system of wrong or robbery to be fixed on any part of His earth.

Well, no attempt was made to break this "final compromise" between the slave-states and the free until that which is our subject to-night, but between 1820 and 1854 (the passing of the Kansas-Nebraska Bill) the question of slavery had changed its aspect in the States. As must always be the case, the plague-spot which was not cut out had spread and festered. In the South, instead of being any longer regarded as an evil to be only tolerated for a time, slavery was now already looked upon as a divinely appointed institution. Moreover, the South had grown reckless from continual success. They had managed, by threats of breaking up the Union on more than one occasion, and by the concentrated action which they could bring to bear on all political questions, to hold a most decided lead in the Central Government. The North had for a long time acquiesced in their virtual supremacy, and tolerated their overbearing habits and principles, for the sake of peace and the Union. But at the time of the Mexican war (a war waged wholly for the benefit of the South), a change of feeling was beginning to be apparent in the Northern States. The slave-states, always vigilant, knew this well. The change was dangerous, because, notwithstanding the admission of Texas as a slave-state, the free states numbered already sixteen to fifteen slave states.

In 1853 it had become clear to the statesmen of the South that their power in the Union could not last, unless they kept pace with the North in extending their territories. They must have at least as many states as the North. This had been the motive for the Mexican war. There was no further opening in the direction of Mexico for the present. The North had found out, even before the excitement of victory had died away, what was the real meaning of such wars, and was not in the humour to bear its portion of the burthen and cost of "extending freedom's area" any further down South by means of bayonets. The chances of annexing Cuba were by no means promising. The unoccupied territories of the West remained, and to these the attention of all parties in the United States was now turned.

Until the discovery of gold in California carried a huge tide of emigration westward across the continent, the Missouri river was regarded as the boundary of all possible settlement by whites. The land beyond was believed to be a worthless waste, which might be left to the Indians. Indeed, many of the remnants of the old Indian tribes—the Delawares, the Wyandots, the Kickapoos, Kaws, and others—had been moved from the more easterly states, and located here on reserves, with the promise that they should never be disturbed. But as the stream of keen-eyed citizens passed backwards and forwards along the great tracks—or roads, if they can even yet be called roads—to California and Santa Fe, the richness and beauty of this Kansas land began to be appreciated and talked of all over the States. Kansas is, in fact, well worthy of the name which has been given it—"The Italy of America." It is the richest rolling prairie country, the undulations often rising into hills, the soil a deep-black virgin loam from two to three feet deep, resting on porous clay and limestone. The timber is plentiful, and remarkably fine along the banks of the streams, which are numerous. Beside the great Missouri, the Kaw river runs through the territory, and the headwaters of the Osage and Arkansas rivers are in it, with the numberless small tributaries of these. The climate is said to be peculiarly invigorating, and as favourable for pulmonary diseases as the table-lands of Mexico. Coal was discovered by the emigrants on the banks of several of the streams. Altogether, Kansas offered every advantage which settlers could desire.

So in 1852, and in February, 1853, petitions were presented in Congress for organising the territories of Nebraska and Kansas; and after the autumn recess, in December 1853, a bill was introduced in the Senate with the same òbject. Into this bill, Douglas of Illinois, and others, introduced clauses which had the effect of repealing the Missouri Compromise, and of establishing the principle that slavery was not to be restricted by arbitrary geographical lines. It seems almost doubtful whether the repeal would have been carried if it had been openly proposed. Mr. Dixon, of Kentucky, moved a direct clause for the repeal of the Missouri Compromise in committee. But it was abandoned. Men more skilful in parliamentary tactics than the straightforward Kentuckian were wanted for this business, and were forthcoming. They put forward the plausible doctrines of "non-intervention by Congress with slavery in the States and territories," and that every State and territory should be left "perfectly free to form and regulate their domestic institutions in their own way, subject only to the Constitution of the United States." These doctrines are commonly known by the name of "Squatter Sovereignty;" but in this instance they were not carried out to their legitimate conclusions, for

Mr. Chase failed in an attempt to give the people of the territory the right of choosing their own governor. This appointment was given to the President, and the slavery party thus gained an enormous advantage, as President Pierce was entirely in their hands.

Night after night, in committee, in the whole Senate, and afterwards in the House of Representatives, the bill was fought with great earnestness. The whole people of the United States was moved to its depths during the struggle. At last "the Act to organise the territories of Nebraska and Kansas" was passed in both Houses, and approved by the President at the end of May.

The name of Mr. Seward, the present Secretary for Foreign Affairs of the United States' Government, has become notorious in England during the last year. He is looked upon, and I think justly, as one chief cause of the ill-feeling which now prevails between England and the United States. But let us do justice even to our enemies. In the struggle of 1854 he was senator for New York, and the leader of the opposition to the Kansas-Nebraska Bill. And well and gallantly he led that opposition; and when all opposition had failed, on the last reading of that bill in the Senate, it was he who declared that the day for compromises between freedom and slavery was past for ever,* and threw

* "Through all the darkness and gloom of the present hour bright stars are breaking, that inspire me with hope and excite me to perseverance. They show that the day for compromises has past for ever, and that henceforward all great questions between Freedom and Slavery legitimately coming here—and none other can come—shall be decided as they ought to

down the gauntlet to the South, in those words which have become classical in America—" Come on, then, gentlemen of the slave-states; since there is no escaping your challenge, I accept it on behalf of freedom. We will engage in competition on the virgin soil of Kansas, and God give the victory to the side that is stronger in numbers as it is in right." If he had only acted up to this language, we should have seen another state of things in the United States, in my judgment, before this time.

The challenge thus given and accepted was the signal for the outbreak of that struggle which has been raging ever since, and has come to a head in the great civil war. As I have said, the people in all parts of the States had been deeply moved by the debates in Congress. In the first months of the year it had become already clear that the Act would pass. The people felt that their representatives were giving over into their hands the battle which had hitherto been fought within the walls of Congress. The question whether Kansas should be free soil was now to be decided on the territory itself, and both sides set to work in earnest. The South got the start. The slave-state of Missouri adjoined the new territory, and within a few days of the passing of the Kansas-Nebraska Act, and as soon as its passage could be known on the border, leading citizens of Missouri crossed over the river into the territory,

be, on their merits, by a fair exercise of legislative power, and not by bargains of equivocal prudence, if not of doubtful morality."

held squatter meetings, passing resolutions in favour of slavery, and then returned to their homes. The following are specimens:—

"That we will afford protection to no abolitionist as a settler of this territory.

"That we recognise the institution of slavery as already existing in this territory, and advise slaveholders to introduce their property as soon as possible."

Those of the Missourians who remained as *bonâ fide* residents in Kansas, and other Southern and Western men favourable to slavery, were undoubtedly the first settlers, and they, and their allies across the river in Missouri, seem to have assumed at once that the question had been settled in their favour. But they were soon roused from this pleasant dream.

Single settlers from the free-states, with their families, very soon moved into Kansas in considerable numbers; and early in July the first company of settlers from the Eastern States, sent by the Emigrant Aid Societies, passed through Missouri. They were shortly followed by other companies, composed of men very unlike the usual coon-hunting, whisky-drinking pioneers of the West. These settlers were educated and intelligent men, and brought with them not only civlised habits, but saw-mills, capital, and other material aid.

Their settlement at Lawrence rose at once into importance, became the capital of the free-soil party, and excited the bitterest wrath of Missouri. The Emigrant Aid Societies, of which the New England Emigrant Aid

Company of Massachusetts was the chief, had been formed in the North during the debates on the Kansas-Nebraska Bill, with the object of organising and facilitating emigration from the free-states. They were managed with vigour, and under their auspices a steady stream of free emigrants was setting in to Kansas. So the border counties of Missouri banded themselves together to stop the emigration, and avowedly to remove from Kansas all emigrants who had gone there under the auspices of the Northern Emigrant Aid Societies.

Before turning to the strife between the white men, we must glance at the vanishing Indian.

The chiefs had been taken to Washington by the Missourians, where they seem to have been persuaded, or forced, into ceding portions of their preference lands. But no regard was soon paid by either party to the arrangement then made. Free-soilers and Southerners indifferently soon settled where they would, regardless of the Red man. The Delaware chiefs protested in the following pathetic manner :—" We, the chiefs, head men and counsellors of the Delaware nation, hereby notify our white brethren, that all settlements on the lands ceded by the Delaware Indians, by treaty at Washington, dated 6th May, 1854, are in violation of said treaty; and that we in no wise give our will or consent to such settlement; and if persisted in by our white brethren, we shall appeal to our great father, the President of the United States, for protection."

Luckless Red men, with Presidents Pierce and Buchanan for their successive " great fathers !"

A. H. Reeder, of Pennsylvania, the first governor, arrived in October, a Government democrat, who had declared at Washington that he had no more scruple in buying a slave than a horse, and regretted that he had not money to buy a number to carry with him to Kansas, but yet a man who would not be a tool in the hands of the slavery party,—too honest to look on quietly while all sorts of injustice and wrong were going on in his district. He came to be governor, and he meant to be governor.

And now the first act of the struggle came on. A delegate to Congress had to be chosen, and the governor named Nov. 29, 1854, as the day of election. The result was in favour of Whitfield (really the slavery candidate, but who gave out that he was in favour of the residents settling the question for themselves) by a very large majority,—the free-state candidate, Judge Wakefield, "no abolitionist," as he described himself, "but free-soiler up to the hub—hub and all," getting only 249 votes.

At this election the Missourians crossed over in large bands, in many cases on the very day of the election, and voted for Whitfield. The Committee of Congress, appointed afterwards to inquire into the state of Kansas and these early elections, reported that 1729 illegal votes had been given. Still this will not account for the very small number of votes given for Wakefield. The fact seems to be, that the free-state settlers were completely taken by surprise in the first instance, and when the real state of the case became plain, were fairly intimidated by the border ruffians, who were led by judges and colonels. Atchison, of Missouri, the ex-Vice-President of the United States, and a senator, if not actually with them, was responsible for the invasion. Just before the election, he urged the citizens of Platte County, Missouri, at a public meeting, to send 500 of their young men to vote "in favour of their institutions," adding, that "if each county of Missouri will now do its duty, the question will be decided quietly by the ballot-box, and, if we are defeated, Missouri and the other Southern States will have shown themselves recreant to their interests, and will deserve their fate." General Stringfellow, of Missouri, is even more explicit, speaking at St. Joseph: "I advise you, one and all," he says, "to enter every election district in Kansas in defiance of Reeder and his vile myrmidons, and vote at the point of the bowie-knife and revolver. Neither give nor take quarter. It is enough that the slave interest wills it, from which there is no appeal."

A story is told in connection with this election, which is, perhaps, worth repeating to you. Together with stout hearts, and teams, and rifles, the New England and other free-state settlers had not failed to bring with them to Kansas a certain dash of Yankee shrewdness. So when they saw the Missourians and others swaming over the border, with the avowed purpose of voting at the election for Whitfield, they began to cast about for some plan of neutralising the effect of the invasion. The bright idea seems to have occurred to some of them of bringing the Indians to the poll. Who could object? Were they not the very *freest* sort of native Americans? A Delaware Chief had been amongst them, and had delivered himself of the following speech: " Good man, heap,—Yankee town. Missouri,—slave-man,—bad,—heap heap,—damn um!" This looked promising. The Delawares were clearly free-soilers; so an enterprising canvasser was sent post-haste to their principal village to bring them in. Unluckily for the success of this ingenious device, it was only hit upon on the very eve of the election, and a conclave of chiefs could only be got together on the very morning of the voting. However, the free-soil ambassador made his statement, and waited for some hours while the chiefs debated. At last he was obliged to press for an answer, which was given by the oldest chief. He rose up, and stood before the impatient Yankee, pointing with the forefinger of his right into the palm of his left hand, and moving it up and down, tapping the palm, as he delivered the answer of the collective chiefs in these words :—

"Tink um four days,—den vote heap, heapum! some time,—may be."

Thus the plan of running the Indians against the border ruffians at the polling places failed.

The united action and great success of the slave party in this opening trial of strength is attributable in great measure to a secret society, known as the "Blue Lodge," or "Sons of the South." All such organizations, even Freemasonry and Oddfellowship in

England, are in my belief objectionable. Men of the same nation do not want an *imperium in imperio*,— they ought to be good fellow-citizens and brethren already, without the ties of secret oaths, signs, grips, and passwords. I say these secret organizations are objectionable even when they have no direct political aims. How atrociously mischievous they may become when they have political objects, Kansas can witness. The Blue Lodge kept that fair land in a state of siege, in constant terror, and bleeding at every pore, for four years.

You will probably all remember the notices in our papers of August last, of a similar secret society called "The Order of the Lone Star," established in the South for the conquest of Mexico and Cuba, the reduction of the whole peon population of Mexico to slavery, and the re-opening of the African slave-trade. The operations of the order in Mexico were to have commenced on October 6th, 1861. The members have now other work on their hands. These secret societies are, amongst many bad features, almost the worst, to my mind, in the Southern States. In Kansas, the free-states' men tried to imitate their enemies, and organised a secret society called the "Kansas Legion," which, I am happy to say, fell into disrepute within a few months, and died out soon after. The atmosphere of freedom did not suit the plant.

The pro-slavery party in Kansas and Missouri waxed fiercer after their first success. I will not detain you with particulars of the doings of rampant border-ruffianism under which the emigrants now suffered. Many of those who had come into the territory " right on the goose" (as the slang phrase went for indicating sound pro-slavery principles), were converted by the insolent and swaggering tyranny of Missouri; while the principles of the old free-states' men were burnt into them by violence and cruelty, such as one could not have believed in but for the evidence of the pro-slavery papers, and the speeches of the Missouri leaders. They not only do not deny the facts, but glory in the commission of the atrocities they have been accused of. The free-soil emigrants were in many instances driven back; their claims of land were seized; leaders, even clergymen, were tarred and feathered; their cabins were plundered and burnt down, and, before the breaking out of open war, murders of great atrocity were committed with perfect impunity.

In the midst of such sayings and doings as these, Governor Reeder appointed March 30th, 1855, for the first elections. Under the organisation provided for the territory by the Kansas-Nebraska Act, a council or upper house of thirteen, and a house of representatives of twenty-six had to be chosen. Reeder was accused by the Missourians of free-soil leanings for delaying the elections so long. Had he been really a free-soil partisan, he would have served his party by holding them earlier or later. In March, the spring emigrants from the West and Missouri, mostly pro-slavery men, had already arrived, while none had yet had time to arrive from the East.

THE BOGUS ELECTIONS.

These elections of the first Kansas Chambers, in March 30th, 1855, were of course more important than any subsequent ones, as they gave the winners such a start in the territory as they could have got in no other way. There are, fortunately, unimpeachable materials for ascertaining precisely what *did* happen at them.

In obedience to the Kansas-Nebraska Act, Governor Reeder took a census of the population between the 20th of January and the end of February. The result shown by the returns was, that there were at that time in Kansas 8501 persons (exclusive of Indians). Of these 5128 were males, 3373 females, and 7161 citizens of the United States, and 409 foreigners; 242 were slaves, and 151 free negroes. Out of the total of 8501 there were 3469 minors; and the whole number of persons entitled to vote was returned at 2905.

When the affairs of Kansas came before Congress, a committee of inquiry was appointed, to report, amongst other matters, on these March elections. Remember that Governor Reeder's census found 2905 voters only in the territory. The report of the Committee of Congress reduced this number slightly, giving a total of 2892 voters. But it went on to find that 5427 votes had been cast for the pro-slavery candidates, and 791 for the free-states' men; that of the whole number of votes given, 1310 only were legal, and that 4908 illegal votes had been consequently cast. And, that no doubt might be left as to the side to which the illegal voting must be charged, they proceeded to state, that in Missouri, " companies of men were arranged in regular parties, and sent into every council district in the territory, and into every representative district but one. The numbers were so distributed as to control the election in each district. They went to vote with the avowed design to make Kansas a slave-state."

One specimen of the kind of evidence, repeated over and over again, on which the report of the committee was founded, will be useful. The witness was a tall, rough-bearded Missourian, named Tom Thorpe, a cattle-dealer, who was summoned to give evidence as he was driving cattle through Kansas, in 1856, and entered the committee-room with an ox-whip six feet long in his hand. He carefully described himself as a pro-slavery man, but admitted that "a heap of respectable people" went and persuaded "the boys" to go over and vote. "There's my own nephew," he said, "he came all the way from Howard County with a company to vote. He came over to see me and our folks as he went along. I says to him, 'Jem Thorpe, han't you nothin' better to do than to come up to vote in the territory?' Well, he told me that they wan't busy to home, an' that they got a dollar a day, an' their expenses an' liquor."

Tom Thorpe's, and other evidence of the same kind, throws light on the real state of the case. The truth seems to be, that the "Blue Lodge" and the wealthier Missouri citizens would gladly have sent *bonâ fide* white settlers into Kansas if they could have found them; but in default of *bonâ fide* white settlers, they excited, and, when necessary paid, all the reckless loafers they could lay hands on, and any young Missourians who were ready for a lark, and not "busy to home," to go over and vote in the territory, in the belief that if the first elections could be carried, the free-soilers would leave, and Kansas be left in the undisturbed possession of the slave power.

The difference between their action and that of the New England Emigrant Aid Societies was, that the latter helped *bonâ fide* settlers into the territory, who brought their families and goods with them. We must try both the Blue Lodge and the Emigrant Aid Societies by the same test, and I think we shall come to the conclusion that the action of the one (apart from all question of open violence) was wholly illegal and unconstitutional —that of the other in strict conformity with the law and Constitution of the United States.

The results of such elections may be easily guessed. Out of the council of thirteen, there was just one man, Mr. Conway, who was not a violent pro-slavery partisan. There was also one free-soiler in the house of representatives, Mr. Houston. Of the rest, many were actual residents in Missouri. The notorious Dr. Stringfellow was chosen speaker of this precious house of representatives—the bogus legislature, as it was at once called.

The indignation of the free-state settlers, who were by this time almost three to one in Kansas, was strong and deep. They memorialised Congress and began to organise themselves regularly in military companies. There was a period of four days for protesting against the elections, and, notwithstanding the extent of the territory, and the want of roads and organisation, they managed to get in a number of protests, six of which the Governor admitted to be legal and to have proved cases of fraud. He consequently annulled the first, and called for special elections in these districts, which resulted in the election of free-state candidates for five of them. In the sixth, Leavenworth, there was again an incursion from Missouri, the polls were seized, free-state voters driven off, and the pro-slavery candidate carried.

The bogus legislature, however, proceeded to deal in their own way with the members returned at these special elections. On July 4th the five free-soil members were expelled, and their places filled by the pro-slavery men whose elections had been declared void by the Governor, on the ground that he had no power under the organic act to declare elections void for fraud. They then proceeded to expel Mr. Conway from the Council, and to declare his pro-slavery opponent duly elected; on what ground I have not been able to ascertain. Mr. Houston, the only free-soil member left in either House, then withdrew. Thus purified, the bogus legislature went to work in earnest. They began by passing an Act, adjourning the sittings to the Shawnee mission, the head-quarters of the pro-slavery party, one mile from the Missouri border, and four from Westport. The Governor vetoed the adjournment, and when, notwithstanding his veto, it was carried, declared the legislature dissolved. But the Governor's declaration was no more heeded than his veto. The legislature adjourned to the Shawnee mission, and there, in the space of a few weeks, passed a code of laws for the territory, of many hundred printed pages. All the most violent acts of Missouri and the slave states were adopted verbatim, with interpretation clauses tacked on to them, providing, that in "the said act" the word "state" was to mean "territory." They had neither leisure nor patience to go through the decent form of having the words altered to meet the actual case.

This code punished with death, not only any "attempt to raise, or to aid or assist, by speech or writing, rebellion amongst slaves," but any attempt to aid a slave to escape. Any person printing or circulating any book or paper "*calculated to produce* a disorderly, dangerous, or rebellious disaffection amongst the slaves of the territory, or to induce such slaves to escape from their masters," was declared guilty of felony, punishable by *not less* than five years' imprisonment with hard labour. Printing or circulating any book or paper "containing any denial of the right of persons to hold slaves in this territory," was felony, punishable by not less than two years' imprisonment and hard labour. No person "conscientiously opposed to holding slaves" was eligible to the bar or bench, or could "sit as a juror on the trial of any prosecution for any violation of any of the sections" of the "act to punish offences against slave property." They excluded every resident from voting who would not swear to support the fugitive slave law, and with a provident view to future invasions at election time, declared every "inhabitant of full age who shall have paid a territorial tax" an elector. Upon which last enactment the committee of Congress comment, "any man of proper age who was in the territory on the day of election, and who paid one dollar as a tax to the sheriff, who was required to be at the polls to receive it, could vote as an inhabitant, although he had breakfasted in Missouri, and intended to return there to supper. There can be no doubt that this unusual and unconstitutional provision was inserted to prevent a full and fair expression of the popular will in the election, or to control it by non-residents."

They appointed a Board of Commissioners by joint ballot of the two Houses, to which board they gave the appointment of all sheriffs, coroners, &c., in short, of all the officials within the territory. They located the capital at Lecompton, and, unless they are much libelled, divided almost all the area of the future capital in town lots amongst themselves. They created joint-stock land companies, and chartered possible railroads, with extraordinary privileges; appointed members of their own body to every place worth having; in short, jobbed as, so far as I know, no legislative body ever did before, or, it is to be hoped, ever will do again; and, to crown all, petitioned the President to remove Governor Reeder, on the ground of his connection with some land speculation.

This petition was backed by a clamour from Missouri. It prevailed at Washington. Reeder was superseded on a charge of having speculated in Kaw lands, and Wilson Shannon, of Ohio, was appointed Governor. Under his rule the war broke out. He is described as a man who could never look *into* himself for a principle, but was always looking *out* for what others said and would pay for. A most unlucky character for a Governor of Kansas just now; besides which, he was already a mere tool of the pro-slavery party, and, if report speaks truly, a drunkard. He set out for his government at once; and, on his road through Missouri, accepted a public reception at Westport, and made a speech, pledging himself to support slavery in Kansas, and to uphold the code of the bogus legislature, on which the veto of his predecessor still rested.

The free-soil settlers were by this time fairly roused to action. They called mass meetings " irrespective of party distinctions." These mass meetings called on the election districts to appoint delegates, which was done. The delegates met at Topeka in September and October, and called a convention, which repudiated the bogus code, settled a constitution, resolved to apply to Congress for admission as a state, and named their late Governor, Reeder, as their delegate to Congress.

The Topeka constitution was essentially a free state one. It contained one article, however, which must not be passed over, I mean that commonly known as the " black law," by which coloured people were excluded from the territory.

THE TOPEKA CONVENTION. 343

This Topeka convention contained a large sprinkling of Southern men from Virginia, Kentucky, Missouri; and one, Mr. Parrott, from South Carolina. The only point on which its members were unanimous was the resolution that Kansas should be free, and should not have laws thrust on her by the citizens of other states. In other respects, they broke into the two great parties of Republicans and Democrats. The Republicans were led by Dr. Charles Robinson, afterwards the first Governor of the state of Kansas; the Democrats (who proved themselves a majority by passing the Black Act), by Colonel James H. Lane, who was elected President of the Convention. The two men were a remarkable contrast. Robinson, a reserved, cautious, cool-headed man, and so little of a popularity hunter that it is strange he should have won so high a place in such a community. Lane, hot-headed, restless, ambitious, and a celebrated stump orator. The one had been a Californian emigrant, the other a volunteer in the Mexican war, and afterwards a member of Congress for his state, Indiana. He had forfeited his seat in Congress by his advocacy of the Kansas Nebraska bill, and came to Kansas a pro-slavery democrat. But he had no idea of being ridden over rough-shod by Missouri border ruffians, or the citizens of any, or all, the other states; and there were many other settlers in the same category, who were converted into resolute free-soil men by the doings of Governor Shannon, Judge Lecompte, Atchison, Stringfellow, and their followers.

Besides framing a state constitution, the Topeka convention appointed officers in the territory, and sent Reeder as delegate to Washington. There were thus at one time in the territory two legislatures and two sets of officials, and at Washington two delegates, keenly hostile to one another, and each assuming to represent Kansas. The President answered the appeal to him in a special message, declaring that the people of Kansas had no right to organise as a state without a previous enabling Act of Congress. He appealed to the citizens of the states, and especially of those contiguous to the territory, neither by intervention of non-residents in elections, nor by unauthorised military force, to attempt to encroach upon or usurp the authority of the inhabitants of the territory He declared it to be his imperative duty "to exert the whole power of the Federal executive to support public order in the territory, and to vindicate the laws, whether Federal or local, against all attempts of organised resistance."

This amounted to a recognition of the bogus legislature, and many of the free-soil settlers gave up the contest in despair, and left the ill-fated territory. But their places were filled by others. The story of the doings in Kansas had roused the spirit of the North, and though it had become a service of danger now to cross Missouri, yet both by that route, and round through Iowa and Nebraska, enough free-soil men came in to maintain still a considerable majority of *bonâ fide* settlers, and so to keep up and intensify the hatred of the Blue Lodge and the border ruffians, who found that they made but little progress in forcing the recognition of the bogus laws in Kansas. They held the lead still by the help of the Federal Government, but they felt that the game was very far from being won.

And now the event happened which brought matters to a crisis. There was a valuable track of well timbered land at Hickory Point, on the Santa Fé road, at which a man named Branson had settled, and gathered round him a small band of free-state men. Disputes arose between them and the pro-slavery men in their neighbourhood as to claims. On November 21, Dow, one of the free-state settlers, went to the blacksmith's shop unarmed, carrying a waggon skein to be repaired. While he was at the shop, Coleman and Buckley of Missouri, and another pro-slavery man came up, all armed, and an angry discussion followed. When Dow left the shop, for his own home, he had to pass Coleman's cabin on the Santa Fé road. Colēman walked near him (Buckley and the other following behind), stopped at his own door, levelled his gun at Dow's back, and drew trigger. The gun missed fire. Dow turned at the sound; they were not thirty yards apart. Coleman, who had now put on a fresh cap, raised the gun again, fired, and shot Dow through the heart in mid-day. The corpse lay there till the evening. Meantime Coleman loaded his waggon and started back to Westport in Missouri. In the evening Branson found the body lying in the road. He summoned the settlers, who met, passed a resolution condemning the murder, a second deprecating the burning of the murderers' houses, which was proposed by some of the neighbours, and appointed a committee to bring the murderers to justice.

Meantime, Buckley, who had gone with Coleman to Westport, consulted Jones, a celebrated leader of the border ruffians, who was acting at this time as postmaster of Westport, Missouri, and sheriff of Douglas county, Kansas. On his advice Coleman surrendered himself to Governor Shannon (by whom he was not even detained), and Buckley having sworn that he was in fear of his life from Branson, a peace-warrant was obtained for Branson's arrest. Jones secured a mounted *posse*, broke into Branson's house in the night, dragged him from bed, and carried him off. A young man who had fallen in with the *posse* had given the alarm to the free-state men, fifteen of whom mustered hastily, and, starting at once, occupied a point on the road which Jones, his *posse*, and prisoner must pass. When these came up, the free-state men showed themselves, and Jones halted, shouting, "What's up?"

The numbers were about equal. After a pause, a voice was heard : " Is that you, Branson ? " " Yes." "Well, come this way." "If you move, we'll shoot you." "I am going," said Branson to Jones. "If you do, I'll shoot you." "Come ahead ; d—— them, if they shoot, *we* will." Branson rode the mule he was mounted on across to his friends. No gun was fired. " Whose mule is that ? " " Belongs to them." " Then get off and drive it back." This was done. Jones threatened and remonstrated, but finding the free-state men firm, at last drew off. The bogus laws and officers had at last been openly resisted. The next day Jones applied to Governor Shannon, who had let Dow's murderer escape but now acted promptly, and at once summoned "the territorial militia" to assist the sheriff in executing the law. As the militia had not yet been organised, an express was sent into Western Missouri that "all the volunteers, ammunition, &c., that could be raised would be needed." Western Missouri rose, sending (in Governor Shannon's words) "not only her young men, but her grey-headed citizens," "the man of seventy winters stood shoulder to shoulder with the youth of sixteen." And these men of another state were enrolled, with the Governor's sanction, as Kansas territorial militia. By the 1st of December Lawrence was effectually surrounded by large bands of Missourians, amongst whom were some seventy or eighty *bonâ fide* settlers.

The citizens of Lawrence had had early notice of what was going on, and had at once prepared for the worst. They had appointed Robinson their Commander-in-Chief, who at once named Lane, his political opponent, to conduct the purely military operations. A committee of safety was appointed, who soon got the name of "the safety valve," from the more resolute of the free-state men, for the anxiety which they showed to prevent a fight. Settlers flocked in from the country, amongst them John Brown, who came in in a lumber waggon with his five sons, "armed with broadswords and revolvers, and long poles surmounted by bayonets standing upright round the waggon-box." Altogether some 800 men, thoroughly-armed, and drilling night and day, were in Lawrence. The town was open. Sheriff Jones rode in from the Wakarusa camp more than once, and others of the Missouri leaders, and inspected everything without any molestation, so the "committee of safety" decreed. On the whole, though far superior in numbers, the Missourians hesitated to attack.

Shannon was now frightened by the Frankenstein he had himself raised. He applied to Colonel Sumner, commanding the United States' troops at Fort Leavenworth, to aid him, but that officer, whose conduct throughout the Kansas struggle was that of a thorough soldier and gentleman, declined to act without definite orders from the Government. Shannon, on the 16th of December, came to the Wakarusa camp, the sight of which frightened him still more. His attempt to call in the troops had made him unpopular with the border ruffians. He notified his coming to Robinson, who sent an escort, and brought him into Lawrence, where he remained three days negotiating. Then "articles of adjustment" were signed, but not published, and the Governor made a conciliatory speech to the Lawrence citizens outside the free-state hotel. The audience were not satisfied. Brown got up amidst vehement applause, mixed with strong signs of disapproval. "If he understood the Governor's speech, something had been conceded, and the territorial laws were to be recognised. Those laws they denounced and spat upon, and would never obey." Then the cry of "Down with the bogus laws, lead us out to fight first," rose. But the leaders interposed, and quieted the people, by the assurance that there had been no concession.

This was scarcely true. The articles are vaguely worded, but seem to imply a recognition of the territorial laws, though the last sentence runs, "That we wish it understood that we do not herein express any opinion as to the validity of the enactments of the territorial legislature." But for this time the danger was passed. The Missourians had already begun to disperse. The bold front of the free-state men, the Governor's negotiations with the enemy, and very bad weather, which now came on, carried off all but the most resolute. These, too, after a few days, withdrew to Missouri, their leaders openly declaring, "Shannon has played us false. The Yankees have tricked us." They had only to bide their time.

A week after the raising of the siege the Topeka constitution was submitted to public vote. At the voting places near the border, the ballot-boxes were mobbed, and voters kept away by armed men; at Leavenworth the poll-books were destroyed. The weather and fear kept back many. But, in spite of all, 1778 votes were cast for the free-state constitution. A party caucus was then held to nominate the officers of the future state of Kansas. Robinson was named for Governor, and Roberts for Lieutenant-Governor. The 1st of March was named for the assembly of the state legislature, by which time it was hoped an answer would come from the President to the memorial for protection against "armed invasion." The answer came in February, in the shape of a message from President Pierce, in words denouncing invasion, but sanctioning the territorial (bogus) legislature which had been elected by the Missourian invaders, and declaring that the territorial (bogus) laws would be sustained by the whole force of the Government.

The message was received with delight in Missouri, where Colonel Buford's regiment from Alabama and Carolina had just arrived, and preparations were going on for another invasion. The Missourians were ready to march "shoulder to shoulder with the South" (as resolutions passed at Lexington and Independence naïvely avowed) "to the last struggle for Southern rights in the contest now going on in Kansas."

On March 1st, 1856, the free-state legislature met. Governor Robinson, took the oaths of office, and delivered his inaugural address. Lane and Reeder were elected senators. A committee was appointed to frame a code of laws, and the legislature memorialised Congress for the admission of Kansas as a state under the Topeka constitution. No further steps were taken, with the view of avoiding, if possible, a collision with the territorial government, which they would not acknowledge but were anxious to put down constitutionally. Then the legislature adjourned till the 4th of July.

Missouri and her allies were now ready for another invasion, and it was time to act. The committee appointed by Congress, as mentioned before, had now come to the territory, and were examining witnesses. Oliver, of Missouri, was doing what he could in the interests of slavery to hinder the true state of things from coming out, but evidence was too abundant. The facts of the invasion, and the real nature and composition of the bogus legislature could no longer be concealed if the committee were not disturbed in some way. They were sitting at the hated Lawrence, in the very centre of the free-soil men, most of whom could themselves give very awkward testimony. But they might be cowed into silence, thought Judge Lecompte, Sheriff Jones, and others. Accordingly, after several ineffectual attempts to get up a disturbance, Sheriff Jones hit upon the device of appearing in Lawrence on Sunday morning, and summoning people going to church to act as his *posse* for making arrests in the town. In the articles signed by Shannon, Robinson, and Lane, in December, one of the stipulations was that the people of Lawrence would aid the Governor in securing a *posse* for the execution of legal process. The people of Lawrence denied Jones's authority altogether, would probably, with the exception perhaps of a few members of "the safety valve"—the peace-at-any-price men—have refused to recognise or assist him on any day of the week in any matter whatever; how much more on a Sunday, and when his avowed object was the arrest of Wood, one of their best citizens, and others, on the worn-out plea of the rescue of Branson.

Jones got no *posse*, not a man to help him in his arrests; went straight to Governor Shannon, and from him to Colonel Sumner with the Governor's requisition for troops. What could the soldier do? He had had positive orders to furnish Federal troops to sustain the bogus officers, so he sent a troop with Jones, and, at the same time, wrote to the Mayor of Lawrence :—

"HEAD-QUARTERS,
"Fort Leavenworth, April 22, 1856.

"SIR,—A small detachment proceeds to Lecompton this morning on the requisition of the Governor, under the orders of the President, to assist the sheriff of Douglas county in executing several writs, in which he says he has been resisted. I know nothing of the merits of the case, and have nothing to do with them; but I would respectfully impress on you and others in authority the necessity of yielding obedience to the proclamation and orders of the general Government. Ours is emphatically a government of laws, and if they are set at naught, there is an end of all order. I feel assured that, on reflection, you will not compel me to resort to violence in carrying out the orders of the Government.

"I am, sir, very respectfully,
"Your obedient servant,
"E. V. SUMNER, Col. First Cavalry Com."

Jones entered Lawrence, made his arrests, and confined his prisoners in a tent, treating them with much indignity. The people of Lawrence submitted in silence when they saw the Federal troops, but there were others besides them in their town. One night Jones was fired at and wounded in his tent. He was carried into the Free State Hotel—the citizens of

Lawrence vied in attentions to him—indignation meetings were held—Robinson at once offered a reward of five hundred dollars for the apprehension and conviction of the offender, and wrote to Colonel Sumner:—
"The cowardly attack upon Mr. Jones receives no countenance whatever from the citizens of Lawrence, but on the contrary meets with universal condemnation, and if the guilty party can be found, he will most certainly be given up to justice. It is and always has been the policy of the people of Lawrence to yield prompt obedience to the laws and officers of the Federal Government, and as Mr. Jones was acting with the authority of that government on the day of the assault, the guilty party was an enemy to the citizens of Lawrence, no less than a violator of the laws," &c.

The free-state men were thoroughly resolved to keep the peace if possible, petitioned Governor Shannon to protect them with the troops at his command, refrained from arming, offered a *posse* of three hundred to make arrests in Lawrence, and gave evidence of the mustering of bands for the destruction of the town. But the Governor sent only ambiguous answers. He was in direct communication at the very time with Buford and Titus, and other Southern leaders, whose bands were drawing round Lawrence, plundering farms and waggons, and murdering men. About the 20th of May, Atchison of Missouri, crossed into Kansas with two pieces of artillery and the Platte rifles; and on the next day, feeling themselves at length strong enough, the united forces marched on Lawrence, led by Donaldson, the United States marshal.

One last protest was made by the citizens of Lawrence to Donaldson, as marshal of Kansas territory. It went further than any previous one:—"We make no resistance," it ran, "to the execution of the laws, national *or territorial;* we ask protection of the government, and claim it as law-abiding American citizens. For the private property already taken by your *posse* we ask indemnification, and what remains to us we throw upon you for protection." They would recognise even the bogus legislature in this hour of trial. They might have saved themselves the useless humiliation. Donaldson entered the town and made three arrests. He then dismissed his *posse*, which was at once summoned by Sheriff Jones, who had recovered from his wound. He produced an order from Judge Lecompte for the abatement of the Free State Hotel and Journal as nuisances. Under him the invaders collected all the arms in the place, battered with cannon the Free State Hotel, and the printing office of the "Free State" journal, and then set fire to them, Governor Robinson's house, and other buildings. They plundered stores, and destroyed 150,000 dollars worth of property, amidst scenes of wild drunkenness and licence, while over the rifled office of the "Free State" a flag was hoisted; "its colour was a blood red, with a lone star in the centre, and S. Carolina above. Thus floated in triumph the banner of South Carolina, that single white star, so emblematic of her course in the early history of our sectional disturbances. When every Southern state stood almost on the verge of ceding their dearest rights to the North, Carolina stood boldly out, the firm and unwavering advocate of Southern institutions."*

The policy of non-resistance had now been fairly tried, and had broken down. Old Captain Brown's warning had come true. There was nothing to be done with these Missouri border ruffians, Buford red-shirts, and Kickapoo rangers, but to fight them. And so the mass of the free-soil settlers felt, though many still were for waiting till July 4th, when the free-soil legislature were to meet at Topeka, and all might be redressed. In the towns the latter feeling was strong enough to preserve a nominal peace, but through all the country districts there was war from the date of the sack of Lawrence.

The free-soil settlers rose, but their first efforts were desultory. There were plenty of flying skirmishes, made by small bands of young men, who came together one day, and broke up the next, generally purposeless even when successful. But little impression was likely to be made thus on rampant border ruffianism. The weakness and desultory character of these first efforts of the free-state settlers may be laid chiefly to the fact that their leaders were gone. Governor Robinson had been seized and was in prison; Reeder had narrowly escaped arrest, and was on his way to Washington;

* The above quotation is from an article in the Lecompton Union, headed " Lawrence taken. Glorious triumph of the law and order party over fanaticism in Kansas."

Lane had had to fly the territory; other prominent men were prisoners or fugitives. Only in the south of the territory, far away from the strongholds of the free-state party, in a frontier district, peculiarly open to the raids from Missouri, a regular system of organised warfare was beginning to show itself, and the eyes of the free-soilers of Kansas turned for encouragement to the Pottowotomie valley, the little town of Ossowotomie, and old Captain Brown.

Brown had a camp near Prairie City, carefully concealed in the woods, and guarded night and day, which served as a rallying point for the free settlers of the neighbourhood, who still, notwithstanding the frequent presence of hordes of Southern banditti, continued to till their farms in companies of from five to ten, armed to the teeth. This secret camp is thus described by one who visited it:—" Near the edge of the creek a dozen horses were tied, all ready saddled for a ride for life, or a hunt after Southern invaders. A dozen rifles and sabres were stacked against the trees. In an open space, amid the shady and lofty woods, there was a great blazing fire, with a pot on it; a woman, bare-headed, with an honest sunburnt face, was picking blackberries from the bushes; three or four armed men were lying on red and blue blankets on the grass; and two fine-looking youths were standing leaning on their arms, on guard, near by. One of them was Brown's youngest son, the other Charley, a brave Hungarian, subsequently murdered at Ossowotomie. Brown himself stood near the fire, with his shirt sleeves rolled up, and a large piece of pork in his hand. He was cooking a pig. He was poorly clad, and his toes protruded from his boots. He received me with great cordiality, and the little band gathered about me. But it was for a moment only, for the Captain ordered them to renew their work. In this camp no manner of profane language was permitted; no man of immoral character was allowed to stay, except as a prisoner of war. He made prayers, in which all the company united every morning and evening; and no food was ever tasted by his men until the Divine blessing had been asked on it. Often, I was told, he returned to the densest solitudes to wrestle with his God in secret prayer. One of his company subsequently informed me that, after these retirings, he would say the Lord had directed him in visions what to do; that for himself he did not love warfare, but peace—only acting in obedience to the will of the Lord, and fighting God's battles for his children's sake. It was at this time he said to me, ' I would rather have the smallpox, yellow fever, and cholera all together in my camp, than a man without principles. It's a mistake, sir, that our people make when they think that bullies are the best fighters, or that they are the men fit to oppose these Southerners. Give me God-fearing men—men who respect themselves—and with a dozen of them I will oppose any hundred such men as those Buford ruffians."

The movements of the border ruffian bands were well known to Brown, who, under the disguise of a government surveyor, often himself drove lines through their camps, and heard them speak of an old man named Brown settled there, whom they hated "like a snake," and that if this man and his sons could be disposed of, the other settlers would give no further trouble.

Just at this juncture the "Times" correspondent arrived in Kansas. He had come up the river with a western pioneer, who, when they parted, gave him this advice: "Now that you're settin' foot in these here Western diggin's, Colonel, don't let a soul of 'em know that you're an Englishman; should it get out, it's just as much as your life's worth, mind that. That's the state we're in just now all along side of this cursed slavery question. If you're an Englishman, it's all the same as being a Yankee, not a bit better. And a Yankee is a nuisance, and nuisances must be abolished. That's what they all say there; so you mind, Colonel, and don't forget what I say."

The correspondent to whom his kind acquaintance thus gave at once brevet rank and wholesome advice, followed it, and got home safely. He states deliberately, that while in Kansas he knew of *no* instance of an outrage committed by the free soilers of a kindred character to those of the border ruffians, with which his letters, and every book, pamphlet, and report on the subject teem. I cite this witness of his here, because I must now refer to the only instance I know of such an outrage, and I wish to give you some evidence beyond my mere statement, that you may not set this down as an example of what the free-soil men were in the habit of doing.

Wilkinson, the magistrate of Pottowotomie, and a member of the bogus legislature, a violent pro-slavery man, had, with others of his neighbours of like opinions, taken advantage of the triumph at Lawrence. A band of them had brutally ill-used a free-state man; had visited farms where women only were at home, and insulted them; had openly boasted that they would kill the men if they did not at once leave the territory. A party of men from Brown's camp attacked the houses of these men in the night. Five pro-slavery men, including Wilkinson, were killed. It is said, and I believe truly, that two of these were taken alive, tried by Lynch law, and shot in cold blood after the fight. Brown was away, twenty-five miles off, at Middle Creek, when the act was done, but he accepted it, and stated that, had he been present, and known the circumstances, he should have ordered it. As I cannot, amidst the conflict of statement, make out what the exact circumstances of provocation, and of the relations of the opposing factions in the district actually were, I can neither justify nor condemn the deed. It may have been a wise and necessary act, but it will take a great deal to justify night attacks and shooting men after drum-head courts-martial.

A force of militia and dragoons under a Captain Pate, a Virginian, resident in Missouri, a well-known leader of the border ruffians, at once started for Ossowotomie. They seized two of Brown's sons while working on their farms, failed to find the father or his camp, burned the house and library of John Brown the younger, and those of some other settlers, and after driving the young Browns about in chains in a burning sun till one of them went mad, handed them over to the dragoons, and themselves encamped near Hickory Point, to overawe the neighbourhood and "wipe out" the free soilers.

Pate was encamped with his company of sixty men at a place called Black Jack, on June 2nd, with a breast-work of waggons round his camping-ground, and stores of arms and ammunition, and spoil of free-trade homesteads. Here he was attacked by twenty-eight men under Brown and Shore, another free-state captain. For three hours Pate and his men held out. Then they sent a lieutenant with a flag of truce. Brown insisted on Pate's coming himself, which he did, and began to explain that he was an officer acting under the United States marshal. "Captain," said Brown, "I understand exactly what you are. Have you any proposition to make to me?"

"Well, no: that is ——"

"Very well, Captain, I have one to make to you—your unconditional surrender."

Pate, after some demur, consented; and he and twenty-one of his men, besides wounded, surrendered prisoners of war, with all their horses, arms, ammunition, and spoil. Three only of Brown's men were wounded. The prisoners were well treated by Brown, and allowed the use of their camp-equipage. A few days afterwards, Colonel Sumner, with the United States dragoons, arrived at Ossowotomie, ordered a band of border ruffians out of the territory, who retired a few miles, and appeared again in force as soon as his back was turned; dispersed Shore's company; and then coming to Prairie City, where Brown met him, and conducted him to his camp, released the whole of the prisoners, and took the ammunition and spoils of the fight. "Old Bull of the Woods," as Sumner was called, gave the deputy-marshal who accompanied him, and Pate's men, a sound rating; but it availed nothing. He himself was honestly bent on dispersing armed bodies on both sides, but his instructions were such, and he was so hampered by Shannon and the pro-slavery officials of the territory, that the action of the Federal troops under his command was always one-sided, and effected little beyond crippling the action of the free soilers.

Sumner returned to Leavenworth, having, as he thought, dispersed the rival forces in the South. A few days afterwards, Whitfield, the delegate for Kansas, with three companies, carefully picked and organised in Missouri, made a rapid inroad into the territory, and burnt and plundered Ossowotomie.

But why multiply instances of the crusade of the border ruffians for the establishment of law, order, and slavery in Kansas? The patience of the free soilers was not yet exhausted. Governor Shannon resigned in June. The acting governor (late secretary) Woodson, was as bad as his master; but a new governor might, perhaps, do justice. Still many of them looked hopefully forward to the 4th of July. The 4th of July came.

The free-state legislature met at Topeka, round which Sumner, urged by Woodson and Donaldson, had collected a large force of United States troops. The more resolute of the free-soil men, after vain protests had been sent to the so-called authorities, were for warning Sumner that an attempt to enter the town and disperse the legislature would be resisted, and for barricading the streets and fighting to the last. But again prudent counsels prevailed. Donaldson was allowed to enter Topeka, and Woodson's proclamation was read in the House of Assembly, that any attempt of persons " to organise, or act, in any legislative capacity whatever," " was illegal, and should be put down." At noon Sumner followed, with his dragoons, posting them round the hall, and entering himself. He walked up to the platform, where a chair was offered him, which he pushed aside, saying, " Do you want to make speaker of me ? " And then the roll of members having been read, addressed them :—

"Gentlemen,—I am called on this day to perform the most painful duty of my whole life. Under the authority of the President's proclamation, I am here to disperse this legislature; and therefore inform you that you cannot meet. God knows I have no party feeling in this matter, and will hold none so long as I occupy my present position in Kansas. I have just returned from the borders, where I have been sending home companies of Missourians, and now I am ordered here to disperse you. Such are my orders, and you must disperse. I now command you to disperse. I repeat, that this is the most painful duty of my whole life."

Judge Schuyler.—" Colonel Sumner, are we to understand that the legislature are driven out at the point of the bayonet?"

Sumner.—" I shall use all the force at my command to carry out my orders."

Thus " Old Bull of the Woods " did his duty, and all chance of a free-state organisation was over for the time.

And now the free-state settlers of Kansas had reached the lowest point of their humiliation. The bogus legislature was recognised by the President, and backed by the United States forces; their attempt to constitute a state legislature had been put down by force; their chosen leaders were prisoners or fugitives; their chief town, and every settlement within reach of Missouri, had been plundered; the Governor of Missouri had formally closed that state and the river against Northern settlers bound for Kansas; the Southern regiments of Buford and Titus, and the border ruffians, backing up the pro-slavery settlers at every point, were lords of Kansas, except in John Brown's camp, and those of Shore and some few other guerilla leaders. Never was cause more hopelessly down to the eyes of man than that of the free-state party in Kansas in July, 1856.

" Providence is on the side of the strongest battalions " is a saying which is much believed in here and elsewhere; in other words, " might, and not right, rules in God's world." That there are specious appearances to justify the belief I will not deny, but it is a lie for all that. At any rate the providence that sides with strong battalions broke down in Kansas. By the end of July the free-soil men had risen and were holding their own. Lane was back in the territory at the head of several hundred men. Stevens was out with another band round Topeka, and Brown at Ossowotomie. The free-soil leaders who had hitherto shunned the resolute old abolitionist, now began to acknowledge his worth and adopt his method. "As politicians," he says, "they thought every man wanted to lead, and, therefore, supposed I might be in the way of their schemes. But politicians and leaders soon found I had different purposes, and forgot their jealousy."

Brown joined Lane, and took the command of the cavalry, and wherever they appeared the border ruffians were worsted. By the middle of August the tables were turned, and it was clear that, unless some great effort were made, Kansas would yet be free. Appeals were therefore made in Missouri for a fresh invasion, and answered, and towards the end of the month 2000 Missourians entered the territory. They divided into two bodies, the larger under Atchison, marching North against Lane, the smaller under Reid, some 800 strong, turning southwards on Ossowotomie. Lane was in force, and drove his opponent back over the river without a fight. Reid found Ossowotomie nearly deserted of men. Brown, with some forty men hastily got together, met Reid at Ossowotomie. His son Frederick and two other free-state men were surprised and murdered in cold blood before the fight began. Brown extended his men in skirmishing order while the enemy were actually in sight, so that the numbers of the free soilers were no secret. The first attack was repulsed, and the Missourians, falling back in confusion, suffered enormously; but after a short time they rallied again. The ammunition of many of Brown's men was now spent. He fell slowly back, fighting, abandoning the town and crossing the river, where the enemy did not follow him. He lost two men killed, three wounded, and several missing; the Missourians, thirty-two killed and fifty wounded. They sacked Ossowotomie again, murdering a Mr. Williams, whom they took there, and who was not even a free soiler, and returned boasting of their triumph to Missouri. But they carried with them their dead and wounded. The number of Brown's company with whom they had fought soon crept out, and his name became a power in Missouri, and a terror to border ruffianism. From the day of that border-ruffian triumph at Ossowotomie, the bands of Southerners began to break up fast, and turn homewards. Many of the respectable inhabitants of Missouri also had become thoroughly ashamed of and disgusted at the doings in Kansas, and the reign of terror on the border. Still, however, the Blue Lodge worked and paid, and Atchison and Stringfellow spouted, and again bands of invaders were poured across the river. On September the 14th Lawrence was again threatened by a force of some 2000 men, and in consequence of the many points at which the free-soil men had to be in force, there was only a small force, less than 200, available for defence.

The enemy were already at Franklin, a large village some four miles distant, when it became known that old Captain Brown was in Lawrence, on his road home from Topeka. He was unanimously chosen to command. The citizens crowded round him in the street. He got on a packing-case and said:—

"Gentlemen,—It is said there are 2500 Missourians down at Franklin, and that they will be here in two hours. You can see for yourselves the smoke they are making by setting fire to the houses in that town. This is probably the last opportunity you will have of seeing a fight, so that you had better do your best. If they should come up and attack us, don't yell and make a great noise, but remain perfectly silent and still. Wait till they get within twenty-five yards of you; get a good object; be sure you see the hind-sight of your gun; then fire. A great deal of powder and lead, and very precious time, is wasted by shooting too high. You had better aim at their legs than at their heads. In either case, be sure of the hind-sight of your gun. It is from this reason that I myself have so many times escaped; for if all the bullets which have ever been aimed at me had hit me, I should have been as full of holes as a riddle."

He then led out the one hundred men who were best armed, and extended them before the town, leaving the rest in reserve. The van of the invaders came on some four hundred strong, and skirmished for some time; till at length the Missourians, finding that they made not the slightest impression on the free-state skirmishers, retired on their main body, and the whole soon afterwards withdrew into Missouri. Geary, the new governor, who was within a few miles of the town with the United States forces, and had been warned by special messengers of the danger, never came up till the enemy had retired.

Though there were many raids of bands of border ruffians into the territory after this time, and the free-state men were obliged to exercise constant and exhausting vigilance, the invasion had been defeated, and the disheartened and broken remnants of the Southern bands went home, leaving Kansas spoiled and scarred, but whole in heart, and more resolved than ever to submit on no terms whatever to the imposition of the bogus code of laws. The border ruffian bands had failed in their special object, but had effected much, for they had opened the eyes of the North to the meaning of "squatter sovereignty" in the territories in Southern mouths; they had converted thousands of Democrats in Kansas and Missouri into free soilers; they had proved the truth of Seward's words, that compromise between freedom and slavery was thenceforth impossible, and had opened the great contest. Bitterly must the unhappy state of Missouri, desolated through all her borders for the last six months, during which she has been the battle-field of the Federals and Confederates in the West, have repented of the game she played in Kansas in the day of her adversity. Her own measure has been meted out to her, not by lawless bands of border ruffians, but by Northern and

Kansas volunteers in league with all her own best citizens. The South now hold but one small corner of that great state, the advanced guard of the slave power. By any mail we may hear that not a Southerner remains in Missouri, and Lane and Montgomery of Kansas have been two of the chief actors in the campaign which has done this good service to the Union.

To return to the autumn of 1856, Governor Geary came declaring that he would oppose all dictation from Missouri, but that he would maintain the territorial laws. Of course no Governor resolved to support the bogus legislature could be acceptable in Kansas, and Geary had no support from the free-state men. On the other hand, he offended the pro-slavery party mortally by opposing Lecompte, the United States Judge for the territory, the worst of all Kansas officials, and mainstay of slavery in the territory. The President sided with Lecompte. Geary found himself unable even to bring murderers to trial, and resigned in disgust after six months.

He was succeeded by Governor R. J. Walker, another sound pro-slavery man, as it was thought, who arrived in May, 1857, and in his inaugural address still upheld the bogus legislature. That body, in June, summoned a convention for framing a state constitution, at which the free soilers refused to vote, and only 2000 votes, including Missourians, were cast. A free-state convention was held in July and August, and the Topeka constitution ratified by more than 10,000 votes of settlers who had been more than six months in the country. Meanwhile, the National Kansas Committee had again appealed to the new president, Buchanan, and had been answered, that "their sufferings were of their own seeking," that "the civil power in the territory must be sustained."

Through the summer, the marauding of border ruffians still continued, accompanied by the usual atrocities, although the invaders never made any serious stand against Montgomery, who had succeeded Brown as the chosen captain of the free-soilers. But the majority of Northern men was every day increasing amongst the *bonâ fide* settlers. A constant stream of them was coming in through Iowa and Nebraska. To punish the settlers for their contumacy, Governor Walker and the United States troops occupied Lawrence. But the citizens took no notice of him or them, and went on with their usual peaceful pursuits. The Governor, after a short occupation, withdrew—a wiser man apparently, as his future conduct showed. In August, another triumph was gained by the free-soil party, by which their best man was restored to them. Robinson was tried for usurping the office of Governor of Kansas, and acquitted.

In October the territorial elections came on, in which the Northern settlers took part. Governor Walker had declared that these elections were held under the laws of Congress, and not under any act of the late territorial legislature. On this declaration of the Governor the free-soilers acted. Both sides put out their whole strength. Although the representatives had been apportioned so as to give a most undue proportion to the border, or pro-slavery, districts, though the old shameless tricks were resorted to, so that in one district (Oxford) 1614 votes were returned as cast for the pro-slavery candidate, where, on examination, there proved to be only 60 voters; though the Governor set aside the elections of free-soilers on frivolous pretexts, and confirmed notoriously irregular returns of pro-slavery men; yet, in spite of all, the free-soilers triumphed, returning a majority of five in the Kansas Council, and fifteen in the House of Representatives. And so, at last, a territorial legislature, fairly representing the people, came into being. Governor Walker honestly accepted the result, and reported at Washington that nine-tenths of the *bond fide* settlers were free-soilers. President Buchanan and the Democrats, however, refused to yield, and, backed by them, the pro-slavery settlers made yet another effort in the territory. Beaten in the territorial elections, they fell back on their convention for framing a state constitution, which met at Lecompton in October and November, and framed a violent pro-slavery constitution, which was forwarded to Washington, without having been submitted to a vote of the people.

The President, in his message, declared his resolution to adhere to this Lecompton constitution. But the house was falling, and the rats beginning to clear out of it. Douglas, of Illinois, seized the occasion to change sides; he saw how the tide of public feeling was turning in the North, and he had an old debt to pay—Buchanan had been a successful rival of his.

Governor Walker now resigned in disgust, leaving his secretary, Stanton, as acting-governor, who summoned the new territorial legislature, and was dismissed by President Buchanan for having done so. But the legislature had time to pass an act, submitting the Lecompton constitution to a vote of the people in January, 1858. It was rejected by 10,226 to 162. They also passed an act to abolish slavery in the territory, but the Governor threw it over by neglecting to approve or veto it before the session was over.

In Congress there was a fierce struggle on that part of the President's message which referred to Kansas, which lasted far into the spring. In April the Houses came to a dead lock. Then English, of Indiana, succeeded in carrying a compromise. His proposition amounted virtually to the admission at once of Kansas as a state with the Lecompton constitution. It included a large bribe in the shape of a land grant of 3,000,000 acres. English's bill was carried in both Houses by means of bribery, and every species of pressure which the Government could bring to bear on members. But the free-soil men of Kansas were too staunch to be bribed, too wary to be tricked. When English's compromise came down to the territory, and was submitted to a vote, they rejected it by a majority of 10,000.

This victory was held to be a decisive one by all but the most extreme border ruffians, and Mr. President

Buchanan and his Government. Many of the Southern settlers moved out of the territory, taking their human chattels with them.

In the northern part of Kansas, where the towns are frequent, and the free-soilers thickly settled, the game was up for the border ruffians. But in the southern parts, in the thinly settled prairies around Ossowotomie, and at Hickory Point, the reign of terror had not come to an end. Notwithstanding the activity and energy of Montgomery and his men, the raids of the Missourians were still frequent and destructive. In May, 1858, a band of mounted Missourians came upon a settlement, known as "The Trading Post," in Lynn county. They seized eleven free-soil men who were quietly at work or in their houses, carried them to an out-of-the-way ravine, and there drew them up in line and shot them. Five were killed, five badly wounded, while one escaped unhurt by falling with the rest and feigning death. The murderers escaped across the border. The new Governor of Kansas, Denver, another rigorous pro-slavery man, was roused by the atrocity of this wholesale murder. He is said to have sent a requisition to the Governor of Missouri for the delivery of the murderers, and proceeded himself to the seat of war with a view to seeing right done. No notice was taken of the requisition, if made, and his zeal soon cooled. But this outrage hastened the return of old Captain Brown from the Eastern states, where he had been to organise the attempt on Virginia, in which he lost his life. The fame of the old

Captain, and the activity of Montgomery, turned the scale again, and kept Southern Kansas comparatively undisturbed for some months, and a sort of armistice was established between the rival factions by Denver just before his resignation, which he sent in in the autumn, after a nine months' experience of ruling Kansas.

This armistice was broken by the pro-slavery men, who seized a free-soiler illegally, and carried him off to Fort Scott, the border ruffian stronghold, situate on the south-east corner of the territory, and close to the Missouri frontier. The free-soilers first asked peacefully for his release. This was refused. In the early morning of December 17th, Montgomery, with seventy men, attacked and entered Fort Scott, and released the prisoner, killing one pro-slavery man in the fight. Next day, meetings were held all along the Missouri border to organise another invasion of Kansas. They were anticipated. It was time,—so thought the freesoilers,—to teach Missouri that if she wanted war, she could have it at home. On the night of December 20th, old Captain Brown (in answer to an appeal from some slaves who were about to be sold), crossed into Missouri with fourteen men, freed and carried off eleven slaves. One pro-slavery man who resisted was killed. The audacity of this deed caused a panic in Missouri. In most of the border counties slaves were sent away from the neighbourhood of the frontier. The Governor of Missouri offered 1000 dollars reward for Brown's apprehension, to which President Buchanan added 250 dollars. Medary, the new Governor of Kansas, sent officers into the southern territory to arrest Brown and Montgomery. But in those parts the feeling was so strong against the one-sided action of the United States Government, and the two free-state leaders were so popular with the free-settlers, so dreaded and hated by the pro-slavery men and their Missourian neighbours and allies, that nothing was done. Governor Medary's emissaries saw full well that it would be hopeless to attempt anything, unless they could secure the help of a *posse* of the settlers, and they might wait long enough before they were likely to manage that. So they hovered about the neighbourhood, while old Captain Brown lived quietly on for a month at the Trading Post with the negroes he had rescued, organising the journey to Canada which he was about to undertake with his convoy. On January 20th, 1859, he started with the negroes, four white men, who had now devoted themselves to his schemes, and a band of some twenty Topeka boys, who would see him safely over the first 300 or 400 miles of his perilous journey.*

* On leaving the territory, he sent the following letter to the editors of the Kansas and some Eastern papers:—

"TRADING POST, KANSAS,
"*January*, 1859.

"GENTLEMEN,—You will greatly oblige a humble friend by allowing the use of your columns, while I briefly state two parallels in my poor way.

"Not one year ago, eleven quiet citizens of this neighbourhood (here he adds their names) were gathered up from their work and their homes by an armed force under one Hamilton, and, without trial, or opportunity to speak in their own defence, were formed into line, and, all but one, shot—five killed and five wounded.

He carried the eleven negroes, and a baby who had been born since their rescue, and christened Captain John Brown, safely through Kansas, Nebraska, Iowa, and Michigan, to Canada, a distance of some 2500 miles, dogged through most part of the way by United States marshals. But the journey, interesting as it is, has nothing to do with our subject. The man who had done more than any other for the liberation of Kansas had now left it for good. But his work was done. From this time there was no more serious outbreak in the southern parts of the territory, though cases of kidnapping of coloured people by Missourians still not unfrequently occurred.

One fell unharmed, pretending to be dead. All were left for dead. The only crime charged against them was, that of being free-state men. Now I inquire what action has ever, since the occurrence, in May last, been taken, by either the President of the United States, the Governor of Missouri, the Governor of Kansas, or any of their tools, or by any pro-slavery or administration man, to ferret out and punish the perpetrators of this crime?

"Now for the other parallel. On Sunday, Dec. 19th, a negro man, called Jem, came over to the Osage settlement from Missouri, and stated that he, together with his wife, two children, and another negro man, was to be sold within a day or two, and begged for help to get away. On Monday (the following) night, two small companies were made up to go to Missouri and liberate the five slaves, together with other slaves. One of these companies I assumed to direct. We proceeded to the place, surrounded the buildings, liberated the slaves, and also took certain property supposed to belong to the estate. We, however, learned before leaving, that a portion of the articles we had taken belonged to a man living on the plantation as a tenant, who was supposed to have no interest in the estate. We promptly returned to him all we had taken. We then went to another plantation, where we found five more slaves, took some property

The last act of the drama in the territory had now come. In February the territorial legislature met and passed a general amnesty for all past offences growing out of the partisan warfare, and an act calling a convention for the framing of a new state constitution. This convention met at Wyandote, and prepared a constitution, in all essentials the same as the old Topeka constitution. It disfranchised the resident coloured people, but an attempt by the Democrats to forbid negroes and mulattoes to enter the state, and to make void all contracts which might be made with any who should come in, was defeated.

and two white men. We moved all slowly away into the territory for some distance, and then sent back the two white men, telling them to follow us as soon as they chose to do so. The other company freed one female slave, took some property, and, as I am informed, killed one white man (the master), who fought against the liberation.

"Now for a comparison. Eleven persons are forcibly restored to their natural and inalienable rights, with but one man killed, and all hell is stirred from beneath. It is currently reported that the Governor of Missouri has made a requisition to the Governor of Kansas for the delivery of all such as were concerned in the last-named 'dreadful outrage.' The Marshal of Kansas is said to be collecting a posse of Missouri (not Kansas) men at West Point, in Missouri, a little town about ten miles distant, to 'enforce the laws.' All pro-slavery, conservative free-state, and dough-face men and administration tools are filled with holy horror.

"Consider the two cases, and the action of the administration party.—Respectfully yours, JOHN BROWN."

I give this letter verbatim, in the belief that it will make you understand the state of affairs and the feelings of parties in the disturbed districts, better than anything I can say. I do not, of course, defend the conduct of the free-state men in the transaction, though I can quite understand, and, to a great extent, sympathize with it.

One cannot but feel disappointed that the free-soil people of Kansas, who had gone through so fiery a trial, should not at last have known how to be thoroughly generous and liberal. But let us make allowances, and try to put ourselves in the place of the men whom we are wont to judge so strictly. Kansas had suffered fearful things for four years and more in the struggle against the slave power. Though her citizens would stand out for their *principles* to the death, very many of them looked on the blacks as the cause of all their miseries, and, ungenerously, no doubt, but very naturally, wished to be rid of them altogether; while the advanced Republicans, though the strongest body in Kansas, still felt themselves on tender ground, and, having gained so much, did not like to push matters too far, and were content to give and take. The new constitution was submitted to the people in October and ratified, and in December the state officers were chosen—Robinson, governor; Lane and Conway, senators; the very men who had been chosen for the same offices under the Topeka constitution four years back.

The state constitution was sent to Washington. In February the territorial legislature again passed a bill abolishing slavery in the territory. It was too early in the session for the Governor to repeat his ingenious plan for throwing it over. Driven to a choice between his masters at Washington and his duty to Kansas, he decided to stand by the former, and vetoed the bill. But the legislature immediately re-passed it by more than the two-thirds majority necessary for over-ruling the governor's veto. And so slavery came to an end in Kansas, and the lie was given to Mr. Buchanan's statement in his presidential message that " Kansas is to-day, by virtue of the constitution, a slave state as much as Georgia or South Carolina."

In Congress in this same February, Mr. Seward in the senate, and Mr. Parrott (Kansas delegate) in the House of Representatives, brought in bills for the admission of Kansas as a free state to the Union. The factious struggle which was made by the Democrats to prevent the passing of these bills is of little interest to us here. I need only tell you that the good cause prevailed at last, and in January, 1861, Kansas was at last acknowledged and admitted to the Union as a free state.

This is the story I had to tell you. I believe I have in no single instance endeavoured to screen or shield the free-state settlers. I am sure that I have not only not over-stated, but have given you a very favourable view of the action of the pro-slavery party, and of the governments of Presidents Pierce and Buchanan. I told you at the outset that the struggle in Kansas was the beginning of the present war. I said so because, though there was a lull of nearly a year between the pacification of Kansas and secession, it was in Kansas that the South came out in its true colours; in Kansas that the North learned finally and thoroughly what they had to expect from the slave power; over the Kansas question of the Lecompton

Constitution (the slave constitution, which its framers had never dared to submit to the people's vote, but had tried to force on the people by the help of the government) that the great Democratic party broke up hopelessly, when Douglas ratted, and the anti-Lecompton Democrats joined their votes to those of the Republicans.

But for the struggle in Kansas, the Republicans would, in all likelihood, have been beaten in the election for President. But for the struggle in Kansas, the platform on which Abraham Lincoln came in, would not have been the accepted one with the North.

What was that platform? I tell you again, as I told many of you before in our common room, that the very essence of it—that without which it would have been meaningless and powerless—was, the limitation of slavery, the deliverance of all the remaining territories from the curse which had cost Kansas four years' war.

The free-trade question which I have heard urged here, as well as elsewhere, as the true cause of Secession, was unheard of in America, and invented by the South for English consumption. Look at all the ordinances of Secession; see what the slave states at home, speaking to their own people, in documents on which everything hung, see what they say as to their own meaning. I ask you only to judge them out of their own mouths, by their own most solemn utterances. The more you will study the question, the more will this truth come home to you, that the Confederate states have seceded because they found that the North would no longer permit the extension of slavery in the territories of the United States. I ask you, therefore, not to let the very natural indignation of the present moment* lead you away from the true bearings, the real merits, of this great struggle. I am quite sure that in a few years—I hope, in a few months—there will not be one of us who will not regret any sympathy which he may have felt for, any aid, however small, which he may have lent by speech, action, or thought, to a confederacy, which, in the year 1861, sets itself up on the avowed corner-stone of Slavery, and comes to the nations of the earth asking to be acknowledged and recognized by them, admitted into their fellowship, with that mark on its forehead.

* December, 1861.

APPENDIX.—THE AMERICAN CENSUS OF 1860.

PART I.—POPULATION AND REPRESENTATION.

STATES.	Whites.	Free Coloured.	Total Free.	Slaves.	Aggregate.	Representatives in 38th Congress.
Alabama	526,534	2,630	529,164	435,132	964,296	6
Arkansas	324,186	137	324,323	111,104	435,427	3
California	376,200	3,816	380,016	......	380,016	3
Connecticut	451,609	8,542	460,151	......	460,151	4
Delaware	90,697	19,723	110,420	1,798	112,218	1
Florida	77,778	908	78,686	61,753	140,439	1
Georgia	591,638	3,459	595,097	462,232	1,057,329	7
Illinois	1,704,684	7,069	1,711,753	......	1,711,753	13
Indiana	1,340,072	10,869	1,350,941	......	1,350,941	11
Iowa	673,925	1,023	674,948	......	674,948	5
Kansas	106,487	623	107,110	......	107,110	1
Kentucky	920,077	10,146	930,223	225,490	1,155,713	8
Louisiana	357,642	18,638	376,280	333,010	709,290	5
Maine	627,081	1,195	628,276	......	628,276	5
Maryland	516,128	83,718	599,846	87,188	687,034	5
Massachusetts	1,221,611	9,454	1,231,065	......	1,231,065	10
Michigan	742,289	6,823	749,112	......	749,112	6
Minnesota	161,793	229	162,022	......	162,022	1
Mississippi	353,969	731	354,700	436,696	791,396	5
Missouri	1,064,369	2,983	1,067,352	114,965	1,182,317	9
New Hampshire	325,622	450	326,072	......	326,072	3
New Jersey	647,084	24,947	672,031	......	672,031	5
Carried over	13,201,475	218,113	13,419,588	2,269,368	15,688,956	117

POPULATION AND REPRESENTATION—continued.

STATES.	Whites.	Free Coloured.	Total Free.	Slaves.	Aggregate.	Representatives in 38th Congress.
Brought over	13,201,475	218,113	13,419,588	2,269,368	15,688,956	117
New York	3,839,544	47,998	3,887,542	......	3,887,542	31
North Carolina	631,489	30,097	661,586	331,081	992,667	7
Ohio	2,303,374	36,225	2,339,599	......	2,339,599	18
Oregon	52,343	121	52,464	......	52,464	1
Pennsylvania	2,849,997	56,373	2,906,370	......	2,906,370	23
Rhode Island	170,703	3,918	174,621	......	174,621	1
South Carolina	291,623	9,648	301,271	402,541	703,812	4
Tennessee	826,828	7,235	834,063	275,784	1,109,847	8
Texas	421,411	339	421,750	180,682	602,432	4
Vermont	314,534	582	315,116	......	315,116	2
Virginia	1,047,613	57,579	1,105,192	490,887	1,596,079	11
Wisconsin	774,392	1,481	775,873	......	775,873	6
	26,725,326	469,709	27,195,035	3,950,343	31,145,378	233
TERRITORIES:						
Colorado	34,153	44	34,197	......	34,197	
Dakota	4,839	......	4,839	......	4,839	
Nebraska	28,755	71	28,826	10	28,836	
Nevada	6,803	54	6,857	......	6,857	
New Mexico	93,447	70	93,517	24	93,541	
Utah	40,236	30	40,266	29	40,295	
Washington	11,548	30	11,578	......	11,578	
Dist. of Columbia	60,788	11,107	71,895	3,181	75,076	
	27,005,895	481,115	27,487,010	3,953,587	31,440,597	

PART II.—RATIO OF INCREASE OF THE POPULATION, AND ALTERATIONS IN THE REPRESENTATION, BETWEEN 1850 AND 1860.

States.	Whites.	Free Coloured.		Total Free.	Slaves.		Aggregate.	Representation.	
								Loss.	Gain.
Alabama	23·45	16·11		23·41	26·92		24·97	1	..
Arkansas	99·88	77·47	Loss	99·22	135·89		107·45	..	1
California	310·54	296·67		310·40			310·40	..	1
Connecticut	24·37	11·04		24·10			24·10	..	..
Delaware	27·44	9·13		23·73	21·48	Loss	22·60	..	..
Florida	64·77	2·58	Loss	63·47	57·09		60·60	..	..
Georgia	13·43	18·01		13·46	21·10		16·68	1	..
Illinois	101·49	30·04		101·04			101·04	..	4
Indiana	37·14	3·49	Loss	36·68			36·68	..	..
Iowa	251·22	207·21		251·14			251·14	..	3
Kansas								..	1
Kentucky	20·84	1·35		20·59	6·87		17·64	2	..
Louisiana	39·98	6·73		37·85	36·03		36·99	..	1
Maine	7·78	11·87	Loss	7·73			7·73	1	..
Maryland	23·49	12·04		21·76	3·52	Loss	17·84	1	..
Massachusetts	23·96	4·30		23·79			23·79	1	..
Michigan	87·89	164·15		88·38			88·38	..	..
Minnesota	2579·58	487·18		2566·15			2566·15	..	2
Mississippi	19·70	21·40	Loss	19·57	40·93		30·48	..	1
Missouri	79·79	13·94		79·50	31·51		73·35	..	2
New Hampshire	2·57	13·46	Loss	2·55			2·55	..	..

RATIO OF INCREASE OF POPULATION, &c.—*continued.*

STATES.	Whites.	Free Coloured.	Total Free.	Slaves.	Aggregate.	Representation. Loss.	Representation. Gain.
New Jersey	39·00	4·77	37·34		37·34		
New York	25·95	Loss 2·18	25·51		25·51	2	
North Carolina	14·19	9·59	13·97	14·74	14·23	1	
Ohio	17·82	43·30	18·14		18·14	3	
Oregon	299·96	Loss 41·54	294·64		294·64		
Pennsylvania	26·20	5·12	25·71		25·71	2	
Rhode Island	18·65	6·76	18·35		18·35	1	
South Carolina	6·21	7·68	6·26	4·56	5·28	2	
Tennessee	9·25	12·66	9·28	15·17	10·68	2	
Texas	173·58	Loss 14·61	173·10	210·66	183·37		2
Vermont	0·36	Loss 18·94	0·32		0·32	1	
Virginia	17·08	5·97	16·44	3·88	12·27	2	
Wisconsin	154·10	133·22	154·06		154·06		3
	37·46	10·68	36·89	23·42	35·02		
TERRITORIES.							
New Mexico	51·83		51·94		51·98		
Utah	254·38		254·64	11·53	254·07		
Dist. of Columbia	60·22	10·41	49·78	Loss 13·72	45·25		
	38·11	10·74	37·52	23·38	35·57		

APPENDIX.

[N.B. From the above tables it would appear that the ratios of increase in population as between the free and slave states and territories, and as between the border slave states—Delaware, Maryland, Virginia, Kentucky, Missouri, and the district of Columbia,—and the remaining states and territories, are as follows :—

	Whites.	Free coloured.	Total free.	Slaves.	Aggregate.
FREE STATES	42·10	13·04	40·94	..	40·94
Border Slave States	33·30	9·09	31·91	6·59	26·13
Other Slave States	29·70	8·22	29·29	29·66	29·44
Slave States generally	31·29	8·84	30·93	23·39	28·14

Thus, 1st. The white, the free, and the total population increase in the free states, as compared with the slave states generally, and with the non-border slave states in particular, in the ratio of 4 to 3, or more.

2nd. The white population increases in the border slave states, as compared with the others, in the ratio of not quite 11 to 9, but the slave population decreases in the ratio of nearly 1 to 5, giving a smaller total increase by about 26 to 29.

3rd. The slave population in the non-border slave states increases more rapidly than the free, and within a trifle as fast as the white.]

INDEX.

ABERDEEN, Lord, on slavery, 208, 209.
Abolitionists, 281, 286, 289; sought to be excluded from Kansas, 327 and foll., 340 and foll.
Adams, John, Vice-President, 54; President, 63 and foll.; his death, 128.
Adams, John Quincy, Secretary of State, 96, 118; President, 122, and foll.; his death, 224.
Address, President's, Jefferson substitutes message for, 68, and see *Inaugural*.
Africa, colonization of, 95-6; United States' squadron on the coast of, 207, 285.
Alabama, admitted as state, 98; protests against high tariff, 135; Indian governments in, disallowed, 169; delegates from, advocate open slave trade, 264; votes for Breckenridge, 300; secedes, 302; and see Appendix.
Algiers, corsairs from, 60; war with, 95.
Alison, Sir A., quoted, 85, 93.
Alleghanies, how slavery came to cross, 47, 48.
Amelia Island, occupation of, 97.
Amendment of constitution, provision for, 37; amendments passed, 39-40; proposed, 230, 290.
American doctrine, the, of Monroe, 120; party, 257, 258; it puts forward Fillmore as candidate, 262.
Anderson, Major, 302.
Annapolis, commissioners meet at, 22.
Anti-slavery societies and efforts, 166, 167.
Appropriations, the struggle as to, under Pierce, 261.

Arizona, slaves introduced into, 286.
Arkansas river, 323; — territory, organised, 98; cession to Cherokees out of, 126; admitted as state, 171; and see Appendix.
Articles of Confederation, 17, 18.
Artillery, permanent, established, 65.
Ashburton, Lord, and his treaty, 207; and see Additions and Corrections.
Astoria, 72.
Atchison (border ruffian), 330, 353, 364, 365.
Attorney-General, see *Crittenden*, *Cushing*.
Augusta convention, 182.
Austria, difficulties with, 243, 244, 254.

BALTIMORE, Lord, and Maryland, 5; — City, riot at, 83; British attempt on, 84; adjourned Democratic convention at, 294, 297; Union convention at, 294, 295.
Barbaresques, see *Algiers* and *Tripoli*.
Bancroft, Mr., Secretary of Navy, 212; referred to, 17 *n*., 45.
Bank of the United States (first), 54; national, Federalists favourable to, 60; (old) Republicans against, 61; dangers of, 156, 157; of the United States, Jackson's struggle with, 158, and foll.; revived as "United States Bank of Pennsylvania," 178, 179; its break up, 203-205.
Banks, Mr., elected Speaker, 258.
Barron, Commodore, 77.
Bay Islands, 254, 255.
Bayonne Decree, 79.

INDEX.

Bear-flag of California, 217.
Bedini, Monsignor, 253.
Bell, Mr., of Tennessee, condemns Buchanan as to Kansas, 276; candidate for Presidency, 294, 295; votes given for, 360.
Benjamin, Mr., of Louisiana, 294.
Benton, Col., 116, 122, 210, 223, 225; his daughter's runaway match, 206; his family, its influence in St. Louis, 281; quoted or referred to, 93, 103, 117, 121, 136, 142, 148, 164, 170, 182, 183, 202, 203, 205, 213, 214, 215, 246; and see Preface.
Berkeley, Vice-Admiral, 77, 78.
Berlin Decree, 79, 83.
Bible, the, and the fugitive slave law, 241.
Biddle, Nicholas, 178, 179, 203, 205; and see "*Bank of the United States.*"
Biglow Papers, 221, 222, 226.
Black Hawk's war, 170; Mr. Lincoln serves in, 296; — Warrior, the, 250.
Blair, republican representative of St. Louis, 298.
Blue Lodge, the, 331, 332, 337, 344, 365.
Bogus legislature in Kansas, 338, and foll. 166, 368; sanctioned by Pierce, 344, 350.
Boone, Daniel, 295.
Border slave-states, at revolution, 8; support protection, 137; antislavery feeling in, 166, 298; — Ruffians (Kansas), 330, 345, 355, and foll.; sack Ossowotomie, 359, 360, 364, 365; their massacre at the "Trading Post," 372.
Boston, Garrison mobbed at, 166, 167; anti-fugitive-slave-law riots at, 242.
Braddock, General, 53.
Branson (Kansas free-soiler), 345-346.
Brazil, differences with, 253.
Breckenridge, Mr., Vice-President, 261; candidate for Presidency, 297; votes given for, 300.
Bright, Mr., of Indiana, 200.
Broke, Captain, 86 and foll.
Brooks, Mr., assailant of Mr. Sumner, 259, 260, 264.

Brown, senator, of Mississippi, 284; — John, 286, 347, 348, 363; organises free-soilers in Kansas, 356, 357; two of his sons seized by border-ruffians, 359, 360; defends Ossowotomie, 364, 365; defends Lawrence, 366; succeeded by Montgomery as chief of the free-soilers, 369; his last proceedings in Kansas, 372, and foll.; letter by him, 374, *n.*; his Harper's Ferry attempt, 287, 288; his companions executed, 290.
Buchanan, James, Foreign Secretary, 212; takes part in Ostend Conference, 250 (see Additions and Corrections); elected President, 261, 262; his Presidency, 271, and foll.; his treatment of Kansas, 369, 373; his last message, 300, 301.
Buckley and Coleman (Missourians), murder Dow, 345, 346.
Buena Vista, battle of, 217.
Buford, Col. (Missourian), 350, 353, 363.
Bulwer, Sir Henry, 230, 231.
Burr, Aaron, Vice-President, 68; kills Col. Hamilton, 72; his conspiracy, 72.

CALHOUN, J. C., supports protection, 95; Secretary of War, 96; supports Missouri compromise, 116; Vice-President, 122, 130; advocates low tariff, 123; his toast at the Jefferson banquet, 136; supports Clay's compromise tariff, 145; his nullification resolutions, 146; adopts slavery as ground of southern Union, 148; establishes pro-slavery paper, &c., 165; advocates recognition of Texas, 168, 169; his resolutions against intermeddling with slavery, 183; Secretary of State, 202, 203, 209; refuses nomination for Presidency, 212; speaks against Mexican war, 216; his resolutions on slavery and the territories, 219, 220; threatens disunion, 222, 223; endeavours to carry slavery into territories, 226, 227; his last speech, 229; his death, 230.

INDEX. 389

California (Upper), declared republic by Fremont, 217; annexed to United States, 218; ceded by Mexico, 221; question of slavery as to, 222, 223; excludes slavery, 224; question of admitting as state, 228 and foll.; admission of, 231; Know-nothings carry elections in, 258; vigilance committee of, 260; votes for Lincoln, 299; and see Appendix.

California, Lower, Walker's attempt to revolutionize, 249.

Campbell, governor, of Virginia, 189, 190.

Canada, originally French, 2; invaded by the Americans, 84; fugitive slaves in, and escapes to, 126, 263, 375; insurrection in, and American sympathizers, 184, 185.

Canadian reciprocity treaty, 251.

Canal between Atlantic and Pacific, proposed, 127; Clayton-Bulwer convention as to the, 230, 231.

Capitol, congress meets at, 67; burnt by English, 84; Governor Wise threatens to seize, 261.

Carolina, early dominion of Spain over, 2; Locke's constitution for, 5.

Carolina, North, protests against tariff, 135; representation in, 194; committee of legislature of, on slavery, 242, 243; and see Appendix.

Carolina, South, exports of, in 1801, 74; supports first protective tariff, 95; Jackson born in, 131; petitions against tariff, 135; nullification ordinance by, 137, and foll.; cost of slave's keep in, 151, n.; notices of trade of, 1760 to 1832, 182, 183; proportion of churches in, 191; representation in, 193, 194; secession advocated in legislature of, 232; ranks 15th by population in 1850, 240; incensed by opposition to fugitive slave-law, 242, 243; opening of slave trade discussed in, 264, 285; under martial law after Harper's Ferry attempt, 287; votes $100,000 for arms, &c., 289, 290; effects of last census on, 298; Governor of, recommends measures for leaving Union, 299; hoists Palmetto flag, 300; convention of, decrees separation, 301; seizes Fort Moultrie, 302; flag of, hoisted in Kansas, 354; and see Appendix.

Caroline, burning of the, 185.

Carroll, Charles, 172.

Cartwright, Dr., his Dysæsthesia Æthiopica, 108, 109.

Cass, Lewis, Secretary at War, 136; candidate for Presidency, 226; in favour of free Kansas, 263; Secretary of State, 273; resigns, 301, 302.

Census, United States, first, 55; second, 66; third, 95; fourth, 101; seventh, 237; last, 298, and see Appendix; — Kansas, first, 334.

Central America, 230, 261, 289.

Cerrogordo, battle of, 217.

Chapultepec, battle of, 217.

Charleston, negro conspiracy in, 118; decay of, 123; convention at, 182; negroes of "Echo" taken to, 279, 280; democratic convention at, 293, 294; meeting at, votes secession, 300.

Cherokee Indians, treaty with, 19; civilization among, 125; cession to, of territory in Arkansas, 126; coerced into removal, 170; what they got for it, 171.

"Chesapeake," "Leopard" and, 76, 77; and "Shannon," 86 and foll.

Chicago, Republican convention at, 295-297.

Chickasaws, removal of, 170.

Chihuahua, part of, ceded by Mexico, 249; Buchanan recommends protectorate over, 283.

Chippewa, battle of, 84.

Choctaws, removal of, 170, 171.

Church accommodation in South, 191; disruption by slavery of Methodist Episcopal, and Baptist, 229.

Churubusco, battle of, 217.

Cincinnati, democratic convention at, 261, 293.

"Circle, knights of the golden," 298.

Citizens of one state entitled to privileges of citizenship in all, 36;

390 INDEX.

men of colour treated as, by Jefferson, Madison, Monroe, 78; by Jackson, 90; discussion of the question on the admission of Missouri, 116; Indians generally cannot have rights of, 125; Wyandots not allowed to become, 234; free negroes denied to be, in Dred Scott case, 264, and foll.

Clay, Henry, urges war with England, 80; devises Missouri compromise, 116; Secretary of State, 122; combines with Calhoun against Jackson, 136; leads protectionists, 121, 137; defeated candidate for Presidency, 145, 210; his compromise tariff, 148; carries censure on Jackson, 160; Madison's letter to, 164; modifies Calhoun's slavery resolutions, 183; withdraws from public life, 202; trims on Texas question, 210; against annexing whole of Mexico, 221; his "omnibus bill," 228-232; demands increased powers to enforce fugitive slave law, 243; his death, 246; — Cassius M., 298.

Clayton, Mr., Secretary of State, 226, 231;—Bulwer treaty, 230, 231, 254.

Cobb, Mr. T. R. R., of Georgia, quoted, 113, 114, 154, 189, 192; on the labour problem, 314; — Mr. Howell, 243, 273, 285-301.

Code, Bogus, of Kansas, 340, 341, 350.

Coleman, see *Buckley*.

Colour, men of, seized on board "Chesapeake," 77, 78; Jackson's proclamation to, 90; provisions of Missouri Constitution as to, 116; school attendance amongst, at North, 190, 191; dismay of, at fugitive slave law, 242; citizenship of, denied in Dred Scott case, 264, and foll.; provision of Oregon and Kansas Constitutions against, 275, 276, 342.

Columbia district ceded to United States, 55; Congress removed to, 67; Jackson recommends representation of, in Congress, 133;

question of abolishing slavery in, 165, 223, 229; Anti-duelling Act for, 184; — river, descended by Lewis and Clark, 72; military post at mouth of, 119; emigration to, 205; territory, joint occupation of, terminated, 213.

Compromise, see *Missouri, Clay, Crittenden*.

Confederation, the 17-20; Jackson upon, 138; project of forming Southern, with Texas, 209; Walker's proposed, 262; the Southern, formed, 303.

Conference, the Ostend, 250 (and see Additions and Corrections); the Paris, 266, 267.

Congress, under Confederation, 17 and foll.; under Constitution, 24 and foll.; limitations to powers of, 30, 39; first, 52; removes to Washington, 67; Southern, proposed, 232.

Connecticut, emancipates slaves, 46; refuses contingent for war with England, 90; laws of, 240; member from, expelled from House, 271; and see Appendix.

Constitution, the American, growth of, 21, 22; analysis of, 23 and foll.; amendments to, 39-40; why weak, 41 and foll.; tone of, in respect to slavery, 51; Jackson upon, 139 and foll., 175; proposed to be extended to territories, 226, 227; Missouri compromise held contrary to, 265; position of Supreme Court in reference to, 268, 269; amendment to, urged by South, 290; — of the Confederate States, 303; — of Kansas, see *Lecompton, Topeka, Wyandot*.

Consul, Spanish, insulted, 244, 245; dismissal of English, 253, 254.

Consumption in slave states, 150 and foll.

Contreras, battle of, 217.

Conventions, 12; the Hartford, 91; nullification of South Carolina, 137, 146; proposed Southern, for Texas or disunion, 209, 210; the presidential, Benton on, 211, 212; of slave states, at Nash-

INDEX. 391

ville, 1850, 232; abolitionist, at Syracuse, &c., 242; Southern, 243; Know-nothing, 258; Democratic, of Cincinnati, 261; commercial, at Savannah, 264; Democratic, of Charleston, 293; do., adjourned to Baltimore, 294, 297; Union, of Baltimore, 294; Republican, of Chicago, 295; Secession, of South Carolina, 301; Free-soil, of Kansas, 342, 368; Bogus, of do., 368; — Diplomatic, see *Treaties*.

Convicts, in Virginia, 6.
Conway, Mr., of Kansas, 338, 339, 377.
Cornwallis, Lord, surrenders, 19.
Costa Rica, 230, 254.
Cotton, first export of, 63; export of, from South Carolina in 1801, 74; abattis at New Orleans, 90; development of growth and export of, 102; states, condition of, 151, 152; famine, Biddle's attempt to create, 178; districts, condition of slaves in, 192, 193, n.
Covode, Mr., of Pennsylvania, 291.
Crampton, Mr., dismissed, 254.
Creeks, wars with, 56, 57, 94, 131, 170; treaty for removal of, 124; removal of, 171.
Creole, case of the, 206.
Crimean war, 253.
Crisis, financial, under Van Buren, 178; under Buchanan, 277.
Crittenden, Mr., Attorney-General, 230; condemns Buchanan as to Kansas, 274; proposes compromise, 301.
Cuba, piratical expedition against, 228; insurrection in, 244, 245; proposed treaty guaranteeing, 245; question of annexing or purchasing, 249-251, 283, 284, 289; Walker's designs on, 262.
Currency, tobacco, 7; see Specie, Bank.
Curtis, Mr. Justice, 266.
Cushing, Caleb, 248, 249, 251.

DALLAS, Mr., envoy to England, 254.
Davis, Mr. Jefferson, and Missis-

sippi repudiation, 181; protests against admission of California, 231; Secretary of War, 248; is for obtaining Cuba at any price, 251; asks for slavery-protection code for territories, 286; his resolutions on duty of protecting slavery, 290, 291; President of Confederate States, 303; — Mr., of Massachusetts, defeats Wilmot proviso, 218.
Debt, notices of American, under confederation, 20; under Washington, 54; under Jefferson, 71; under Madison, 93; practically extinct under Jackson, 171; of states, Van Buren on, 180; of Texas, 210, 228.
Decatur, Commodore, 92, 95.
Declaration of Independence, 12 and foll.; formulas from, in state constitutions, 46, 99; Jackson upon, 138; death of last signer of, 172.
De Haven, Lieutenant, his expedition in search of Franklin, 235.
Delaware, Swedes in, 4; included in grant of Pennsylvania, *ibid.*; supports protection; 121, 137; republican committees in, 298; votes for Bell, 300; — Indians, 233; protest against encroachments in Kansas, 328; decline to vote in ditto, 331; and see Appendix.
Democratic party elects Jackson, 130; Van Buren, 172; Convention, chooses Polk, 211; puts forward Cass, 226; elects Pierce, 248; elects Buchanan, 261; party broken up at Charleston Convention, 293, 294; Convention at Baltimore, 297; in Kansas, 343, 367.
Denmark, treaty with, 19; refusal to renew Sound Dues treaties with, 253; convention with, 273.
Denvir, Governor of Kansas, 372, 373.
Deserters, search for, 75 and foll.; from Federal army, 142.
Dixon, Mr., of Kentucky, 324.
Dominican republic, treaty with, 252; and see Additions and Corrections.

Donaldson (Marshal, of Kansas), 354, 362.
Doniphan, Colonel, takes possession of New Mexico, 217.
Douglas, Mr., of Illinois, slaveholder, 200; member of order of "Lone Star," 245; brings in Kansas-Nebraska Bill, 255; called the "Little Giant," 259; candidate for Presidency, 261, 293; against Lecompton Constitution, 274, 370; his opposition to Buchanan, 282, 285, 290; breaks up Baltimore Convention, 294; competed with by Lincoln for Senatorship, 296; "goes the stump" through South, 298; defeated, 300;—Frederick, fugitive slave, 242.
Dow (Kansas free-soiler) murdered, 345.
Dred Scott case, 264-269, 273, 274, 282, 294.
Duelling, Act against, 183.
Dutch, the, in New York and New Jersey, 4.
Dysæsthesia Æthiopica, 108, 109.

"ECHO," slaver, taken by "Dolphin," 279.
Education at the South, 189 and foll.
Election of senators and representatives, 24, 25; of President and Vice-President, 31, 32; of Jefferson by House of Representatives, 68; of J. Q. Adams by ditto, 122; the Buchanan, 261, 262; the Lincoln, 293 and foll.; in Kansas, 329 and foll., 369, 370.
Emancipation, early acts for, 46; in district of Columbia, discussed, 165; in Virginia, discussed, 166; in Mexico (including Texas), 168.
Embargoes, 60, 79, 81, 82.
Emigrant Aid societies, 327, 328, 338.
England, colonization of the United States from, 1 and foll.; history of, contrasted with American, 11; treaty with, 19; another rejected by Jefferson, 93; Federalist party leans to, 60; John Adams first ambassador to, 65; differences with, as to search for deserters, 74 and foll.; makes amends for affair of the "Chesapeake," 78, 81; orders in council of, 79; difficulties with (1809), 81; war with, 82 and foll.; peace with, 91; negotiations with, as to slave-trade, 118; convention with, as to North-West Coast, &c., 126, 127; treaty with, as to West India trade, 171, 172; difficulties with (1837-8), 184, 185; recognizes Texas, 185; difficulties with, as to Oregon boundary, 212-214; treaty with, as to ditto, 214; Clayton-Bulwer Convention with, 230, 231; differences with (1852), 245, 246; ditto as to violation of neutrality in Crimean war, 253, 254; ditto as to Vancouver's Island, 289.
English, Mr., his ordinance as to Kansas, 275, 371.
Excise, insurrection against, 58, 59.
Expunging resolution, the, 177, 178.

FAIRFAX, Lord, Washington surveys for, 52;—county, in Virginia, 112.
Federal power under Constitution, 41, 43; party, 60 and foll.; ditto dies out, 96; authority, Jackson upon, 143, 144, 174, 175; officers imprisoned by State courts, 274, 285; courts of justice disregarded by Mormonites, 276; officers ordered to oppose Douglas, 293; employés in South Carolina resign, 300; forts, &c., seized by Secessionists, 302; troops called in, in Kansas, 351 and foll., 363, 364, &c.
"Federalist," the, 80; party, see Federal.
Filibustering, 228, 244, 245, 249, 251, 252, 279, 284.
Fillmore, Millard, his Presidency, 230 and foll.; a candidate in 1856, 262; purpose of his candidateship, 292.
"Fire-eaters," 298, 299.
Florida, originally Spanish, 2; west of Perdido river, taken possession

INDEX. 393

of, 94; encroachments on, under Monroe, 97; negotiations with Spain for cession of, 97, 98 (and see Additions and Corrections); occupied, 118; Jackson, first governor of, 132; treaty for cession of, ratified by Mexico, 127; admitted as State, 225; votes for Breckenridge, 300; secedes, 302; and see *Seminoles*, and Appendix.

Floyd, Mr., Governor of Virginia, 242; Secretary of War, 273; accusations against, 277, 302.

France, share of, in colonizing United States, 1, 2; history of, contrasted with American, 9, 10; treaty with, 19; (old) Republican party leans to, 61; quarrel with, under Adams, 65; Louisiana purchased from, 71; decrees, &c., of, under Napoleon, 79, 81, 82; difficulties with, under Jackson, 161, 162; recognizes Texas, 185.

Franklin, Sir John, the search for, 235, 254; restoration of his ship, the Resolute, 262.

Free-soil party springs up, 224; puts forward Van Buren, 226; resists Kansas-Nebraska Bill, 256; in Missouri, 281; in Kansas, 257, 327, and foll.

Fremont, his exploring expeditions, 205, 206, 217, 224; declares California independent, 217; court-martialed, 224; senator for California, 231; Republican candidate for Presidency, 261, 262; his popularity in St. Louis, 281.

Frenchtown, General Winchester's surrender at, 84.

Fuca, straits of, 214; and see Additions and Corrections.

Fugitive slaves, no provision for recovering under Confederation, 18, 48; provision for ditto under Constitution, 36, 48; negotiations with England as to ditto, 126, 127; slave law, 232; effects of, discussed, 236 and foll.; resistance to, 242, 256, 274; made applicable to Kansas-Nebraska territories, 256; repealed by Massachusetts, 256, 257; set at nought by Vermont, Wisconsin, 286.

Functionaries, mischievous effects of excluding from Congress, 43, 44; elections of, by the slave-power, 188, 200.

GABRIEL, General's insurrection, 73.
Galapagos Islands, 253.
Galveston, buccaneering establishment at, 97.
Garrison, Wm. Lloyd, 166, 167, 301.
Geary, Governor (Kansas), 367, 368.
Genet, the French Minister, 61, 62.
Georgia, early history of, 4, 5; cession by, to Indians, 57; murders of Indians, by citizens of, 58; treaty for removal of Creeks from, 124; protests against tariff, 135; mint for gold region of, 162; Indian governments in, disallowed, 169; church accommodation in, 191; discountenances Southern Congress, 233; Mr. Howell Cobb heads Unionists in, 243; "Wanderer" lands slaves in, 285; secedes, 302; and see Appendix.
Ghent, peace of, 91.
Gold discovered in California, 218.
Great Britain, see *England*.
Great Salt Lake, 225; and see *Mormonites*.
Greytown, 245; bombarded, 251, 253.
Grinnell, Henry, his expeditions in search of Franklin, 235, 254.
Guadalupe Hidalgo, treaty of, 221.
Gwin, Mr., Senator for California, 231.

HABEAS CORPUS, the Constitution on, 30; Jackson's fine for disregarding, refunded, 204; and secession, 307; and see 274.
Hale, Mr., of New Hampshire, 254.
Hamilton, Col., head of Federalist party, 61; writes in "Federalist," 80; killed by Aaron Burr, 72; — General, of South Carolina, 243.
Hamlin, Mr., of Maine, 219.
Hammond, Governor, 313.

394 INDEX.

"Hard-shells" and "Soft-shells," 247.
Harney, General, occupies St. Juan, 289.
Harper's Ferry, John Brown's attempt on, 287, 289, 290.
Harrison, General, defeats Indians at Tippecanoe, 94; his Presidency, 201.
Hartford convention, 91.
Hawaii, see *Sandwich Islands.*
Hawthorne, Mr., his biographical puff of Pierce, 248.
Haydee, slaver, 280.
Hayti, Walker's designs on, 262.
Hazlett, execution of, 290.
Helper, Mr., of North Carolina, 288.
Hickman, Mr., of Pennsylvania, 292.
Hill, Mr., of New Hampshire, 165.
History, character of American, 9 and foll.
Hollins, Captain, bombards Grey Town, 251.
Honduras, English settlement at, 231; republic of, 254.
House of Representatives, constitution of, 24, 25; elects President when, 32; election of Jefferson, 68; J. Q. Adams, 122; supports Jackson against Bank, 160, 161; against receiving petition on slavery, 166; Wilmot proviso carried in, 218, 219; ditto, abandoned by, 224; Republican majority in, 258; expels members for selling votes, &c., 271.
Houston, General, President of Texas, 210; senator from ditto, 223; opposes disunion, 243, 301, 302; — Mr., Kansas free-soiler, 338, 339.
Howison, Mr., historian of Virginia, 190.
Hull, General, surrenders, 84.

ILLINOIS admitted as state, 98; War of Sacs and Foxes in, 170; exodus of Mormons from, 225; Douglas carries elections of, 282; Mr. Lincoln's connection with, 295, 296; and see Appendix.
Import Duties, why relied on, 50; first laid on for protection, 95;
danger of relying on, 123; and see *Tariff.*
Impressment, the question of, 75, 76, 93.
Improvements, internal, the question of, 121, 122, 133, 134; scarcity of, in slave states, 113, 114, 155.
"Inaugural," the, 68; Jefferson's, 69; Madison's, 81; Monroe's, 97; Jackson's, 132, 145; Van Buren's, 177; Polk's, 212; Taylor's, 227; Pierce's, 248; Buchanan's, 273.
Indiana, territory organized, 66; admitted as state, 95; carried by Democrats for Buchanan, 262; and see Appendix.
Indian Fund, the, 302.
Indians, their original condition, &c., 55 and foll.; Washington's policy towards, 58; peace with, under Jefferson, 71; wars and treaties with, under Madison, 84, 94; Monroe suggests removal of, 119; civilization among, dangerous, 124 and foll., 169; removal of, under Jackson, 169-171, 181, 233; in Kansas, 323, 328, 331; and see *Cherokees, Creeks, Kaskaskias, Seminoles, Kansas, Osages, Sacs and Foxes, Choctaws, Chickasaws, Wyandots, Delawares, Kaws.*
Ingraham, Captain, 254.
Insurrections, under Confederacy, 20; under Washington, 58, 59; of coloured men in Virginia, 73.
Iowa, admitted as state, 225; Republicans carry elections in, 282; emigration to Kansas through, 344, 369; slaves rescued through, 375; and see Appendix.
Irish labourers in slave states, 107; riots between, and Know-nothings or Protestants, 258.
Isthmus of Panama, 127, 230, 231, 262, 281, 283.
Iverson, Mr., of Georgia, 301.

JACKSON, General, commands at New Orleans, 89, 90; his proclamation, to men of colour, 90; occupies Pensacola and St. Mark's, 97; his presidency, 130 and foll.;

INDEX. 395

expunging of censure passed on, 177, 178; repayment of fine to, 204; his death, 176.
Japan, expedition to, 246.
Jefferson, Thomas, as to convicts in Virginia, 6; author of Declaration of Independence, 12; would exclude slavery from territories, 47; Secretary of State, 54; Vice-President, 63; discourages secession, 64; President, 68 and foll.; Madison adheres to views of, 80; his death, 128, 129; banquet in honour of, under Jackson, 135, 136; on slavery, 108.
Jessup, General, treacherously seizes Osceola, 182.
Jones, Sheriff (Kansas), 346-353; heads sack of Lawrence, 354.
July, Fourth of, 9, 15; deaths of J. Adams and Jefferson on, 128; of Monroe on, 172; kills General Taylor, 230; toasts, secessionist, 233.

KAMEHAMEHA IV., King of Sandwich Islands, 252.
Kane, Dr., 254.
Kansas Indians, cessions by, 124; — Nebraska-bill, 255, 256, 321, 324, 326, 333, 334; — the contest for, 257, 261, 263, 274, 276, 286, 324 and foll.; its importance, 378; nature of country, 323, 324; Mr. Seward's bill for admission of, 291, 292, 295; free-soilers triumph in, 369 and foll.; admitted as free state, 378; and see Appendix; — legion, 332.
Kaskaskias, cede rich territory, 71.
Kaw Indians and river, 323.
Kearney, General, annexes New Mexico, 217.
Kentucky, growth of, 46; admission of, as state, 54; supports protection, 121; negro conspiracy extending to, 263; Abraham Lincoln born in, 295; Republican committees in, 298; votes for Bell, 300; and see Appendix.
Kickapoo rangers, 343, 355.
King, Mr., American Minister in London, 76.

Know-nothings, 257, 258; become "Native American" party, 262.
Kossuth, 243, 244.
Koszta, Martin rescued, 254.

LABOUR, free and slave contrasted, 106 and foll.; hours of slave, 192, 193; Mr. Cobb on advantage of making capital, 314.
Lafayette, General, his visit, 128.
Lamar, the slave-trader, 285.
Land, price of, in free and slave states contrasted, 111; exhausted by slave labour, 110 and foll.
Lane, James H., of Kansas, 343, 347; elected senator by free state legislature, 350; has to fly, 355; heads free-soilers, 364; senator, 377; — General, of Oregon, 297.
Lawrence, Captain, 87 and foll.; — city (Kansas), 327, 347-349, 351, 352, 365-369; sacked by Missourians, 354.
Lazaretto of Staten Island, destroyed, 278, 279.
Leavenworth (Kansas), elections disturbed at, 339, 349.
Lecompte, Judge (Kansas), 368.
Lecompton, Bogus capital of Kansas, 341; pro-slavery constitution of, 274, 275, 370, 371.
"Leopard" and "Chesapeake," 76, 77.
Lewis and Clarke's expedition, 72.
"Liberator," the, 166, 301.
Liberia, 96; slaves from "Echo" sent to, 280.
Lincoln, Abraham, candidate for Presidency, 295, 296; elected, 299, 300.
Lingan, General, killed, 83.
"Little Belt" and "President," 81.
Livingston, Secretary of State, 136.
Loanda, American squadron on coast of, 285.
Lobos Islands, 246.
Locke, his constitution for Carolina, 5.
Lone Star, order of the, 245, 332.
Lopez, General (filibuster), 244, 245.
Louisiana, French, 2; purchase of,

by United States, 71 ; Jackson's proclamation to coloured men of, 90 ; admitted as state, 95 ; claims of, on Texas, ceded, 98 ; partition of territory, between freedom and slavery, 99 ; education in, 190 ; hours of labour in, 192 ; negro conspiracy extending to, 263 ; votes for Breckenridge, 300 ; vigilance committees in, 301 ; secedes, 302 ; ordinance of secession of, 303 ; and see Appendix.

Louisville and Portland Canal Bill, 134.

Lowell, Mr., his "Biglow Papers," 221, 222.

Lowndes, Wm. (South Carolina), 95.

McCLELLAN, General, commissioner in Crimean war, 253.

McDowell, Mr. (Virginia), 225.

"Macedonian," the, and "United States," 92.

McGillivray, Alexander, 57.

McGregor, Gregor, 97.

McLeod, Mr., trial of, 185.

Madison, James, Secretary of State, 78 ; President, 80 and foll ; on the slavery agitation and secession, 164, 165 ; his death, 172.

Maine, admitted as state, 99 ; and see Appendix.

Majority, Jefferson urges acquiescence in decisions of, 70.

Marcy, Mr., Secretary of State, 248, 249, 251.

Maryland, its administration by Lord Baltimore, 5 ; growth of tobacco in, 7, 8 ; its share in constitution, 21, 22 ; cedes district of Columbia to United States, 55 ; war-riot in, 83 ; senators from, support protection, 137 ; votes for Fillmore, in 1856, 261 ; Republican committees in, 298 ; and see Appendix.

Mason, Mr., of Virginia, reads Calhoun's last speech, 229 ; takes part in Ostend conference, 250 ; presides over committee on Harper's Ferry affair, 290.

Massachusetts, insurrection in, 20, 21 ; slavery held abolished in, 46 ; public school system of, 63 ; refuses militia for war with England, 90, 91 ; Northern, becomes state of Maine, 98, 90 ; in favour of free trade till 1824, 121 ; school attendance of coloured people in, 191 ; free-soil party in, 224 ; repeals fugitive-slave law, 256 ; Republicans carry elections in, 282 ; emigrant aid company of, 328, 329 ; and see Appendix.

Maysville Road Bill, 133.

Medary, Governor of Kansas, 373, 374.

Memminger, Mr., 289, 290.

Message, President's substituted for address, 68 ; and see names of Presidents.

Methodism, Wesleyan, 4, 5, 229.

Mexico, Burr's project to attack, 72 ; boundary treaty with, 127 ; Texas separates from, 168, 169 ; Van Buren treats with, 185 ; Tyler's defiance to, 210, 211 ; war with, 215 and foll. ; treaty with, 221 ; new boundary treaty with, and cession from, 249 ; Walker's designs on, 262 ; Buchanan complains of, 283 ; he asks for leave to occupy part of, 289 ; his treaty with, rejected, 292 ; designs of South on, 298, 332.

Mexico, New, see *New Mexico*.

Miami, battle of, 57.

Michigan territory invaded by English, 84 ; admitted as state, 171 ; repudiation by, 181 ; rescues of slaves through, 375 ; and see Appendix.

Milan decree, 79, 83.

Militia, Congress provides for calling out, 28 ; President, Commander-in-Chief of, 33.

Minnesota admitted, 275 ; scandals 277, and see Appendix.

Mississippi river, originally in control of France, 2 ; ascended, 72 ; secured by purchase of Louisiana, 71, 72; Indians to be removed beyond, 169, 170 ; on, 296 ; — territory organized, 66 ; admitted as state, 98 ; protests against tariff, 135; repudiation by, 181; Act of, to promote Southern Congress, 232 ; Governor of, asks for duty on

INDEX. 397

Northern manufactures, 288; votes for Breckenridge, 300; vigilance committees in, 301; secedes, 302; and see Appendix.
Missouri river, explored, 72; long held boundary of settlement by whites, 323; territory, 98; state admitted, 116; enlarged, 167; emigration from, to Pacific, 205; to Kansas, 326 and foll.; abolitionist elected in, 281; free-soil party in, 286; votes given in for Lincoln, 300; and see Appendix;—border-ruffians of, and voters from, in Kansas, 330 and foll.; 345 and foll. (and see *Border Ruffians*);— compromise, 99, 100, 104, 105 and foll., 321; devised by Clay, 116; Calhoun declares against, 183; line of, extended to Texas, 211; ditto, not extended to Pacific, 222; repealed, 256, 257; declared unconstitutional by Pierce, 263; held unconstitutional by Supreme Court, 265.
Monomania, moral, of benevolent slave owners, 312, 313.
Monroe, James, Minister in England, 78, 93; President, 96 and foll., 116 and foll.; death of, 172; —doctrine, the, 120.
Monterey occupied, 217.
Montgomery, city (Alabama), Southern Confederacy formed at, 303; —Captain, of Kansas, 369, 372, 373.
Mormonites, 225, 276, 277.
Morrill tariff, 306.
Mosquito coast, 330, 231, 254.
Moultrie, Fort, Osceola's death in, 182; South Carolina seizes, 302.

NAPOLEON, his decrees, 79, 81, 83.
Nashville (Tennessee), 131, 176, 232, 263.
"National Era," riot against, 223.
"Native American" party, 262.
Navy, commenced under Washington, 55; impulse given to, under J. Adams, 65; increase of, under Jefferson, 79, 80; in war with England, 85, 92; fostered by J. Q. Adams, 122; neglected by Jackson, 134; inquiry into abuses of, 285; committee on, 297; —secretary of, see *Secretary*.
Navy Island, seizure of, 184, 185.
Nauvoo, 225.
Nebraska-Kansas Bill, see *Kansas*; emigration to Kansas through, 344, 369; rescue of slaves through, 375, and see *Appendix*.
Negroes, serve in revolutionary war, 45; conspiracy of, in Charleston, 117; ditto, at Nashville, &c., 263; citizenship of free, denied in Dred Scott case, 264 and foll. and see *Colour, Slaves, Slave Trade, Slavery*.
Neutrality, American, proclaimed by Washington, 60; complaints of violation of, by England, 75 and foll., 82 and foll., 253, 254; of Pacific canal, guaranteed, 230, 231; rights of, conferences of Paris as to, 266, 267.
Newark, riot at, 258.
New England, colonization of, 4; not prominent in colonial period, 7; war with England unpopular in, 90, 91; in favour of free-trade till 1824, 121; M. Elisée Reclus on society in, 315; emigrants to Kansas, 327, 330, 338.
New Granada, 251, 262, 273.
New Hampshire, insurrection in, 20; and see Appendix.
New Jersey, Dutch and Swedes in, 4; labour and land in, contrasted with Virginia, 110, 111; Republicans carry elections in, 282; irritation of manufacturers of, 298; and see Appendix.
New Mexico, trade-road to, 122; annexed and ceded, 217, 221; question of slavery as to, 228; territorial government for, 232; slaves introduced into, 286; and see Appendix.
New Orleans, Burr's projected attempt on, 72; battle of, 89, 90; mint established at, 162; riots at, 244, 258; Walker tried and acquitted at, 279; Federal funds seized at, 302.
New York, the Dutch in, 4; first of states in point of population, 106, 239; labour in, contrasted with Virginia. 110; trade of,

1760 to 1832, 182, 183; anti-popery movements in, 258; members from, expelled, 271; Senate of, its resolutions against slavery, 274; municipal scandals in, 278; Republicans carry elections in, 282; customs, scandals of, 292; and see Appendix.
"New York Herald," the, 202, 277, 282.
"New York Times," the, 281.
Nicaragua, 127, 230, 251, 262, 281.
North and South, divided as to slavery in Missouri, 98; as to the tariff, 103, 104, 123, and foll.; contrasted, as to colonization, 4, and foll.; representation, 48, 49; emigration, 105; population, 106, and see Appendix; cost of labour, 109, 110; price of land, 111; production and consumption, 149, and foll.; trade, till 1832, 182, 183; possession of office, till 1845, 187, 188; education, 191; political ability, 195, 196; struggle between, for Kansas, 257 and foll., 319 and foll.
Northern Democrats, Mr. Douglas leads, 274; oppose slavery protection code, 287; turn scales of party, 293; break up Charleston convention, 293, 294.
Nueces river, 215.
Nullification (South Carolina), 135, and foll.; 143, 146, 147, 164.

OHIO river, slavery excluded N.W. of, 48; state admitted, 71; ranks third by population in 1850, 239; carried by Democrats for Buchanan, 262; rescues of fugitive slaves, &c. in, 274; and see Appendix.
Olmsted, Frederick Law, his works, 270; quoted, 107, 109, 110, 111, 112, 151, 152, 153, 155, 156, 190, 112, 194, 307, 312.
Orders in Council, English, 79, 82, 83.
Ordinance of 1787, 48, 98, 99; —nullification, of South Carolina, 137; — the "English," 275, 371; — secession, of Louisiana, 303.

Oregon boundary question, 212 and foll.; government question, 222, 223; constitution and admission of, 275, 276; votes for Lincoln, 300; and see Appendix.
Osage Indians, 124; river, 323.
Orr, Mr., of South Carolina, 264.
Osceola, Seminole chief, 170, 182.
Ossowotomie (Kansas), 356, 359, 363, 372; burnt by Missourians, 361, 364, 365.
Ostend Conference, 250; and see Additions and Corrections.

PACIFIC, reached by Lewis and Clarke, 72; American dealings on coast of, 119, 120; convention as to coast of, 126; and Atlantic Canal, 127, 230, 231; road to, 273.
Palfrey, Mr., quoted, 48, 193, 194, 200.
Palmetto flag, hoisted, 300.
Panama, 262, 273; and see *Isthmus*.
Paraguay, 253, 280.
Paris, Conferences of, 266, 267.
Parrott, Mr. (Kansas rpresentative), 378.
Passports, refused to persons of colour, 266.
Pate, Captain (Kansas), 359, 360.
Paulding, Commodore, stops Walker, 279.
Peel, Sir Robert, speech of, 211.
Pensacola, Jackson occupies, 97; restored, 98; fort, seized by Secessionists, 302.
Pennington, Mr., elected Speaker, 291.
Pennsylvania, colonization of, 4; emancipates slaves, 46; insurrection in, under Washington, 58, 59; opposition to direct taxation in, under J. Adams, 66; price of land in, compared with Virginia, 111; repudiation, 180, 181; notice of trade of, in, 1760, 182; repeals Slave-sojournment Act, 220; ranks second of states by population, 239; carried by Democrats for Buchanan, 261; Senate of, declares Dred Scott decision unconstitutional, 274; Republicans carry elections in, 282;

978-3-74463-767-1

Die Lusiaden des Luis de Camoens ist ein unveränderter, hochwertiger Nachdruck der Originalausgabe aus dem Jahr 1869.
Hansebooks ist Herausgeber von Literatur zu unterschiedlichen Themengebieten wie Forschung und Wissenschaft, Reisen und Expeditionen, Kochen und Ernährung, Medizin und weiteren Genres. Der Schwerpunkt des Verlages liegt auf dem Erhalt historischer Literatur. Viele Werke historischer Schriftsteller und Wissenschaftler sind heute nur noch als Antiquitäten erhältlich. Hansebooks verlegt diese Bücher neu und trägt damit zum Erhalt selten gewordener Literatur und historischem Wissen auch für die Zukunft bei.

ISBN/EAN: 978-3-74463-767-1
www.hansebooks.com

hanse

ironmasters of, dissatisfied, 298; and see Appendix; — United States Bank of, see Bank.
Perdido river, 94.
Perry, Commodore, 85.
Personal Liberty Acts, 301.
Peru, differences with, 246.
Philadelphia, Congress sits at, 67; anti-fugitive-slave-law riots at, 242.
Pierce, Franklin, President, 248, and foll.; sanctions Bogus legislature of Kansas, 344, 350.
Pike, Lieutenant, 72.
Pinckney, of South Carolina, 14, 65, 93.
Piracy, slave trade declared, 118.
Pittsburg, Mr. Buchanan's letter to, 282.
Poinsett, Mr., of South Carolina, 243.
Polk, James R., elected President, 210; his Presidency, 211, and foll.; his death, 230.
Polygamy, in Utah, Republicans against, 276, 277.
Population, increases faster in free states, 105, 106, 239 (see Appendix), and see *Census*.
Potomac, proposed convention as to, 21; bridge over, burnt by English, 84.
Powhattan, 56.
Presidents of United States, their share in legislation, 26, 27; their election and powers, 31, and foll.; their appointments to office, 33, 34; Jackson's views as to election of, 133; the mediocre, 186, and foll.; two, proposed by Calhoun, 230; and see *Washington, Adams, Jefferson, Madison, Monroe, Jackson, Van Buren, Harrison, Tyler, Polk, Taylor, Fillmore, Pierce, Buchanan*; — (ship) and "Little Belt," 81.
Princeton explosion, the, 202.
Printing system, the, exposed, 291, 292; and see 297.
Protection, first duties laid on for, 95; Monroe in favour of, 121; Webster turns in favour of, 123; Clay leads for, 121, 137; how tariffs for, have been passed, 306, 307; and see *Tariff*.

Protestant and Roman Catholic riots, 258.
Prussia, treaty with, 19; education in, referred to, 191.

QUAKERS, grant to, of Pennsylvania, 4; memorial of, for abolition of slavery in Columbia district, 165.

RAMBOUILLET decree, 81.
Randolph, John, 117, 172.
Rape, none, by master on slave, 192.
Reeder, Governor of Kansas, 329, 333, 334, 341, 342, 344, 350, 355.
Reid, border-ruffian (Kansas), 364.
Representation, the principle of, under Constitution, 24.
Representatives, House of, see *House*.
Republican form of government guaranteed by Constitution, 37; party (old), 61; dies out, 96; party (new) formed, 258, 259; puts forward Fremont as candidate, 261, 262; against polygamy in Utah, 276, 277; reforms New York municipal government, 278; carries elections in 1858, 282; convention at Chicago, 295-297; carries Lincoln's election, 299, 300; in Kansas, 343, 377.
Repudiation, 180, 181; by Confederate states, 300, 302.
Rescues of fugitive slaves arrested, 242, 273; see *Brown, John*.
"Resolute," restoration of, 262, 263.
Rhode Island, foundation of, 4; refuses contingent for war with England, 91; and see Appendix.
Richmond (Virginia), coloured men attempt to take, 73.
Rio Grande, 215, 216, 221, 228.
Riots, war, at Baltimore, 83; pro-slavery, 167; Anti-fugitive-slave Law, 242; at New Orleans, against Spaniards, 244; of Irish and Know-nothings, 258.
Roberts, Lieut.-Governor of Kansas, 349.

400   INDEX.

Robinson, Dr. Charles, Governor of Kansas, 343, 347, 349, 350, 352, 354, 355, 369, 377.
Rocky Mountains, safe pass through, discovered, 224.
Roman Catholic and Protestant riots, 258.
Rush, Dr., 19.
Russia, treaty with, 19; convention with, as to northern coast, 119, 120; and see *Crimean war*.
Rutledge, of South Carolina, 45.

SACS and Foxes, war with, and removal of, 167, 170.
Sailors, impressment of, &c., 74, 76, 92.
St. Juan, island of, occupied, 289.
St. Louis, riot at, 258; abolitionist elected for, 281; abolitionists strong in, 286; Blair re-elected at, 298.
St. Mark's, Jackson occupies, 97; restored, 98.
Sandwich Islands, treaty with, 252.
San Jacinto, battle of, 168.
Santa Anna, President, 216, 217.
Savannah, commercial convention at, 263; forts at, seized by Secessionists, 302.
Schell, Mr., 293.
Scott, General, his successes in Mexico, 217; candidate for Presidency, 247, 248; sent to settle St. Juan difficulty, 289; his plans for defending Washington rejected, 301.
Seabrook, Governor of South Carolina, 242.
Search, right of, for deserters, 75 and foll.; mutual, against slave-trade, 118.
Secession, unconstitutional, 41 and foll.; Jefferson on, 64; mooted at Hartford Convention, 91, 103; Jackson on, 139 and foll., 145, 173; Madison on, 164, 165; advocated in South Carolina, 233, 242; the present, 299-303; considerations on, 304 and foll.
Secretary of State, the Prime Minister, 54; foremost politicians rise no higher than, 187; and see *Jefferson, Madison, Monroe, Adams*,

Clay, Van Buren, Livingston, Webster, Upshur, Calhoun, Clayton, Marcy, Cass, Everett; — of Treasury, see *Hamilton, Taney, Walker, Cobb*; — of War, see *Calhoun, Cass, Davis, Floyd*; — of Navy, see *Bancroft, Toucey*; — of Interior, created, 226.
Seminole Indians, 97, 131, 170, 181, 182, 207.
Senate, Constitution of, 24, 25; elects Vice-President when, 32; consent of, to treaties, 33; majority in, against J. Q. Adams, 122; against Jackson, 136, 137, &c.; supports Bank against President, 160, 161; rejects nomination of Taney, 162; expunges censure on Jackson, 177, 178; rejects Texan annexation treaty, 210; adopts boundary line for Oregon, 214; Wilmot proviso defeated in, 218, 219; refuses citizenship to Wyandots, 233, 234.
Seward, William Henry, 291, 295; opposes Kansas-Nebraska Bill, 325, 326; moves admission of Kansas as a free state, 378.
Seymour, (English) Attorney-General, 6-7.
"Shannon" the, and "Chesapeake," 86 and foll.; — Wilson, Governor of Kansas, 342 and foll., 353, 361.
Shore, free-soiler (Kansas), 360, 361, 363.
Slade, Mr., of Vermont, 184.
Slave-power, the, 48, 189 and foll.
Slave-representation, under Constitution, 24, 48 and foll.; effects of, 193, 194.
Slave-Sojournment Act, of Pennsylvania, 220.
Slave-states, increase of power of, 103; cultivation of, 109 and foll.; production and consumption of, 149 and foll.; education and church accommodation in, 189 and foll.; manifesto of members from, 227; programme of, rejected in Charleston Convention, 293; Republican committees in, 298; and see *Appendix*.
Slave-trade, Virginia seeks discon-

INDEX. 401

tinuance of, 6; declaration of independence, and the, 16, 17; resolution against, by Confederation, 18; provision as to, in Constitution, 30; prohibited under Jefferson, 73; Treaty of Ghent as to, 91; declared piracy, 118; internal, in Columbia district, 165, 229; Ashburton Treaty, as to African, 207; Tyler's insinuations as to, against England, 211; opening of, discussed at Savannah, 264; proceedings against, under Buchanan, 279, 280, 285; reopening of, necessary to Confederate States, 311, 312.

Slavery and the declaration of Independence, 16, 17; unpopular at the revolution, 45-47; ordinance of 1787 as to, 48; Constitution as to, 49, 51; as respects Louisiana, 98; Missouri Compromise as to, 99; question of territorial extension of, 104 and foll.; Missouri Constitution as to, 116; effect of, on consumption, 150 and foll.; discussions on, under Jackson, 164 and foll.; abolished in Mexico, 168; question of, under Van Buren, 177, 183, 184; Lord Aberdeen and Calhoun on, 202, 208, 209; question of, as to Texas, 211; as to Mexican cessions, 218, 219; as to Oregon, 222, 223; proposed extension of, to territories, 227; question of, as to California, 224, 228-31; Clay on, 229; question of, as to Kansas and Nebraska, 256, 257, 327 and foll.; Walker re-establishes, in Nicaragua, 262; prohibition of in territories, held unconstitutional, 265; contest as to, becomes political solely, 269; excluded from Oregon and Kansas, 275, 276; Mr. J. Davis seeks protection for, 286; Democratic and Republican Conventions on, 293, 296, 297; how far involved in Secession, 309 and foll.; and see *Fugitive Slave Law, Kansas, Slave-Power,* &c.

Slaves, carried to Virginia, 6; not mentioned in Constitution, 51; increased value of, through cotton, 102; labour of, see *Labour;* cost of consumption of, 150, 151; liberation of, in British ports, 184; condition of, at South, 192; of "Echo" sent to Liberia, 280; introduced into Arizona and New Mexico, 286.

Slidell, Mr., 215, 284.
Sloat, Commodore, takes Monterey, 217; annexes California, 218.
Smith, Joseph, 225.
Sonora, part of, ceded by Mexico, 249; Buchanan recommends protectorate over, 283.
Soulé, Mr. Pierre, 231, 246, 249-251.
Sound dues, 253, 273.
South, see *North and South.*
Southern Confederacy, prospects of English trade with, 156; with Texas, proposed, 209; with Mexico, Cuba, &c., 298; the present, formed, 303; — rights volunteers, 299.
Sovereignty, the question of, 13 and foll., 19 and foll., 29, 41-3, 141, 146-7, 174.
Spain, share of, in colonizing United States, 2, 3; treaty with (1783), 19; American aggression on, in Florida, 94; Florida Treaty with, 97, 98, 129; and see Additions and Corrections; difficulties with, as to Cuba, 244, 245, 249-251.
Specie circular, Jackson's, 162.
Spence, Mr., his book, see Preface.
Squatter Sovereignty, 293, 298, 324.
Stanton, acting Governor of Kansas, 371.
State, Secretaries of, see *Secretary.*
Staten Island Lazaretto destroyed, 278, 279.
States, the thirteen original, 18, *n.*; limitations to powers of, under Constitution, 30, 31; new, how admitted, 37; admission of new, 54, 71, 95, 98, 116, 171, 214, 225, 231, 275; ten new ones by 1820, 101; free and slave, at time of Kansas struggle, 322; list of present ones, 309, 310, *n.*; and see Appendix.
States' rights doctrine, the, 14 and foll., 61, 80, 135, 146, 147.
Stephens, Mr., of Georgia, in favour of slave trade, 285; Vice-President of Confederate States, 303.

D D

402 INDEX.

Stevens, boatswain of Shannon, 88; — (another) John Brown's companion, 364, 290.
Stony Creek, battle of, 84.
Stringfellow, Dr., of Missouri, 330, 338, 365.
Sub-Treasury Act, the, 180, 181; and see Additions and Corrections.
Sumner, Charles, outrage on, 258, 259; — Colonel (Kansas), 348, 352, 353, 360.
Sumter, Fort, taken, 302.
Supreme Court, its functions, 35, 36; and see 268, 269; judgment of, in Dred Scott case, 265, 267; effects of such judgment, 268 and foll.
Sweden, treaty with, 19.
Swedes, the, in New Jersey, &c., 4.

TANEY, Roger, disallowed as Secretary of Treasury, 162; Chief-Justice, 204; his judgment in Dred Scott case, 265 and foll.
Tariff, first protective, 95; North and South divided on, 103, 104, 123; debates on, under Monroe, 121, 123; petitions and protests against, by South, 135; nullified by South Carolina, 137; Clay's compromise, 145, 148; question of, between North and South considered, 149 and foll.; Whigs cajoled by prospect of protective, 214, 215; Buchanan recommends high, 283, 289; Northern high, rejected by Senate, 298; question and secession, 306, 307.
Taylor, General, and Mexican war, 215, 217; elected President, 226; his Presidency, 227, and foll.; his death, 230.
Taxation, principle of, under constitution, 24; direct, rarely applied, 50; opposition to, under J. Adams, 66; J. Q. Adams on, 122, 123; what, possible in Southern confederacy, 306.
Tecumseh, 94.
'Telegraph,' the 'United States,' newspaper, 165.
Tennessee, admission of, as state, 54; Jackson's connection with, 131; ranks ninth by population in 1850, 239; negro plot in, 263; republican committees in, 298; votes for Bell, 300; and see Appendix.
Territories of United States, regulated by congress, 37; Jefferson proposes to exclude slavery from, 47; Mississippi and Indiana organised as, 66; Arkansas do., 98; question of slavery as to, 104 and foll.; do. discussed in senate, 219, 220; constitution proposed to be extended to, 226, 227; prohibition of slavery in, held unconstitutional, 265; protection of slavery in, asked by J. Davis, 286, 290; the question discussed in Charleston and Chicago Conventions, 293, 296, 297; the present, 310, n.; and see Appendix.
Texas, early invasions of, 95, 97; claims on, ceded, 98, 127; consumption in, 153, n., 155; independence of, 168; question of recognising and admitting, 168, 169, 183, 207, 209 and foll.; convention and boundary treaty with, 185; Lord Aberdeen as to slavery in, 208; treaty for annexation of, rejected, 210; admission of, 210, 211, 214; claim of, on New Mexico, 228; boundary Act, 231; delegates from, advocate open slave trade, 264; secedes, 302; and see Appendix.
Thames, the battle of, 84, 94.
Thompson, Mr., of Kentucky, 284; — George, English abolitionist, 167.
Thorpe, Jan, the Missourian, 337.
Times correspondent in Kansas, 358.
Tippecanoe, battle of, 94.
Titus (border-ruffian), 353, 363.
Tobacco, growth of, in the south, 5, 7, 8.
Tocqueville, referred to, 56, n., 157, 158.
Topeka constitution of Kansas, 342 and foll., 368; free-soil legislature at, dispersed, 361-363.
Toucey, Mr., Secretary of Navy, 299.
Trade, notices of American, in colonial times, 7, 8; under Con-

INDEX. 403

federation, 20, 21; under Washington, 55, 63; under Adams, 66; under Jefferson, 74; under Madison, 93; under J. Q. Adams, 123; till 1832, 182, 183.
"Trading Post" (Kansas), massacre of the, 372; and see 374.
Treaties, early, with France, &c., 19; how made under constitution, 33; with England, &c., 54; with England, rejected by Jefferson, 93; of Ghent with England, 91; with Indians, 54, 94, 124, 182; with Spain for Florida, 98, and see Additions and Corrections; with Russia, 119; with Mexico, 127; with England, as to West India trade, 171; with Texas, 185; the Ashburton, 207, and see Additions and Corrections; rejected, for annexing Texas, 210; second, of Washington, for North Western boundary, 214, and see Additions and Corrections; of Guadalupe Hidalgo, 221; the Clayton-Bulwer, 230; with Wyandots, 233, 234; with Sandwich Islands, 252; with Dominican republic, rejected, 252, and see Additions and Corrections; Sound dues, with Denmark, 253, 273; Canadian reciprocity, 253; with New Grenada, 272; Buchanan's, with Mexico, rejected, 292; with Delaware Indians, 328.
Tripoli, war with, 74.
Tyler, John, his Presidency, 201 and foll.

"UNCLE Tom's Cabin," 246, 247.
Union, Jackson on, 143, 173; — newspaper, 292; — convention, 294, 295.
Unionists, of Georgia, headed by Mr. Howell Cobb, 243.
United States, original colonization of, 1-8; character of history of, 9-12; declaration of Independence of, 12 and foll.; articles of confederation of, 17 and foll.; constitution of, 21 and foll.; view of growth of, to Missourri Compromise, 100 and foll.; refuse to accede to principles of Paris conferences, 266, 267.
Upshur, Abel P., Secretary of State, 202, 207.
Utah, question of slavery as to, 228; territorial government for, 232; Brigham Young, Governor of, 276; bill against polygamy in, 292; and see Appendix.

VAN BUREN, Secretary of State, 132; disallowed as minister to England, 136, 137; Vice-President, 145; elected President, 172; his Presidency, 176 and foll.; free-soil candidate for Presidency, 226.
Vancouver Island, 214, 289.
Van Rensselaer, General, surrenders, 84.
Vermont, growth of, 47; admission of, as state, 54; memorial from, against admitting Texas, 183; sets at naught fugitive slave law, 286; and see Appendix.
Vice-President of United States, 25; his election and powers, 31, 32; and see *Adams, Jefferson, Burr, Calhoun, Van Buren, Tyler, Fillmore, Breckenridge, Lane.*
Vigil, Father, 254.
Vigilance committees of California, 260; of South, 298, 301.
Virginia, colonization and early greatness of, 5-8; her share in constitution, 21, 22; opposed to slavery and slave trade, 6, 45; state constitution of, 46; cessions of, to United States, 47, 55; Washington a burgess in, 53; Indians in, their original condition, 56; excise insurrection extends to, 59; insurrection of coloured men in, 73; report of legislature of, 80; falls behind New York in population, 106; labour and land in, 109-12; protests against tariff, 135; emancipation discussed in, 166; notices of trade of, 182, 183; education in, 189, 190; representation in, 194; the slave trade advocated by delegate from, 264; 'fire-eaters' triumph in, 287; Memminger deputed to, 289, 290; effect of

last census on, 298 ; votes for Bell, 300; offers mediation, 301; and see Appendix.
Votes, sale of, in Congress, 271 ; manufacture of, in Kansas, 334, 335.

WAKEFIELD, Mr., free-soil candidate for Kansas delegacy, 329.
Walker, R. J., on Texas and tariff, 215 ; Secretary of Treasury, 212 ; Governor of Kansas, 368 ; — Mr., of Wisconsin, 226 ; — Wm., the filibuster, 249, 251, 252, 262, 279 ; — Mr., of Alabama, withdraws from Charleston convention, 294.
"Wanderer," the, slaver, 285.
War, small importance of, in history of United States, 9-11 ; of Independence, 8, 19 ; with Indians under Washington, 56, 57 ; under Adams, 68 ; under Madison, 82, 94, 131 ; with England, 82 and foll.; with Tripoli, 74 ; the great Continental, 60 and foll., 74 and foll., 81 and foll., 91, 92 ; with Seminoles, 97, 131, 170, 181-2 ; with Sacs and Foxes, and Creeks, 170 ; with Mexico, 215 and foll., 322; the Crimean, 253, 254.
Washington, George, his views, 19, 21 ; President, 52 and foll. ; farewell address of, 62 ; death of, 67 ; — city of, laid out, 55 ; Congress removes to, 67 ; taken by English, 84; Calhoun's pro-slavery paper at, 165 ; treaty of (Lord Ashburton's), 207, and see Additions and Corrections; second ditto, for North Western boundary, 214, and see Additions and Corrections; pro-slavery riot in, 223 ; Governor Wise threatens to march on, 261 ; threatened by Secessionists, 303.
Webster, Daniel, leads free-traders till 1824, 121 ; combines with Calhoun against Jackson, 136 ; his resolutions on the Constitution, 147 ; his conduct with reference to bank, 159 ; in office, but withdraws, 202 ; Secretary of State under Fillmore, 230 ; his efforts against disunion, 243 ; his correspondence with Austria, 244 ; his death, 246 ; and see Preface, and Additions and Corrections.
Wendell, Mr., official printer, 292.
Western Virginia, why faithful to union, 111, 112; representation of, in state, 194.
Whig party, 96 ; opposes Jackson, 136, 159 ; elects Harrison, 185; quarrels with Tyler, 201, 202 ; abandons opposition to admitting Texas, 214 ; elects Taylor, 226 ; puts forward General Scott, 247.
Whitfield, Mr., pro-slavery delegate from Kansas, 329, 330 ; burns Ossowotomie, 361.
Whittier, Mr., the poet, 222.
'Wide-awake committees,' 299.
Wilkinson, of Pottowotomie, 358, 359.
Williams, Mr., murdered in Kansas, 365.
Wilmot proviso, 218, 219, 224.
Winchester, Brig.-General, surrenders, 84.
Wisconsin admitted as state, 225 ; sets at naught fugitive slave law, 286 ; and see Appendix.
Wise, Governor, 261, 274.
Wood, Fernando, Mayor of New York, 278.
Woodson, Acting Governor, Kansas, 361, 362.
Wyandot Indians, 233, 234, 323 ; constitution of Kansas, 292, 376.

YANKEE, the, and the Delawares, 330, 331.
Young, Brigham, 225, 276.
Yulee, Mr., of Florida, 245.

THE END.

BRADBURY AND EVANS, PRINTERS, WHITEFRIARS.

www.ingramcontent.com/pod-product-compliance
Lightning Source LLC
Chambersburg PA
CBHW020544300426
44111CB00008B/792